HERMES' LYRE
Italian Poetic Self-Commentary from
Dante to Tommaso Campanella

SHERRY ROUSH

Hermes' Lyre

Italian Poetic Self-Commentary from
Dante to Tommaso Campanella

UNIVERSITY OF TORONTO PRESS
Toronto Buffalo London

© University of Toronto Press Incorporated 2002
Toronto Buffalo London
Printed in Canada

ISBN 0-8020-3712-7

Printed on acid-free paper

Toronto Italian Studies

National Library of Canada Cataloguing in Publication Data

Roush, Sherry
   Hermes' lyre : Italian poetic self-commentary from Dante to
Tommaso Campanella / Sherry Roush.

(Toronto Italian studies)
Includes bibliographical references and index.
ISBN 0-8020-3712-7

1. Italian poetry – History and criticism.   2. Hermeneutics.
I. Title.   II. Series

PQ4066.R68 2002   851.009   C2002-902114-6

This volume was published with the financial assistance of the Research
and Graduate Studies Office of the College of the Liberal Arts and the
Department of Spanish, Italian and Portuguese, Penn State University.

University of Toronto Press acknowledges the financial assistance to
its publishing program of the Canada Council for the Arts and the
Ontario Arts Council.

University of Toronto Press acknowledges the financial support for
its publishing activities of the Government of Canada through the
Book Publishing Industry Development Program (BPIDP).

Contents

PREFACE: THE LYRE OF HERMES   vii

INTRODUCTION. Beyond Explication: Poets and Their Own Commentaries   3

Part One. Dante and Boccaccio: The Emergence of Italian Poetic Self-Commentary

1 'You might call it something of a commentary': Defining Terms in Dante's *Vita Nuova* and *Convivio*   25
2 'Only the ploughshare aided by many clever talents cleaves the soil of poetry': Boccaccio's Earthly Vision of the Text and the Requisites for its Interpretation   52

Part Two. Poetic Self-Commentary Reborn in Quattrocento Florence

3 'Know thyself': Self-knowledge and New Life in Lorenzo de' Medici's *Commentary on My Sonnets*   71
4 'Distorted in contrary senses': Girolamo Benivieni's Self-Commentative Reformation   96

Part Three. Poetic Self-Commentary at the End of the Renaissance

5 'It is neither formed nor form': Reading Beyond the Lines of Bruno's Dialogic Self-Commentary, the *Heroic Frenzies*   119

6 'Did we not prophesy in Your name?': Settimontano Squilla as the Apocalyptic Seventh Trumpet in Tommaso Campanella's Vatic Project   134
7 Invocation, Interpretation, Inspiration   153

NOTES   163
BIBLIOGRAPHY   217
INDEX   239

Preface

The Lyre of Hermes

This study's emblem, Hermes' lyre, aims to invoke the mythic, original union of the hermeneutic and the lyric spheres. The lyre, symbol of poetry, traditionally falls under the aegis of Apollo, god of light and reason, whose laurel crown honours the greatest poets. According to the *Homeric Hymn to Hermes*, however, it was the playful newborn Hermes who created the lyre and played it so well that he left Apollo marvelling. Only after Hermes and Apollo struck a bargain did Apollo come to possess the instrument.

On the very day of his birth, playful Hermes leapt from his crib and went in search of Apollo's sacred cows. Hermes, whose name will lend itself to 'hermeneutics,' interpreted his encounter with a tortoise along the way, as a 'very propitious sign' (*Homeric Hymn to Hermes*, l. 30, my translations). He foresaw that the reptile's shell could prove useful even after the animal's death, since that shell, expertly strung, could protect its possessor through its enchanting sound. The mercurial god killed the tortoise and created his new stringed instrument, but the improvised toy did not occupy his full attention for long. The protector of wanderers quickly ventured out again to effect his initial quest, and promptly led away Apollo's herd of cows, disguising their path and hiding place with ingenious subterfuges.

Apollo soon discovered both the theft and the perpetrator's identity and summoned the feisty, young Hermes to defend his actions before Zeus. Hermes had to return Apollo's cows, despite his eloquent, albeit untruthful, defence. When Apollo realized that Hermes had slaughtered two of his sacred animals, he seethed in rage and disbelief. Only when Hermes drew out his lyre and began to pluck its strings was he able to placate Apollo's wrath. Apollo finally said to Hermes: 'Killer of cattle, rascally one, friend of the banquet, what you have invented is worth fifty cows easily! From now on I suppose we will get along well' (ll. 436–8). Apollo proposed that Hermes give him the lyre and teach him his musical art; in exchange, Apollo would leave Hermes the offices of guide of souls and keeper of herds. Hermes agreed. Hermes, 'who conceals his thought' (l. 413), became god of secrets, as well as being the god of exchanges and fecundity. Alone in his calling as guide of souls, Hermes could transgress all boundaries. He also received from Apollo the capacity of divination by pebbles.

Poetic self-commentary, like Hermes' lyre, contains both hermeneutic and lyric dimensions. The authors of poetic self-commentary also seem to take on decidedly hermetic traits. The symbolic form of their poetic visions suggests that they are both inventors of their own music and carriers of messages and secrets. Poetic self-commentators are ostensibly guides, but will show themselves to be players as well. They are boundary crossers, violating the established poetic notions of genre and the role of the commentator. Each of the six authors treated in this study deliberately goes beyond the boundary of his role as poet to explore new expressive potentials at the liminal spaces of his text. A number of these poetic self-commentators – especially Dante, Giordano Bruno, and Tommaso Campanella – also recognize a vatic (a divinatory or poetic-prophetic) motivation for their work. To study the poetic self-commentator, as I hope to show, is to face a Hermes-like figure of complexity and paradox. Perhaps most importantly, the study of self-commentary draws attention to an understanding of works that somehow precede or wilfully oppose an Apollonian rationality.

The present book departs in important ways from the doctoral dissertation (Yale University, 1999) on which it is based. My understanding of self-commentary has evolved through a struggle to understand the self vis-à-vis literature over time. Poetic self-commentary also unites in a personal and efficacious way my profound interests in the proximity of poetry and hermeneutics, the expression of spiritual conversion, the open forms of literary and philosophical texts, and the understanding of prescriptive versus Socratic or other dialogic approaches to pedagogy.

My heartfelt thanks go to my doctoral dissertation adviser Giuseppe Mazzotta, and thoughtful readers Paolo Valesio, Ernesto Livorni, and

Deanna Shemek. I benefited greatly from the weekly encounters with the members of Yale University's Whitney Humanities Center, 1997–8. Other colleagues at Yale provided provocative and useful feedback. I am most grateful to Thomas Greene and Olivia Holmes.

At the Pennsylvania State University I have enjoyed the generous advice of colleagues Alan R. Perry, Beno Weiss, Terry Peavler, Robert Edwards, Caroline Eckhardt, John Buck, Michael Wolfe, Marica Tacconi, Djelal Kadir, Kit Hume, and John Lipski. Olga Zorzi Pugliese at the University of Toronto also provided much appreciated guidance.

It has been a pleasure working with the ever-insightful and commendably efficient Toronto Italian Studies series editor Ron Schoeffel. I also thank Allyson N. May and the University of Toronto Press's anonymous readers for the time they took in offering useful, constructive criticism.

Finally, I am grateful for the financial support of Richard J. Franke, the Giles Whiting Foundation, the Beinecke Rare Books and Manuscripts Library, the John Perry Miller Research Fund, and the Folger Institute/Folger Shakespeare Library.

Pictured on the book jacket is the 'Self-portrait in a Convex Mirror' (c. 1524) by Parmigianino (1503–1540). I thank the Kunsthistorisches Museum, Wien, for permission to use it.

HERMES' LYRE
Italian Poetic Self-Commentary from
Dante to Tommaso Campanella

Introduction

Beyond Explication:
Poets and Their Own Commentaries

*Con orrore
la poesia rifiuta
le glosse degli scoliasti.
Ma non è certo che la troppo muta
basti a se stessa.*
　　　　　　– Eugenio Montale

With horror
poetry refuses
the exegetes' glosses.
But, too mute, it may not
be enough in itself.

When commentators gloss a poetic text, they typically do so in order to make the poetry more accessible. Standard commentaries have predominantly utilitarian purposes. Commentators may define obscure terms, note literary allusions, explain the verses' moral or ideological import, or make any of a number of other, largely pedagogical contributions. While commentators can have multiple and varying intentions, one widely shared aim is to mediate between their own readership and the oftentimes temporally and culturally remote context of the poem's composition. As reader needs shift over the course of time, commentators respond by reviewing, revising, and writing explications that supersede previous interpretive interventions. However, one special kind of commentary radically defies this utilitarian purpose: the poetic self-commentary.

Poetic self-commentators tend to subvert pedagogical intent and frequently avoid straightforward explications of the meaning of their poetry. Dante, for example, remarks in his prosimetrical account of love and poetic development, the *Vita Nuova* (1292–5), that there is really no need for his self-commentary. Those of his readers who have experienced love already understand his meaning and those who have not cannot be helped by his notes:

> Vero è che tra le parole ove si manifesta la cagione di questo sonetto si scrivono dubbiose parole ... E questo dubbio è impossibile a solvere a chi non fosse in simile grado fedele d'Amore; e a coloro che vi sono è manifesto ciò che solverebbe le dubitose parole. E però non è bene a me di dichiarare cotale dubitazione, acciò che lo mio parlare dichiarando sarebbe indarno, overo di soperchio. (7.14)[1]

> [It is true that among the words that expound the cause of this sonnet are written obscure words ... This doubt is impossible to solve for those who in the same degree are not the faithful of Love; and for those who are, the solution to the obscure words is clear: and so it is not fitting that I explain those obscurities, for my written explanations would be in vain, or in truth superfluous.] (14.14)

Poetic self-commentators may also flaunt their freedom from providing purely utilitarian commentaries and assert the kind of absolute personal judgment that no standard commentator would ever dare. Thus Tommaso Campanella, in expounding one of his most difficult philosophical poems, states: 'Il sonetto è chiaro: desidera attenzione e osservanza, riconoscimento e imitazione' ['This sonnet is clear; it yearns for attention and comment, recognition and imitation'] (21n).[2]

In these two brief examples it is already possible to see a striking contrast between externally imposed commentary and the poet's self-commentary. Yet little critical scholarship explores the development of medieval and Renaissance poetic self-commentaries and the theoretical implications of the form. The present study aims to open just such a critical inquiry, to address why significant numbers of important poets bother to write their own ostensibly interpretive prose, to hypothesize possible models for their procedure, and to note the formal problems inherent in self-commentary. This undertaking requires a critical look at certain self-commentative preconceptions.

The first problem arises in defining poetic self-commentary, since widely differing conceptions of it exist. On the one hand, the definition cannot be so broad as to offer no hope of providing a basis for theoretical appreciation of the form's specific motivations and contributions. Gianfranco Folena, who wrote the preface for the proceedings of an international conference in Bressanone (1990) on *autocommento*, defined self-commentary as: 'l'esegesi applicata dall'autore a tutti i livelli della propria opera' ['the exegesis applied by the author to all levels of his/her own work'].[3] Given this definition, it is not surprising to find in this collection of essays vastly disparate contributions on self-citation, prose/prose commentaries, and various forms of metapoetic discourse. Distinguishing the specific attributes of poetic self-commentary becomes difficult. On the other hand, the definition cannot be so focused on the minute formal variations of its paratextual manifestation as to lose sight of the unifying literary nature of the poetic work. This is the risk incurred in otherwise useful formalist treatments of generic categories like Gérard Genette's study *Paratexts*, for example.[4]

Provisionally defined, poetic self-commentary consists of a unified work of poetry and the poet's own paraphrase, gloss, or other ostensibly interpretive prose intervention. It is a specific subcategory of metacriticism or autoexegesis and differs from apologies, defences of poetry, personal statements of poetics, confessions, and autobiographies. Poetic self-commentary is a mixed genre in which the author deliberately combines poetic and prose expression. Frequently, poetic self-commentary is the result of a poet's elaboration of an earlier work in single-genre form to create an entirely new poetic vision. For example, Dante redeployed some of his early love lyrics in his *Vita Nuova*. In doing so, however, he changed the way readers would understand the poems forever. Moreover, he created a work that is much more than the sum of its parts (poetry + prose). By its very form the *Vita Nuova* succeeds in communicating a uniquely illuminating articulation of its message.

To all outward appearances, poetic self-commentaries mimic in significant ways standard commentary. However, commentary and self-commentary differ greatly in their motivations. Self-commentary, unlike the successful standard commentary, does not necessarily clarify the poetic word. The act of clarification frequently calls for a limiting or delimiting of textual significance. This purpose is especially prevalent in, but not exclusively restricted to, juridical and biblical commentary. In such commentary the interpretation serves to fence in the text by excluding undesirable readings and by sanctioning a narrower application of the law or guarding the inner depository of sacred significance.

Poetic self-commentators, on the other hand, tend not 'to fix the text's message unequivocally for posterity.'[5] Rather, they themselves highlight the ways in which the poetic text will always elude attempts to define it absolutely. Thus Boccaccio, in a gloss on his *Teseida delle nozze d'Emilia* (The Book of Theseus, 1339–41) states, 'So che assai più cose e meglio sopra questa materia si potrebbono dire; lasciole a coloro che con più diletto partitamente le vorranno ancora raguardare e scrivere' ['I know that many more things could be better said about this matter. I leave them to those people who with greater delight would want to go over them again and write about them in detail'].[6]

This understanding should lead us to reconsider a widespread assumption concerning poetic self-commentaries: that they at least partially preclude any other interpretive contributions. It is not difficult to find examples of this assumption. Alberto Limentani, editor of Boccaccio's *Teseida*, remarked: 'Il compito di preparare per il *Teseida* una serie di note esplicative è per certi aspetti semplificato dalla presenza delle chiose del B[occaccio]' ['The task of preparing a series of explicative notes for the *Teseida* is simplified to a certain degree by the presence of Boccaccio's glosses'].[7] In fact, modern studies of poetic self-commentaries typically call attention to the supposed sufficiency of the poet's 'critical' contribution. James Wyatt Cook, translator of Lorenzo de' Medici's self-commentary (Commentary on my Sonnets, 1473–91), thus stated: 'Given L[orenzo]'s own Neoplatonic exposition of the allegory of these sonnets, one hardly needs to supply more elaborate speculation.'[8] Robin Kirkpatrick reached similar conclusions about the ultimate reliability of the self-commentary: 'Dante combines prose and verse in the *Vita nuova*, writing here – as Boethius did in the *Consolation of Philosophy* – a "prosimetrum," in which the single moments of insight expressed in verse could be developed in a narrative and discursive form which established, as Petrarch never does, *an unambiguous understanding* of intellectual goals and spiritual purposes.'[9]

Underlying each of these examples is a belief that self-commentary is peculiarly authoritative precisely because the poets themselves present it. According to this line of thinking, poets have a privileged knowledge of their poetry's truth, a truth that would not be otherwise transmissible. Some poetic self-commentators considered within this study, such as Lorenzo de' Medici, even appear to encourage the reader in this regard: 'nessuno il può fare [commentare i versi] con più chiara espressione del vero senso che io medesimo' ['No one can (comment on the poetry) with a clearer expression of its true sense than I myself'].[10] I will return to the broader context of this passage in chapter 3. In the end, Lorenzo, like other poetic self-commentators, acknowledges the limits of the conscious drawing out of the poetic significance and of its clear or strictly logical expression. Moreover, the most sophisticated of these self-commentators – especially Dante, Lorenzo, and Campanella – demonstrate an awareness of the necessary cooperation between their own commentary and that provided by others.

The idea that self-commentary is especially authoritative and true – or reliable – has gone surprisingly unquestioned. Studies in deconstruction and reader reception theory have ably pointed out the limitations of the strict authorial intentionalist position. However, poetic self-commentary, which would seem most relevant to those debates, has somehow not received the attention it deserves. Critics indicate their reliance on the supposed authoritative status of self-commentary by beginning their observations with a variation on the statement 'As Lorenzo himself affirms in the proem, ...' or by citing poetic self-commentary in support of historical fact or the absolute validity of the poet's interpretation.[11] Such treatment rests on the fallacious assumption that the work of art must communicate factual knowledge or information. What is more, some critics take the poets to task for a perceived lack of factual material: 'The sole event of [Lorenzo de' Medici's] *Comento* which is both real and non-amorous is the Pazzi conspiracy.'[12]

It should come as no surprise that critics have endeavoured to discover the poets' 'truths.' However, the lesson self-commentators can teach concerns not the final determination of poetic significance but a new understanding of the way people think about and express truth. In particular, the self-commentators can point out *why* readers look for the poet's truth and *how* they can understand and communicate it. Actually, if what were important about the self-commentary were the truth content of the poet's statement, it would make no difference if poetic self-commentary came in any other self-interpretive form. Perhaps this accounts, at least in part, for the sustained non-individuation of poetic self-commentary as a unique literary category that presents theoretical issues in ways that no other forms do. If the content of the self-commentary is its raison d'être, it does not matter at all if that clarification appears in the margins of the poetic text or outside the work altogether. On the contrary, one could argue that a separate text may even be preferable, since it might better avoid the possible contamination of poetic fictions with the supposed truths of poetic analysis.

The term *autocommento* is relatively recent, coined with a decidedly pejorative significance by Giosuè Carducci: 'Un signore mi scrive da Genova, domandandomi una spiegazione del verso tale della strofa tale. E questo vezzo del chiedermi autocommenti l'hanno preso da un pezzo molti in Italia' ['A man wrote to me from Genoa, asking me for an explanation of such-and-such a verse of such-and-such a stanza. And many in Italy for some time now have taken up this habit of asking me for self-commentaries'].[13] Of course, the nineteenth-century poet did not have the same understanding of self-commentary that the medieval and Renaissance poets of the present study developed, even as they lacked a term for their procedure. The earlier poets used a variety of terms, including 'quasi commento' [perhaps best rendered as 'something of a commentary'], 'commento' [also spelled 'comento,' commentary], and 'la mia interpretazione' [my interpretation]. I cite Carducci not to define the term, but as representative of the more general resistance among poets to forms of self-interpretation. Understanding the underlying premise for the resistance to ostensibly explicit self-interpretation allows us to comprehend more effectively the remarks of those poets who create self-commentaries.

One could argue that what disturbs Carducci is the implication that there is a single, correct explanation for any given stanza. According to this view, poetry would be but the code, the medium for a ciphered communication. The code writers would need only provide a one-to-one correspondence key to their privileged addressees for their messages to be clearly and unequivocally understood. An even more fundamental objection might be to the idea that an overarching meaning of poetry is contained in any given verse or stanza. Poets might object to the notion that the full comprehensibility of their poetic visions may be contained in any random pieces of them.

Alternatively, Carducci perhaps shudders at the assumption that poetry makes sense only according to the significance the poet confers on it. In this case, his Genoese correspondent perceives poetry not as being animated by a life of its own, but as a dull possession of the poet, which the reader can acquire only by confirming its perceived rudimentaries. The Genoese letter writer would not dream that poetry would require its reader to engage in a living, dynamic act of interpretation. The demand for an effortless – and perhaps precisely because of this, a hopelessly wrong – understanding of poetry is shown to be worthy of scorn. These various hypotheses for Carducci's impatience should be kept in mind throughout this study as we encounter the uncertainty, disdain, curiosity, and perplexity of poets' excuses for and critics' analyses of the self-commentary.

The assumption that poets provide a uniquely authoritative explanation of truth in their self-commentaries often accompanies the supposition that the self-commentary must be taken at face value. Usually, although not always, prose appears less coded and more transparent or monosemous than poetry. Accustomed to conventional commentaries, the reader of self-commentary may trust that it presents a plain, simplified exposition of the poetry's significance. The reader perhaps assumes that the only difference between commentary and self-commentary is simply that the poet writes the latter. Self-commentary becomes an approximation to commentary, without any consideration of the possibilities that the self might instead mark a point of radical differentiation.

Moreover, readers of poetic self-commentary have sometimes held that the form generally succumbs to inherent risks of over-determination, assuming that by their self-commentaries poets say too much. Thus many early editors of Dante's *Vita Nuova* took the liberty of cutting his *divisioni* [divisions], which they perceived as needlessly tedious.[14] After all, what need is there of accompanying prose if the poetry can successfully convey its vision? On the other hand, if the poet's vision may be stated just as effectively in prose, the ontological necessity of the poetry is placed in doubt. However, given that the two do indeed coexist in a work of art, the reader must reach an understanding of the text's poetics that purposefully foregoes the rational explication generally characteristic of an outside commentary in favour of an enduring, internal implication of ultimate significance.

Saying too much turns out to be a fault of varying degree and consequence. Criticism can rest on the elitist or purely aesthetic argument that the poet simply renders banal an aspect of the verse by making it too easily understood. Alternatively, the accusation can veer into theological territory and become a reproach of the poet for betraying sacred truths by casting pearls (of poetic wisdom) before (the uninitiated) swine. On this view the self-commentary may appear of ambivalent value, even somehow distasteful. Already in Boccaccio's time, the self-commentator wrestled with the issue of precisely what poetic revelation meant:

> Verum non ob id, ut isti volunt, iure damnanda, cum inter alia poete officia sit non eviscerare fictionibus palliata, quin imo, si in propatulo posita sint memoratu et veneratione digna, ne vilescant familiaritate nimia, quanta possunt industria tegere et ab oculis torpentium auferre. Et si, quod ad eos spectat, fecere solertes, non execrandi, sed commendandi potius poete venient.

> [Surely it is not one of the poet's various functions to rip up and lay bare the meaning which lies hidden in his inventions. Rather where matters truly solemn and memorable are too much exposed, it is his office by every effort to protect as well as he can and remove them from the gaze of the irreverent, that they cheapen not by too common familiarity. So when he discharges his duty and does it ingeniously, the poet earns commendation, not anathema.] (*Genealogia* 14.12)[15]

Given what has been said thus far, it is hardly surprising that poetic self-commentary has, more often than not, encountered the harsh condemnation of various critics. Readers may view self-commentaries as maddeningly unhelpful. Viewed with the expectations of commentary, self-commentary may seem at best 'pseudoscientific,' 'remarkably banal,' even a 'torture!'[16] Perhaps it is possible to put forward a more radical view, however: a medieval or Renaissance poet who purposefully incorporates an unorthodox self-commentary within the poetic sphere of a work of art may have in mind a startlingly modern, wholly creative literary vision.[17]

To date, the only critical considerations of poetic self-commentary in the Renaissance focus on isolated works. Two studies, however, have laid some of the groundwork for the approach I propose. In *Verse with Prose from Petronius to Dante: The Art and Scope of the Mixed Form*, Peter Dronke establishes a starting point for the classical and medieval study of the *prosimetrum*, which he sees as stemming from the mixed form of Menippean satire. However, Dronke does not distinguish between any given *prosimetra* and those that contain the ostensibly interpretive dimension that make them poetic self-commentaries.[18] In the other study, *Renaissance Theory of Love: The Context of Giordano Bruno's* Eroici Furori, John Charles Nelson dedicates a chapter to 'Prose Commentaries on Verses.'[19] In some ways, Nelson's approach is the complete opposite to that of Dronke, since Nelson emphasizes the commentative aspect of poetic study. Nevertheless, he makes no theoretical differentiation between the commentary and the self-commentary and selects his examples exclusively with a view to illuminating Bruno's work. By contrast, I hope to reveal the common ties between 'verse with prose' works and 'prose commentaries on verses,' and to demonstrate that the deliberate choice of formal composition adds a dimension of poetic significance to these works. This consideration of genre enables us to recognize how the early self-commentators rebel against a demand for adherence to literary dictates. These thinkers overtly refuse to conform to the generic precepts of the early determinists of poetic categorical purity.[20]

Even before Giordano Bruno made the dialogic nature of the poetic self-commentary explicit in his *Heroic Frenzies*, it was evident that this mixed genre strives both to draw together multiple voices and to maintain their distinctive timbres. Dialogue marks a space of divergent perspectives in which readers must negotiate for themselves a position to take. Unlike the moral or didactic tract, dialogue relegates certainty to a realm of possibilities. In Bakhtinian terms, truth is not given in an official version, but unfolds in the play of countering positions. Personal investment on the part of the reader in the playing out of dialogue becomes the only means of approaching the truth of the text. Dialogue highlights the importance of the contending voices. One interlocutor continually endeavours to persuade another of the relative merit of his or her own position, always trying to absorb the opposing view, even while asserting the differences that remain between the two.[21]

This same ambivalence animates self-commentary, particularly prosimetrical self-commentary. On the one hand, the poets, aware that their poetic visions exceed their capacity to convey them within the lyric sphere, resort to self-commentative prose. But this prose can never be extricated from its ties to the poetry, and risks being entirely absorbed by it. Precisely because prosimetrical self-commentary is not a treatise that has dispensed with any contending voice, it retains a tension between the divergent perspectives of verse and prose. The reader must arrive at an understanding that the author never preordains.

A similar analogy might aid our understanding of the self-gloss. The primary distinction between the two manifestations of self-commentary (prosimetrical and glossorial) resides in the more pronounced hierarchical relationship between verse and prose found in the self-gloss form.[22] The verse occupies the central place on the page, while the prose gloss is displaced to the margins. Another mode that is dependent upon the central text, but marginalized by it in its own way, is translation. Commentary, as I have said, is an explication, a kind of translation into some form of more explicit language of what is left implicit in the poem. Latin writers typically translated the Greek *hermeneía* as *interpretatio*, by which they intended 'interpretation' but also 'commentary' (or expounding of other senses of the text) and, significantly, 'translation.' Interpreters bring to light the hidden – usually allegorical – senses of the text by translating the poetic language into other words. In rhetorical terms, poetic self-commentary seems more like a laconic mode that masquerades as a Ciceronian one. Poetic self-commentary can appear excessively prolix, redundant, or pedantic. But self-commentaries are in fact evasive, and call attention to a gap in understanding at the heart of each of these projects. Unlike the standard commentary-by-another, self-commentary reads many more ideas into the poem.[23] Self-commentators read and translate what is in the poetry, it is true, and in this way they formally mimic the critic's procedure. But the self-commentator's translation enriches the poetic text with another dimension that itself demands interpretation.

The very act of translating the implicit into the explicit renders external criticism temporary, since this procedure aims at mediating the experience of a text to a reader of a given historical and cultural context. It is, in fact, dated, and destined to be discarded, mutated, or circumscribed by subsequent commentators and critics. In this regard, criticism shares the same fate as translation in its conventional sense of the rendering of a text in a foreign language.[24] What poetry expresses can only be contained in the form it embodies. What readers perceive to be poetry's infinite ambiguity is what sustains it as such. The poetry that distinguishes itself as an enduring revelation partially reveals its essence and continually alludes to what remains veiled. Poetic self-commentary further complicates, but does not violate, the ontological basis of the verse. If, as one scholar observed, one of the most effective methods for conveying meaning in translation is, paradoxically, to leave a key word untranslated, 'so that the reader has to pick up its contextual associations in the original language from his own,'[25] then by extension, it is interesting to consider whether the closest understanding of poetic self-commentary might not lie in this notion of leaving a key word untranslated.

Apart from believing that self-commentary must be viewed as something other than commentary, perhaps rather more akin to dialogue or translation, I am inclined to question the assumption that it is primarily a *self*-centred project. Some of the narrated accounts may be autobiographical, and self-commentators may betray some measure of egoism in admitting that they fear being negatively perceived as egoistic. Nevertheless, self-commentaries are seldom primarily about the poet's self-memorialization, authorization, or aggrandizement. On the contrary, those who write self-commentaries appear to be unusually concerned with that which exceeds them, with that which they cannot ultimately possess in lyric expression, and with those readers who understand differently than they do. In choosing an authorizing – and authority-conferring – form such as commentary to conjoin to their verse, these poets strike at the heart of what it means to construct authorship. Almost paradoxically, they suggest in both theory and practice that authorship and authority depend on a reader who can enter into the same spirit of the text. True authorship, these self-commentators implicitly argue, can never be merely a rhetorical or political issue.

In studying poetic self-commentary, we confront the issue of the stability of the grounds on which the commentative voice – in this case, my voice – intervenes. According to the dictates of post-Cartesian methodology, objective questioning and verifiable evidence must serve as the basis for analysis. The result is a factual, certain knowledge. Literature, now more than ever, has become the handmaiden of science in attempts to demystify the text by viewing it through the lenses of history, linguistics, anthropology, politics, or sociology. An entirely different epistemology, however, emerges from the works of the poets treated in this study. Faith more than scientific inquiry impels these poets' hermeneutic quests. While it may strike some readers as decidedly less rigorous, a faith-motivated hermeneutics can also be less reductive. In this spirit poets, to borrow Dante's phrase, 'open [their] verse by means of prose.'

My research thus departs from an assumption concerning the nature of poetry, or a medieval and Renaissance Italian Christian poetry, if one prefers. It is an assumption that I must ask the reader, if not to accept, at least to allow: the poet's inspiration participates in the transcendent Spirit infusing the ultimate Author and His Word. The study of poetic self-commentary illuminates in an extraordinary way an underlying Trinitarian view of the poetic text. There is in these works a three-dimensional dynamic between poetry, self-commentary, and a reflective acknowledgment by the two of the otherness of their inspiration. Poetry and self-commentary in their non-correspondence and incomplete complementarities succeed in pointing beyond the letter of the text and the author's intention to a locus of meaning (i.e., the Word) that is not *merely* what each reader perceives to have received. Not a means to objective certainty, the reflections made in these pages rejoice precisely in the work's ultimate incomprehensibility and inexplicability and view the sincere interpreter's failure as a kind of happy fault indeed. Moreover, and of keen importance, these poet-commentators argue implicitly for a view of wisdom that is not most quickly or completely grasped through demystification.

Study of how each poetic self-commentary explicitly treats the relationship between the distinct realms of poetry and interpretive discourse enables a greater understanding of what it means to approach the poetic work as a scholar today. The Trinitarian conceptualization of the poetic self-commentary – (1) poetry, (2) self-commentative prose, and (3) the *quid*, that is, the acknowledged otherness of their inspiration – becomes the ideal for my own procedure. Analogously, to that same *quid* (3) now point the literary work as a whole (1) and my intervening commentative voice (2). According to this view, no longer does mine remain an outside commentary, in the sense that the conventional critical contribution today rigorously defends its position as providing a perspective on the text-as-a-whole from without. The critic who approaches the poetic self-commentary cannot accept the poet's own commentary as the ultimate, or even simply the deservedly privileged, interpretation of the poetry, since this would lead to a strictly one-dimensional or otherwise overly limited view of the work. Likewise, the critic's interpretation depends upon the other two dimensions for the fullest possible understanding of the poetic work.

Poetic self-commentary demands, to borrow two terms from T.S. Eliot, understanding rather than explanation. This is to say, commentators cannot and should not feign a position of totalizing perspective of the poetic self-commentary from outside of it (explanation). Instead, they are called to enter into a communion of and with the work. In understanding, readers become guides as they are guided. The hermeneutic purpose shifts from learning some supposed actual intent of the work, or defending what the critic sees as a valid interpretation (both authorial intentionalists and supporters of strict reader reception focus on an answer to the text's implicit question), to valorizing the process of poetic contemplation and enrichment. In this mode of interpretation, it is not the end that counts, although the reader's eyes never waver from the promise of the work's understanding. What matters is the realization of every point along the way of the sincere endeavour.

Although this study does not belong to the growing corpus of recent textual studies scholarship, I am not unaware of the potential of poetic self-commentary within such a critical perspective. Leah S. Marcus's book, *Unediting the Renaissance*, made a particularly persuasive case for the hypothesis that today's published editions of literary texts often influence the interpretation of Renaissance works in subtle and profound ways. She asserted: 'No single version of a literary work, whether Renaissance or modern, can offer us the fond dream of unmediated access to an author or to his or her era; the more aware we are of the processes of mediation to which a given edition has been subject, the less likely we are to be caught up in a constricting hermeneutic knot by which the shaping hand of the editor is mistaken for the intent of the author, or for some lost, "perfect" version of the author's creation.'[26] This process of mediation can be an especially thorny issue when it comes to poetic self-commentary. Anyone reading the *Vita Nuova* in the popular Renaissance versions without Dante's divisions or the *Teseida* without Boccaccio's glosses, or who is predisposed to believe that the exposition of Campanella's philosophical poems was written by his first editor, Tobia Adami, can attest to an understanding of the text that is not merely formally different.

Italy is a particularly fertile ground for poetic self-commentaries, although examples of them exist in other national literary traditions. John Gower's Latin commentary on his Middle English *Confessio amantis* (The Lover's Shrift, c. 1390) is especially interesting for the way in which it carefully distinguished between the *auctor* of the work as a whole and the *persona* of the confessing lover.[27] The most famous and most contested example of poetic self-commentary in the English Renaissance is probably Edmund Spenser's *The Shephearde's Calender* (c. 1580), the glosses for which were written by a mysterious 'E.K.,' whom some critics identify as Spenser himself.[28] In the Spanish tradition, St John of the Cross's spiritual works, including the *Ascesa del Monte Carmelo [Ascent of Mount Carmel]*, the *Noche obscura del alma [Dark Night of the Soul]*, and the *Llama de amor viva [Love's Living Flame]*, all composed between 1582 and 1588, represent poetic self-commentative masterpieces.

Likewise, poetic self-commentary does not begin with Dante and end in the Baroque. Verse-with-prose forms, as Peter Dronke has shown, trace their origins back to classical times, and before the Renaissance it is common to find didactic treatises written in the same form.[29] Prosimetra by Alan of Lille and Bernardus Silvestris, or self-glossed encyclopedic poems by Cecco d'Ascoli or Francesco da Barberino, to name but a few, are justly famous, although not all verse-with-prose compositions are poetic self-commentaries. I am not suggesting, however, that the *Vita Nuova* had no poetic self-commentative precedents in Latin. In fact, a few works, while differing significantly in their projects from Dante's book, contain the seeds of poetic self-commentary, particularly Martianus Capella's *De nuptiis Philologiae et Mercurii* (The Marriage of Philology and Mercury, probably written between 410 and 429). The *incipit* of the first book should suffice to illustrate the point. Capella's work opens with an invocation to the 'sacred principle of unity amongst the gods,' which continues in verse in the original Latin:

> Tu quem psallentem thalamis, quem matre Camena
> progenitum perhibent, copula sacra deum,
> semina qui arcanis stringens pugnantia vinclis
> complexunque sacro dissona nexa foves,
> namque elementa ligas vicibus mundumque maritas
> atque auram mentis corporibus socias,
> foedere complacito sub quo natura iugatur,
> sexus concilians et sub amore fidem.

> [You bind the warring seeds of the world with secret bonds and encourage the union of opposites by your sacred embrace ... Mind is breathed into bodies by a union of concord which rules over Nature.] (1.1–11)

The narrator eventually switches to prose and recounts that, upon reciting these first verses of his new composition, he was interrupted by his son, Martianus. Martianus derisively compared his father to the 'sleepy priest' who begins chanting a hymn before opening up the portals of the temple, and demanded that he tell 'the burden and the meaning of [his] utterance' (1.2). The father responded preliminarily indicating the importance of both his theme and the form of his work, a *Satura*:

> '... Si vero concepta cuius scaturriginis vena profluxerint properus scrutator inquiris, fabellam tibi, quam Satura comminiscens hiemali pervigilio marcescentes mecum lucernas edocuit, ni prolixitas perculerit, explicabo.' (1.2)

[If, however, your question is serious, when you ask from what source my ideas have flowed, I shall unfold to you a story which Satire invented in the long winter nights and taught me by the dimming lamplight.']

The *Satura*, a dish of mixed ingredients that Latin writers took to be a mixture of prose and verse on miscellaneous topics, suggests the conscious effort with which some poetic self-commentative forerunners considered the formal presentation of their works.[30]

Boethius's prosimetrical *De consolatione philosophiae* [The Consolation of Philosophy] is also a significant precedent of Italian poetic self-commentary, not only because subsequent authors of the mixed form explicitly cite the sixth-century work, but also because there is an evident tension building within the two forms of the text, which points to a central concern for a revelation of poetic-philosophic significance. Near the end of the second book, for instance, Philosophia, faced with a string of paradoxes about Fortuna's nature, set up an important, exegetical discourse: 'Nondum forte quid loquar intellegis; mirum est quod dicere gestio, eoque sententiam verbis explicare vix queo' ['What I am about to say is so strange that I scarcely know how to make my meaning clear'] (2.8). Self-commentative cruxes, such as this one, recur frequently in subsequent imitators.

Ultimately, I am distrustful of hard and fast distinctions between historically imposed temporal categories; in particular, I find little value in distinguishing between medieval and Renaissance modes of poetic self-commentary. Such a distinction, for example, would make Dante's *Vita Nuova* appear more antiquated than its highly experimental nature would permit, or Benivieni's *Commento* seem more modern than its allegorizing line-by-line commentary can actually be considered.

In this book I place the works of six poetic self-commentators in three representative historical contexts: the emergence of exemplary vernacular forms in the late-thirteenth to mid-fourteenth centuries (Dante and Boccaccio), the humanistically innovative and spiritually charged backdrop of high Renaissance Florence (Lorenzo de' Medici and Girolamo Benivieni), and the unorthodox Catholic Reformation milieu of the turn of the seventeenth century (Giordano Bruno and Tommaso Campanella). Each pair of authors in question utilizes self-commentative approaches that contrast in form: prosimetrical (Dante, Lorenzo, and Bruno) and glossarial (Boccaccio, Benivieni, and Campanella). I consider each work on its own terms, as well as exploring the way in which each poetic self-commentary presents itself with respect to its contemporaries and with respect to generic precedents. In pursuing this approach I hope to demonstrate that poetic self-commentary is not an individual and isolated phenomenon, but one that has its own sense of participation in a wider literary line of development, albeit a discontinuous and non-teleological line.

In the first chapter, I consider the vernacular founding of the prosimetrical poetic self-commentary by Dante. In his *Vita Nuova* Dante endeavoured to 'aprire per prosa' ['open by means of prose'] his poetic vision, which in form and content ultimately pointed to a transcendent purpose and destination. He provided more than just an autobiographical account of his poetic and emotional development, more than a writing of his own troubadour *chansonnier*, containing his own *vida* and *razos* along with his lyric. Textual clues in his *libello* suggest that Dante found his way of thinking about poetic self-commentary in Christ's 'clarification' of His parables. In Dante's subsequent *Convivio* [The Banquet, 1304–7], what he haltingly defined as 'scritto, che quasi comento dir si può' ['that writing that could be called something of a commentary'] further developed the poet's vocation to distribute wisdom to all, even to those who did not sit at the philosophers' table. In *The Banquet* Dante significantly adopted the same vocabulary used to describe Christ's multiplication of the fish and loaves (John 6). Dante's procedure continually represented itself as a sign of a greater *mysterium*, calling the reader to renewed exegetical meditation on its as yet obscure truths.

Chapter 2 considers how Giovanni Boccaccio inaugurated the self-gloss form of poetic self-commentary with the marginal notes appended to his *Teseida*. Boccaccio created an epic with a commentary as part of a mimetic strategy intended to confer authority on a vernacular poet, but also to encourage other commentative interventions: 'solo il bomere aiutato da molti ingegni fende la terra' ['only the plowshare aided by many clever talents cleaves the soil [of poetry]']. His earthly vision of the poetic text stands in marked contrast to Dante's, a fact made all the more evident by an examination of Boccaccio's editing of his predecessor's *Vita Nuova*. Boccaccio's editorial decision to relegate Dante's divisions to the margins of the poetic text (following his own procedure in the *Teseida*) upset the co-equal status of the *Vita Nuova*'s three voices (of poetry, prose narrative, and divisions). Boccaccio's work thus highlights crucial differences between commentary and self-commentary.

The third chapter focuses on Lorenzo de' Medici's *Comento alli miei sonetti* [*Commentary on My Sonnets*, 1473–91].[31] Lorenzo's work formally follows the prosimetrical Dantesque precedent. His search for truth also takes the path from death towards an ascendant new life. However, while Dante's self-commentative procedure in the *Vita Nuova* was ruled by the god of Love, Lorenzo invokes Apollo, the god of light and reason. Lorenzo sets up in his proem to the *Comento* no less than the originary Amor-Apollo conflict over the poetic laurel addressed by Ovid in another way in the *Metamorphosis*. Like Apollo's failure to win the mortal Daphne, Lorenzo's self-commentative 'failure' marks the very transformation into something invested with further significance (like that of the laurel tree into poetic wreath). Thus Lorenzo compared his own poetic-interpretive sufficiency with that of Dante, and marked his difference by means of textual divergence from his model.

Chapter 4 presents the other side of the ideological coin in the *Canzoni e sonetti con commento* [*Songs and Sonnets with a Commentary*, 1500] of Lorenzo's longer-living contemporary, Girolamo Benivieni (1453–1542). Benivieni originally circulated his poetry without the prose apparatus, and the prose in this edition had the intent of limiting or closing down its potential poetic significance, perceived as being too open to readerly interpretation. The strictly devout follower of Girolamo Savonarola attempted to recast his youthful lyrics praising earthly love into an encomium of divine Christian love. However, even in a comparatively prescriptive, line-by-line, moralizing allegorization of his hundred lyrics, Benivieni added another veil of significance to the poetic text, by invoking Dante's journey in the hundred cantos of the *Divine Comedy*. Benivieni's work also demanded, by means of its form, not the reader's passive understanding of the poet's spiritual conversion, but an active engagement in re-experiencing that conversion.

It is significant that Benivieni did not entirely succeed in his project. The inclusion of the *Canzoni* in this study is vitally important because it reveals the risks self-commentators run when they try to prescribe a single textual meaning, thereby drawing the life force from the poetic word. The implications of this failure are decidedly counterintuitive for the critic who reads self-commentary as an approximation to commentary, since the success of each depends on diametrically opposed procedures. While a compelling outside commentary may carefully demarcate and mediate a specific reading of the poetry for the commentator's reading audience, the same procedure conducted by the poet can obviate the very reading of the poetry.

The fifth and sixth chapters discuss two late Renaissance experiments with poetic self-commentary: Giordano Bruno's prosimetrical *Eroici furori* [Heroic Frenzies, 1585] and Tommaso Campanella's *Scelta di poesie filosofiche* [Selection of Philosophical Poems, 1613]. Each work radically transforms the mixed genre by drawing the realms of philosophy and prophecy within the scope of poetry in ways not seen before or since then. Bruno's further fragmentation of the poetic-commentative self in dialogue form turns out to be appropriate for this syncretic thinker: the dialogue form, as I have shown, attempts to transcend the narrow demarcations of a subjective perspective while simultaneously seeking to encompass the differing voices it openly acknowledges. In opting to present his philosophic poetry within this Socratic mode, Bruno responds to the dictum, 'know thyself.' The *Heroic Frenzies* also poses important questions about the contamination of self-commentary and interpretive analysis on or by others, especially those attributed to Bruno's contemporary, the poet Luigi Tansillo.

Campanella's philosophical poems, on the other hand, assert an unceasing, implicit questioning of the point of intersection between the poetic and the prophetic word. Fundamental in this regard is the poet's choice of the pseudonym Settimontano Squilla. This choice is motivated less by a desire to conceal his identity than by Campanella's need to create a conceptual space between the poet and the prophetic message. In my reading of Campanella's self-commentary, I argue that the traditional view of his glosses as politically motivated falls short of the mark. Campanella is not solely interested in self-commentary as offering a possible defence of his poetry from misinterpretation by Catholic Reformation authorities. Instead, the pen name Settimontano Squilla, among its other purposes, would seem to liken the poet's function to that of the apocalyptic angel of the 'settima tromba' [seventh trumpet], an identification he cryptically suggests in his glosses on the poetic verses containing variations on his pseudonym.

A brief seventh chapter considers how poetic self-commentary changed after the Renaissance. Campanella's contemporary Alessandro Tassoni (1565–1635) penned a self-commentary in the form of *Dichiarazioni del Signor Gaspare Salviani alla 'Secchia Rapita'* [*Declarations by Mr Gaspare Salviani on 'The Rape of the Bucket,'* 1630]. Certainly by the late Baroque and Enlightenment age of Benedetto Menzini (1646–1704) and Antonio Conti (1677–1749), a special defining characteristic of the Renaissance spirit of poetic self-commentary no longer endured. The self-commentary took on satirical and parodic tones, paralleling the ascendant tone acquired, according to Anthony Grafton, by the literary footnote: 'From Rabelais and Cervantes on, as Walter Rehm showed long ago, the tendency of many writers to support every sentence in their own texts and illustrate every sentence in those of others with some sort of gloss or reference has provided a fruitful source of satirical pleasure. In the eighteenth century, literary footnotes burgeoned and propagated like branches and leaves in a William Morris wallpaper.'[32] With the rise of the new sciences came a push to attain a more objective perspective on one's poetry, entailing a split in the originally non-differentiated role of the poet-prophet implicit in this study's emblematic title, *Hermes' Lyre*.

Part One

Dante and Boccaccio:

The Emergence of Italian Poetic Self-Commentary

1

'You might call it something of a commentary': Defining Terms in Dante's *Vita Nuova* and *Convivio*

> Knock and it will be open unto you.
> – St Augustine

Dante is the touchstone for any study of Italian poetic self-commentary. In fact, one could go so far as to say that Dante is the first theorist of the unique mixed genre. He develops his thought both descriptively and by example in the *Vita Nuova* – Dante's story of his love for Beatrice – and the *Convivio* the unfinished banquet of his glossed philosophical canzoni. Dante's way of composing these works suggests that the whole form – the poetry, together with the self-commentary – becomes a vehicle for poetic expression.

In fact, few issues could be of more central concern to Dante's early *libello* than its consideration as poetic self-commentary. The work opens by pondering its status as a notably different kind of commentary, and the issue of the relationship between poetry and its commentary arises repeatedly and insistently throughout the *Vita Nuova*, manifesting in various ways problematic facets of its nature. These include the risks inherent in speaking of oneself; the different mode that self-commentators, as opposed to commentators on another, follow; the qualitative difference between the true poet and the mere poetaster; what inspires the commentary in the first place; and the circumstances which can affect its outcome. In the *Vita Nuova* we find the earliest formation and development of a self-commentative procedure that will vault Dante's collection of rhymes to the status of the 'first book of Italian literature.'[1]

The famous proem of the *Vita Nuova* sets the stage for an innovative treatment of reading, writing, and commemorating one's life.

> In quella parte del libro della mia memoria dinanzi alla quale poco si potrebbe leggere, si trova una rubrica la quale dice *Incipit Vita Nova*. Sotto la quale rubrica io trovo scripte le parole le quali è mio intendimento d'asemplare in questo libello, e se non tutte, almeno la loro sententia. (1.1)

> [In that part of the book of my memory before which little could be read, a rubric is found that says: *Incipit vita nova* [Here begins the new life]. Beneath this rubric I find written the words that it is my intention to transcribe into this little book: if not all of them, at least their substance. (1.1)

The author's declared intention is to *asemplare* the *sententia* of the words that follow under the *Vita Nova* rubric of his Book of Memory. By *asemplare* Dante implies both 'to transcribe' and 'to exemplify,' suggesting an Augustinian allusion to the excuse of being able to record remembrances of one's own life without such an act being reprehensible. This record avoids censure if it serves as an *exemplum*, imparting to the readers a clear understanding of the evils to be avoided and the good to be embraced. 'Sententia' is also difficult to translate. A rendering of 'essence' or 'substance,' the essential significance, may be the closest approximation. Thus: I find written the words which it is my intention to exemplify in this little book, if not all of them [the words], at least their essential significance.

Dante's role is therefore that of scribe or copyist of the Book of Memory, but his task is a bit more complicated.[2] His actions represent more properly those of a translator (etymologically speaking) of meaning, one who rephrases, that is, a commentator, because he first edits from the whole of words that are present to him and determines the substance of what is written in this 'book,' and then transfers what he has understood to the *Vita Nuova*. Dante emphasizes the locus of his work in memory and the mind (*mens, cum-mente*, with the mind, i.e., comment).[3] The whole of the *Vita Nuova*, then, in its triune formal presentation of narrative, divisions, and poetry, is one: a poetic self-commentary on an intangible book, the 'word' of which it surrounds and to which it continually points. Unlike any other commentary, however, the *Vita Nuova* has entirely incorporated into itself the text on which it should be dependent. This is to say that the New Life has seemingly circumscribed within itself the Old Life of the book of memory, of which 'little could be read.'[4] It is only through a sort of faith in the originary book of memory that readers can make any sense of the way in which Dante defined his *Vita Nuova*.

The relationship between the book (of memory) and its commentary (the *Vita Nuova*) is reflected in, and seeks to be illuminated by, the structure of the *Vita Nuova* itself, between the poetry and the prose that surrounds it. In this prose the traditional conceptualization of Dante as self-glossator or self-interpreter is most evident. However, the purpose of his commentative procedure has not always left his readers unperplexed. Studies that have taken into account aspects of Dante's self-commentary in the *Vita Nuova* have focused almost exclusively on the divisions. More often than not these studies conclude, in a tradition that reaches back to the work's first editor, Giovanni Boccaccio, that the divisions somehow fail to achieve their perceived purpose of making obvious the lyric significance of the poems. It may be possible to view the divisions in a less negative light, however, by taking into consideration interpretive procedures that function somewhat differently from the reader's expectations of commentary.

Boccaccio launched the debate surrounding the formal presentation of the *Vita Nuova* when he moved the divisions from their original position within the body of the text to the margins. The renowned medieval storyteller and Dante exegete justified his decision in the oft-cited postscript of the *Vita Nuova*:

> Maraviglierannosi molti per quello che io avvisi, perché io le divisioni de' sonetti non ho nel testo poste come l'autore del presente libretto le pose. Ma a ciò rispondo due essere state le cagioni. La prima, perciò che le divisioni de' sonetti manifestamente sono dichiarazione di quegli, per che piú tosto chiose appaiono dovere esser che testo; e però chiosa l'ho poste, non testo, non stando l'un con l'altro mescolato bene. Se qui forse dicesse alcuno: – E le teme de' sonetti e canzoni scritte da lui similmente si potrebbon dir chiosa, conciosiacosa che esse sieno non minore dichiarazione di quegli che le divisioni, – dico che, quantunque sieno dichiarazioni, non son dichiarazioni per dichiarare, ma dimostrazioni delle cagioni che a fare lo 'ndusse i sonetti e le canzoni; e appare ancora queste dimostrazioni essere dello intento principale: per che meritamente testo sono e non chiose.

[Many wonder, from what I can tell, why I did not put the divisions of the sonnets in the text as the author did. But to this I answer that there are two reasons. The first is that since the divisions of the sonnets are manifestly declarations of them, they more readily seem to be glosses not text, since the two do not mix well together. If someone were perhaps to say here: 'And the themes of the sonnets and canzoni written by him could similarly be called a gloss, since they are no less declarations of those than the divisions.' I say that, in as much as they are declarations, they are not declarations intended to declare, but proofs of the reasons that induced him to compose the sonnets and canzoni; and so it appears that these proofs are part of the principle intention: thus they are deservedly text and not glosses.][5]

Boccaccio draws a careful distinction between the divisions, which he claims are simply there to declare the poems, and the rest of the prose, the explication of the themes of the poems, which he views as the principle intention of the work. According to Boccaccio, then, the work aims to explain the inspiration of Dante's lyric poetry and the declarations thus somehow detract from this endeavour.

Subsequent editors continued to marginalize the divisions, remove them entirely, or reintegrate them haphazardly into the text until the publication of Michele Barbi's 1907 critical edition.[6] Barbi's reconstitution of the work inspired renewed questioning of the purpose of the divisions. They became a favourite point of example of Crocean *non-poesia*.[7] One popular but mistaken understanding of the divisions emphasizes Dante's ultimate intention to clarify poetic signification.[8] Other influential critics have considered the divisions of little importance or see them as a sign of Dante tending towards an overly prosaic mode.[9]

Charles S. Singleton suggests the first holistic approach to the work, making a convincing argument for the integral manifestation of lyric, narrative, and divisions according to a theologically sub-structured paradigm of the Book of Memory. Antonio d'Andrea goes on to provide the most comprehensive consideration of Dante's *divisio textus* to date. D'Andrea concludes that the divisions were part of the 'significato ultimo del libro, del suo significato poetico: la creazione da parte dello scrittore-protagonista di un'immagine complessa ed elusiva di se stesso, in continuo progresso verso una meta ancora avvolta nel mistero del futuro' ['ultimate significance of the book, of its poetic significance: the creation on the part of the writer-protagonist of a complex and elusive image of himself in continual progress towards a goal still concealed in the mystery of the future'].[10] Mark Musa's passing remark that the divisions perhaps serve a formal, rather than a purely explicative purpose, cannot readily be dismissed.[11] Finally, Robert M. Durling and Ronald L. Martinez advance in *Time and the Crystal* a thought-provoking argument that underscores a Neoplatonic order behind the divisions.

In addition to these perceptive hypotheses, I would like to suggest the possibility that Dante's procedure of dividing his lyrics does precisely what he says it should do: 'la divisione non si fa se non per aprire la sententia della cosa divisa' (7.13) ['Division is made only to open up the meaning of the thing divided'] (14.13). This is to say that the divisions open up the reasoning behind the verse. In other words, were Dante to have attempted to reduce his lyric to an explicitly defined statement of significance, the result would have been a sort of closing of the lyric essence by means of prose. This non-declarative function of the lyric significance the *divisioni* perform helps to explain why the presence of 'doubtful words,' from the passage cited in the Introduction, does not require self-interpretive intervention. Instead, Dante chooses to open his poetry by pointing to numerous other textual settings for plurisignificant interpretive hints.[12] This is the crucial, defining distinction between self-commentary and commentary-by-another, and it comes as no surprise that Dante explicitly draws attention to this separation of roles.

Dante asserts a clear distinction of duties between what he, as glossator of his own text, can say, as opposed to what the 'altro chiosatore' [other glossator] can contribute to the margins. For example, upon Beatrice's passing, Dante discusses the reasons why he does not speak about her death. In the first place, to do so would mean departing from the work's proposal, as evidenced in the proem. Dante implies that to dwell on the actual death would not fit his intention to 'asemplare' its essential significance, that is, how its effect makes Dante an example. It is this essential significance that Dante proceeds to expound, rather than the details of her death. Second, even if it were his intention to speak of those details, Dante states that he does not possess the linguistic means to treat the subject with the proper respect. Lastly, to speak of Beatrice's death would require this self-commentator to be a 'laudatore di [se] medesimo' (19.2) [praiser of himself] (28.2), and not a praiser of his lady, as he had earlier vowed to remain. Therefore, he continues in this same paragraph, 'lascio cotale tractato ad altro chiosatore' ['I leave this matter to some other glossator'].

For Dante, at this point, treating of Beatrice's passing would require him to praise himself, an action 'postrutto biasimevole a chi lo fa' (19.2) ['at all times reprehensible to whoever does it'] (28.2). The excuse that he implicitly makes in the proem, as I have noted, insists on an Augustinian mode of confession as example. Dante will later make explicit this Augustinian connection in the *Convivio*, which asserts that the models for not speaking reprehensibly of oneself are found in Boethius and Augustine. At this time, nevertheless, the threat of reprehension signals a perceived necessity to separate the roles of self-commentator and other commentator. These roles differ also in that Dante and the other glossator are commenting on different texts. Dante expounds, of course, the meaning of the words written in the Book of his Memory. The other glossator, who lacks that 'Book,' works instead to open the *Vita Nuova*'s sense. Given that the other glossator's perspective lies outside the Dantean self, the other commentator does not run the risk of empty boasting and is not constrained to follow the proem's intention. At the same time, however, the other glossator occupies a less privileged vantage point in Dante's hierarchy of textual views: he does not possess the global viewpoint that a familiarity with the original text affords. The scholar of the *Vita Nuova* is yet another step removed from the originating source of the narrative that is the Book of Memory.

The limitation on what self-commentators can say relates to other ways in which they must follow a certain measure in explaining a poem's significance. Fear of revealing too much is proper to the self-commentator: 'io temo d'avere a troppi comunicato lo suo intendimento pur per queste divisioni che facte sono' (10.33) ['I fear having communicated its meaning to too many people already through the divisions made'] (29.22). A rich rhetorical trove is available to Dante as he takes up the challenge of both revealing and guarding the perceived significance of his poems. Two of these ambivalent techniques include the invocation of *dignitas* and of *utilitas*.

The appraisal of worthiness, in fact, determines fundamentally the development and direction of the *Vita Nuova*'s self-commentary. Dante implies that he follows a program in which he expounds what is worthy and passes over or avoids that which lends no merit to, or detracts from the worthiness of, his endeavour. In particular, Dante cites worthiness as a defining factor in the manner in which Love exhorts him to speak to Beatrice; that is, in a manner that is not unmediated: 'Queste parole fa che sieno quasi un mezzo, sì che tu non parli a llei immediatamente, che non è degno' (5.15) ['Let these words be like an intermediary, so that you do not speak to her directly, which is not fitting'] (12.8). Here Dante's words should act as a sort of intermediary, to sanction the discourse that he dares address to his beloved. But given that the mediator is, paradoxically, that very discourse of erotic desire, the unworthiness of Dante's speech to her is unmasked. The mode of discourse, which echoes motifs of *retorica ornata*, nevertheless serves *Eros* in this case and is inscribed within a *trobar clus* economy.[13]

Dante moves from the realm of *eros* to that of *charitas* in his resolution to write verse in praise of Beatrice rather than to address her even with 'mediating words.'[14] The transition is not an easy one. At the end of the *Vita Nuova* Dante recognizes that he falls short of having treated appropriately this 'blessed one.' The wording of his promise – to treat of her 'more worthily' in the future – remains charged with significance.

For the examination of the relationship between the concept of worthiness and Dante's adoption of poetic self-commentary, let one further example suffice. Dante divides the canzone 'Donne ch'avete intelletto d'amore' ['Ladies who have understanding of love'] much more elaborately than the other poems contained in the *Vita Nuova*. He goes on to say that more divisions might help to open further the meaning of the song: 'Questa canzone, acciò che sia meglio intesa, la dividerò più artificiosamente che l'altre cose di sopra' (10.26) ['This canzone, to be better understood, I will divide more subtly than the other things above'] (19.15). But those who do not comprehend its significance with the divisions already made are not of great concern to the poet, since, as I have begun to discuss, Dante fears that its meaning would be too much exposed were the poem to be widely circulated:

> chi non è di tanto ingegno che per queste [divisioni] che sono fatte la possa intendere, a me non dispiace se la mi lascia stare, ché certo io temo d'avere a troppi comunicato lo suo intendimento pur per queste divisioni che fatte sono, s'elli avvenisse che molti le potessero audire. (10.33)

> [Those who have not enough wit to understand it through these [divisions] already made do me no displeasure if they let the matter drop, because in truth I fear having communicated its meaning to too many people already through the divisions made, should it come to pass that many were to hear them.] (19.22)

The very next statement is, in fact, confirmation that the poem had a wide divulgation indeed. A friend happens to hear the song and entreats Dante to speak more about the nature of Love. Dante acknowledges in this way that he is aware he has not actually communicated to too many of his readers the song's recondite meaning. There seems to be a tongue-in-cheek tone to his remark that his reader had 'forse per l'udite parole speranza di me oltre che *degna*' (11.1, emphasis mine) ['perhaps, through the words he heard, more hope in me than I deserved'] (20.1). It is in mediated language that Dante will then *worthily* speak of Love, that is, in the poetically ornate lyric that follows, 'Amor e 'l cor gentil sono una cosa' ['Love and the gentle heart are one thing']. This passage is a sort of paradigm for Dante's 'opening' procedure. First he expresses his fear that he has revealed too much through his exposition of the secrets beneath the poetic veils, then he suggests by means of a narrative example that his readers do not fully comprehend the poem's essence, and finally he demonstrates that the poem can be interpreted indefinitely by exactly the same procedure of ambiguous poetic-self-commentative expression that led to the friend's request in the first place. Dante's procedure effectively blurs every boundary between poetry and its supposed dialectical opposite, the prose commentary, when the prose presents an inventive fiction and the poetry is said to be intended to further explain a previous lyric.

Like the issue of worthiness, that of *utilitas* helps to define how Dante presents the 'explicative' prose, since Dante invokes the usefulness objection for the purpose of underlining the limits of the interpretive contribution. Of possible examples I will cite only two in which Dante effectively calls into question the commentary's usefulness and ontological status. In the first example, the protagonist finds that he is denied an explanation of Love's obscure words because further explanation would not be useful to him. In the second instance, Dante the self-commentator questions the readership of his work and wonders if the self-commentary can be at all useful for such an audience.

After Beatrice denies Dante's *saluto* (both the greeting and the wellbeing of his soul), Love appears to Dante the protagonist and sighing states that it is time for them to put aside their *simulacra*. Love begins to weep, and Dante asks him why. He replies with the sentence, now famous for the interpretive difficulties it presents: 'Ego tamquam centrum circuli cui simili modo se habent circumferentie partes; tu autem non sic' (5.11) ['I am like the centre of a circle, to which all the points of the circumference bear the same relation; you, however, are not'] (12). Dante's use of the Latin is meant to draw the reader's attention specifically to the issue of interpretation and to the differences in understanding between the outsider and the *fedele d'amore*. Dante finds Amor's words difficult to understand and does not receive an explanation because it is not deemed useful: 'Non dimandar più che utile ti sia' (5.12) ['Ask no more than may be useful to you'] (12).[15] Given the resonance this passage has with St Paul's Epistle to the Romans 12:3 – 'non plus sapere quam oportet sapere' ['not to be more wise than it behoveth to be wise'] – the inference might be that this passage is a call for faith, rather than a scientific or rationalistic approach, before a divine mystery.[16]

This becomes a more persuasive argument if taken into consideration with the other invocation concerning utility, in which the self-commentator questions the usefulness of his gloss. I have already touched briefly on this passage concerning the 'obscure words' for which Dante's explanation would be 'in vain, or in truth superfluous' for those readers not equally faithful followers of Love (7.14 [14.14]). The passage recalls obliquely another biblical parallel, that of Christ's speaking in parables. My purpose here is not to interpret the biblical parables but to suggest ways in which Dante may be looking to the Gospel text for an interpretive paradigm.

When the disciples ask Christ why He speaks in such a seemingly opaque way before the people, He responds, 'Because to you it is given to know the mysteries of the kingdom of heaven: but to them it is not given. For he that hath, to him shall be given, and he shall abound: but he that hath not, from him shall be taken away that also which he hath' (Matthew 13:11–12).[17] For the people, or rather those who are not the 'fedeli d'Amore,' according to this analogy, an explanation would be superfluous since 'seeing they see not, and hearing they hear not, neither do they understand' (Matthew 13:13). For the disciples, as for Dante's few to whom he is 'pleased to make these things open' (27.5), an explanation is unnecessary.[18] When Christ 'divides' his parables the division does not really help the disciples to understand, but they usually do not require an explanation in any case:

> 'Have ye understood all these [parables]?'
> They said to him: 'Yes.'
> He said unto them: Therefore every scribe instructed in the kingdom of heaven is like to a man that is a householder, who bringeth forth, out of his treasure new things and old.' (Matthew 13:51–52)

It is important to emphasize that what some have seen as Dante's wilfully obscurantistic tendencies may actually serve a very different purpose than to confuse, a purpose perhaps similar to that announced in Paul's second letter to the Corinthians (4:1–4):

> 'Seeing we have this ministration, according as we have obtained mercy, we faint not; but we renounce the hidden things of dishonesty, not walking in craftiness, or adulterating the word of God; but, by manifestation of the truth commending ourselves to every man's conscience, in the sight of God. And if our gospel be also hid, it is hid to them that are lost, in whom the god of this world hath blinded the minds of the unbelievers, that the light of the gospel of glory of Christ, who is the image of God, should not shine unto them.'

While there is little evidence to prove that Dante had at the time of the *Vita Nuova* a Gospel model for what is perceived as his veiled language, the *Convivio* strongly implies such a basis.

Apart from the distinction Dante makes between his own commentary and that of the other glossator, he delineates another separation between poets and mere poetasters. The difference between these two consists significantly in the ability to 'open by means of prose' a lyric composition. Dante presents a sort of defence of vernacular poetry vis-à-vis Latin poetry, and an argument for the underlying rationality of poetic tropes:

> Dunque, se noi vedemo che li poete ànno parlato alle cose inanimate sì come se avessero senso o ragione, e fattele parlare insieme; e non solamente cose vere, ma cose non vere: cioè che detto ànno, di cose le quali non sono, che parlano, e detto che molti accidenti parlano, sì come se fossero sustantie e uomini, degno è lo dicitore per rima di fare lo somigliante; ma non sanza ragione alcuna, ma con ragione la quale poscia sia possibile d'aprire per prosa. (16.8)

> [Therefore, if we see that poets have addressed inanimate things as if they had sense and reason, and have made them speak to each other: and not only of true things but of things not true: that is, they have said of things non-existent that they speak, and said that many accidents speak as if they were substances and human beings; worthy is the vernacular writer in rhyme to do the same, but not without a reason, rather with a reason that is then possible to disclose in prose.] (25.8)

The vernacular writer ('dicitore per rima'), he says, has the same license to speak to inanimate things, to have them speak among themselves, or to employ the rhetorical trope of personification as the Latin poets do. However, like the Latin poets, vernacular rhymers who put things under the veil of a figure or give them a rhetorical colour, must not do so without good reason and must be able to explain their motivations when asked to do so. Dante continues:

> Grande vergogna sarebbe a colui che rimasse cose sotto vesta di figura o di colore rectorico, e poscia domandato non sapesse denudare le sue parole da cotale vesta, in guisa che avessero verace intendimento. E questo mio primo amico e io ne sapemo bene di quelli che così rimano stoltamente. (16.10)

> [A great shame would befall those who put things under the veil of a figure or rhetorical colour and then, when asked, could not unveil their words in a way that would show their true reasoning. And this best friend of mine and I know well some who rhyme so senselessly.] (25.10)

Critics have already pointed out that Dante is not talking here about the versifier's ability to render in a literal exposition the figurative language of the poem.[19] Dante links this stripping away of the figurative veils to the *divisioni*, in particular: 'Questo sonetto non divido in parti, però che la divisione non si fa se non per aprire la sententia della cosa divisa; onde con ciò sia cosa che per la sua ragionata cagione assai sia manifesto, non à mestiere di divisione' (7.13). ['This sonnet I do not divide into parts, because division is made only to open up the meaning of the thing divided; hence, given that it is quite evident through its narrated cause, it needs no division'] (14.13).

At first glance, Dante's prose accompaniments to his sonnets and canzoni in the *Vita Nuova* would seem to address this need to strip away the rhetorical ornamentations of the poetic text to reveal its true, hidden meaning. What is apparent upon closer examination, however, is that Dante draws attention in this way to the very procedure his prose fails to accomplish. Nowhere in the *Vita Nuova* is the meaning of Dante's poetry left naked. This fact has provoked some critics to denounce the *divisioni* as failing to live up to their perceived purpose of denuding the poetry: 'Dante's prosaic practice in the *Vita Nuova* in no way conforms to the agenda of "denudation" called for by chapter XXV. The digression into literary theory is exceptional in the deep sense of the word, for it not only interrupts the narrative but also contradicts the deepest intention of its enterprise. Except for the deliberate decomposition of the lord of love, nowhere does Dante engage in the systematic divestment of figurative language which he recommended in chapter XXV. Yet he would have us believe that in his prose, and especially in the *divisioni*, or subdivisions of his poems, he is actually laying bare the poems' "true meaning." Dante is quite explicit about the function of these *divisioni*: they divest the poems of their poetic dress.'[20] True, Dante does not rephrase in more understandable prose what he expresses in his poems. However, might it be possible that he wishes to allow the form of poetic expression to communicate an inner essence that is *ragionata* (not unfounded)?

Dante acknowledges that various interpretations of a given poem or symbol exist and are possible, but one, his own, is preferable to the others. This is apparent from his discussion of the association between Beatrice and the number nine:

> Questa è una ragione di ciò. Ma più sottilmente pensando, e secondo la infallibile veritade, questo numero fue ella medesima: per similitudine dico, e ciò intendo così ... Forse ancora per più sottile persona si vederebbe più sottile ragione in ciò; ma questa è quella che io ne veggio, e che più mi piace.' (19.6–7)

> [This is one reason for it; but if we consider more subtly and according to infallible truth, this number was herself; I speak by similitude, and I explicate it thusly ... Perhaps a still more subtle person might see in this matter a more subtle reason; but this is the one I see in it, and which most pleases me.] (29.3–4)

Perhaps a more clever person could find other motivations behind all of the occurrences of the number nine, Dante asserts, but he prefers the identification of her with this number, the root of which is the Trinity.

Furthermore, Dante asserts himself to be judge of the truth-content of the contributions of others. When those in his circle of poets and friends offer interpretations of a sonnet describing the dream in which Love feeds Dante's flaming heart to Beatrice, the self-commentator states, 'A questo sonetto fu risposto da molti, e di diverse sententie ... Lo verace iuditio del detto sogno non fu veduto allora per alcuno, ma ora è manifestissimo alli più semplici' (2.1–2). ['This sonnet was answered by many and by diverse interpretations ... The true meaning of the said dream was not seen by anyone then, but now it is perfectly clear to the simplest'] (3.14–15). Dante indicates in language charged with biblical and teleological implications that there is one evident and correct interpretation of the given sonnet, that he is the one with the authority to define it, and that in the end his exegetical reading will be confirmed. Dante's words echo such biblical passages as Matthew 11:25: 'At that time Jesus answered and said, "I confess to thee, O, Father, Lord of heaven and earth, because thou has hid these things from the wise and the prudent, and hast revealed them to little ones"' and Matthew 10:26: 'For nothing is covered that shall not be revealed: nor hid that shall not be known.'[21]

The various interpretive procedures Dante has adopted favour language that, while it suggests the unveiling of poetic significance, guards it from the gaze of the irreverent or from those not chosen to know it. For these reasons it might be possible to consider that Dante models his commentary of the poems not only on the *explication du texte* characteristic of the Scholastic *divisio textus*,[22] but also on the interpretive procedure called for by the Provençal *trobar clus* or by Christ's speaking in parables. These two modes certainly resemble the stylistic distinctions made by classical writers like Theophrastus. The first mode, termed dialectic, presents plain, unadorned language suited to factual statement and logical disputation. The second, rhetoric, is the grand style of ornamental language better suited to the expression or influence of emotion. The bringing together of these two interpretive procedures seems to suggest that in 'opening [his poetry] by means of prose,' Dante somehow had in mind an opening to infinite poetic complexity, which he develops further in the *Convivio*. Thus, Dante's opening by means of prose comes to have a much different meaning than is implied in its use as a Scholastic procedure, that is, rephrasing the metaphorical in non-metaphorical terms.

The divisions also serve a formal purpose, of course, in that when they follow the poems, they are 'wedded' to them, acting as natural and rightful companions. A change takes place after Beatrice's death, however, and to reflect her separation from her faithful one in this life, Dante declares that the poems will be made to seem more widowed by having nothing follow them: 'E acciò che questa canzone paia rimanere più vedova dopo lo suo fine, la dividerò prima ch'io la scriva; e cotale modo terrò da qui innanzi' (20.2) ['And so that this canzone may seem to remain all the more widowed after its end, I will divide it before I transcribe it; and I will hold to such a mode from now on'] (31.2). But the widowed condition of the poems also reflects the condition of the city, as evidenced by the citation of the exordium of Lamentations that interrupts the canzone 'Sì lungiamente m'à tenuto Amore' ['So long a time has Love kept me a slave'] after the first stanza: '*Quomodo sedet sola civitas plena populo! facta est quasi vidua domina gentium*' (19.1) ['How doth the city sit solitary that was full of people! How is she become a widow, she that was great among the nations!'] (28.1). After Beatrice dies, Dante likens the city to a widow stripped of every dignity (19.8 [30.1]). In fact, the larger context of this passage deserves closer examination:

> Poi che fue partita da questo secolo, rimase tutta la sopradecta cittade quasi vedova dispogliata da ogni dignitade. Onde io, ancora lagrimando in questa desolata cittade, scrissi alli principi della terra alquanto della sua conditione, pigliando quello cominciamento di Yeremia profeta *Quomodo sedet sola civitas*. E questo dico acciò che altri non si maravigli perché io l'abbia allegato di sopra, quasi come entrata de la nuova materia che apresso viene.
>
> [After she had departed from this century, the entire aforementioned city was left like a widow dispossessed of every dignity; hence, still weeping in this desolate city, I wrote to the princes of the earth somewhat about its condition, taking the beginning from Jeremiah the prophet, who says: *Quomodo sedet sola civitas* [How solitary lies the city]. And I say this so that no one may wonder why I have cited it above as the introduction to the new matter that comes after.]

'Da questo secolo' suggests 'from this worldly life [to the divine one],' but also, in its temporal resonances, 'from the mortal life [to the eternal].' Later, in fact, Dante will refer to Beatrice as a 'citizen of life eternal' (23.1 [34.1]). The phrase also serves to link this passage with that of the pilgrims, in which Dante refers periphrastically to the city of Florence as 'la cittade ove nacque e vivette e morio la gentilissima donna' (29.1) ['the city where the most noble lady was born, lived, and died'] (40.1). In the same chapter Dante explains that the word 'pilgrim' may be understood in two ways, 'in uno largo e in uno strecto: in largo, in quanto è peregrino chiunque è fuori della sua patria; in modo strecto non s'intende peregrino se non chi va verso la Casa di Sa' Iacopo o riede' (29.6) ['one broad and the other strict: in the broad sense, in that a pilgrim is anyone outside one's country; in the strict sense no one is considered a pilgrim but who goes to the house of Saint James or returns from there'] (40.6). Beatrice is a citizen, because she is in her rightful country of heaven; the pilgrims and Dante, by implication then, are outsiders.

Dante never explicitly mentions Florence by name in the *Vita Nuova*. In the passage quoted above, it is only the 'abovementioned city.' Florence represents, not a specific geographical place or, as in his later works, Dante's beloved homeland in this life, but rather a space of death, and most significantly, of exile. For the young Dante in mourning, the desolate city is his own Old Testament desert. It is precisely when Dante ventures outside the city that he encounters *presence*, such as the presence of his Lord during his first travels:

> Apresso la morte di questa donna alquanti die, avenne cosa per la quale me convenne partire della sopradecta cittade e ... l'andare mi dispiacea sì, che quasi li sospiri non poteano disfogare l'angoscia ... E però lo dolcissimo signore, lo quale mi signoreggiava per la virtù della gentilissima donna, nella mia ymaginatione apparve. (4.1–3)

> [A few days after the death of this lady something happened that made it necessary for me to leave the aforementioned city ... and the journey so displeased me that my sighs could hardly relieve the anguish ... Therefore, the sweetest Lord, who ruled me through the power of the most gentle lady, appeared.] (9.1–3)

Here again Dante associates the city with death, the death of one of Beatrice's companions. When Dante ventures from the city a second time, he is inspired to write his most complex and esteemed canzone, 'Donne ch'avete intelletto d'amore' (10.15 [19.1]). At other times, when the young poet escapes from the city to the most secret chamber of his heart, for example, he may otherwise come into the presence of his Lord. There is a strong opposition, then, between the earthly city and that which God and His citizens inhabit. Dante suggests that he must leave the earthly city in order to come into contact with the beloved ones he seeks.

Dante takes Jeremiah's mode of prophecy as his own beginning ('cominciamento'). Prophecy, like the poetry inspired outside the city, is exiled speech. It does not belong to the present, but stands as the point of conversion between the past – the poet's memories – and the future.[23] The 'entrata' of the phrase 'quasi come entrata de la nuova materia' ['as the introduction to the new matter'] is like the gate to the city and signals the boundary of that space, which is the new material and the new life. At the same time, this 'quasi ... entrata' marks the self-commentary itself, which seeks to 'open' and to serve as an opening to the exiled speech. The 'quasi ... entrata' finds rearticulation in the 'quasi comento' of the *Convivio*, which follows.

Dante devotes most of the first book of his unfinished *Convivio* to an examination of the nature, motivation, and purpose of self-commentary. He does not however, call the exegetical prose that binds together his philosophical lyrics to comprise the *Convivio* self-commentary. His definition of the text is never fixed, in fact, and oscillates between such terms as 'esposizione' ['exposition'] (1.1.18), 'la presente opera' ['the present work'] (1.1.16), 'la presente scrittura' ['the present writing'] (1.2.1), and 'lo mio scritto, che quasi comento dir si può' ['my writing, which one could call something of a commentary'] (1.3.2).[24] Dante critics have taken great pains to inscribe the *Convivio* within the medieval commentary tradition by reading Dante's 'scritto, che quasi comento dir si può' as an approximation of this tradition, sometimes going so far as to say that the work 'is quite clearly based on the medieval genre of the commentary on an author; indeed, Dante calls it 'quasi comento,' a kind of commentary.'[25] Despite the fact that Dante on occasion refers to his exegetical prose as a 'comento' or 'commento,' his reluctance to assign the work to any determinant literary category provides an important indication of his conceptualization of the work. This reluctance informs our understanding not only of the work's formal structure, but also of its thematic content. I argue that while it is true that Dante overtly models his *Convivio* on the *accessus ad auctores*, he does so in order to mark the vitally important difference between his work and that commentary tradition.[26]

Dante's procedure of framing his canzoni mimics to a certain extent the description of *materia, intentio, finis, modus tractandi, titulus libri*, and *ordo* [subject, intent, aim, approach, title of the book, and its order], which exemplify some important aspects of the traditional *accessus ad auctores*. In the first chapter of the proem Dante specifies that he wishes his work to be called the *Convivio*, and that it is to consist of fourteen canzoni, treating of love and virtue, with a prose accompaniment intended to shed some light on the obscurities of the songs. The purpose of the work, he states, is to share wisdom with those who could not otherwise partake of philosophy, the 'bread of angels.' Although Dante offers these and other explications worthy of the most conscientious *accessus* writer, he nevertheless appears aware of the theoretical difficulties inherent in asserting himself as a commentator on his own work.[27]

Dante would hardly fit the definition of commentator typically proffered in medieval treatises, which tend to stress as requisites writing on the works *of others* and illuminating so-called obscure sayings. Conrad of Hirsau, for example, states: 'Commentatores sunt qui solent ex paucis multa cogitare et *obscura dicta aliorum dilucidare*' ['Commentators are those who can work out many ideas, beginning with just a few facts and *illuminate the obscure sayings of others*'].[28] Indeed, Dante anticipates readers' criticism of his prose on both of these points. Rhetoricians, he states, do not allow us to speak of ourselves because we cannot be impartial judges of our own character and cannot avoid praising or blaming ourselves. Dante cites only two exceptions to this prohibition: self-commentary becomes acceptable when great danger or infamy cannot otherwise be avoided, and when useful instruction may be imparted by personal example. The author then declares that he should not be censured for speaking of himself: like Boethius, he must defend himself against the infamy of exile; like St Augustine, he hopes his personal testimony can direct others along a path of human and divine wisdom.

Dante also anticipates that some readers may blame him for not clarifying the obscure sayings of his philosophical canzoni. He compares his prose writing in this context to a man sent with the express duty of breaking up a fight who starts another rift himself:

> Degna di molta riprensione è quella cosa che, ordinata a tòrre alcuno difetto, per se medesima quello induce; sì come quelli che fosse mandato a partire una rissa, e prima che partisse quella, ne iniziasse un'altra. E però che lo mio pane è purgato da una parte, convienlomi purgare dall'altra, per fuggire questa riprensione.

> [Anything is deserving of severe censure which itself brings about the very defect it is intended to remove, as would a person sent to break up a fight who, before he had broken up the first, stirred up another. Now that my bread is purified in one respect, I must purify it in another if I am to escape such censure.] (1.3.1–2)

Similarly, Dante's prose is intended to shed light on the dark and difficult aspects of his verse, but risks itself being accused of obscurantism. The fact that his poetry is cloaked under the veils of allegory, he writes, means that no one can perceive its underlying, true meaning unless he himself reveals it. What is more, Dante admits, the difficulty of his prose is deliberate. This characteristic, which would be particularly reprehensible in a mere commentary, actually seems necessary in a self-commentary.

Dante then explains why his prose is deliberately difficult ('duro,' 1.3.2). The citizens of his native Florence consigned him to wander like a pilgrim through virtually all the regions to which the Italian tongue extends (1.3.4), and Dante believes that his reputation as a man and poet has been greatly diminished. He continues that 'la fama, oltre la veritade si sciampia; e ... la presenza oltre la veritade stringe' ['renown inflates things with respect to the truth, and ... presence diminishes things with respect to the truth'] (1.3.6). To compensate for the damage done to his reputation, 'conviemmi che con più alto stilo dea, [al]la presente opera un poco di gravezza, per la quale paia di maggiore autoritade. E questa scusa basti alla fortezza del mio comento' ['it is fitting that I should add, with a loftier style, a little weight to the present work, so that it may seem to take on an air of greater authority. This should suffice to excuse the gravity of my commentary'] (1.4.13–14).[29]

Establishing authority is central to the medieval poet's project.[30] The tension inherent in establishing poetic authority resides in reconciling the often paradoxical tasks of asserting a degree of creative autonomy while at the same time earning a place for oneself *within* a literary tradition. In the Middle Ages, writing a book was not in itself sufficient to be considered an author, or *auctor*. An *auctor* was one who wrote, it is true, but more specifically one who wrote with authority, according to rigorous notions of authenticity and merited authoritativeness.[31] Until roughly Dante's generation, *auctor* referred exclusively to writers revered over a long period of time.[32] The challenge for writers in the thirteenth, fourteenth, and fifteenth centuries was to somehow transfer *auctoritas* 'from the divine realm to the human.'[33] Commentary provided one of the primary means of explicitly or implicitly assigning a degree of prestige to a work, since this apparatus conventionally accompanied texts of revered *auctoritates*. Some of the hermeneutic glosses written by Dante appear to be imaginative extensions of techniques previously developed in exegetic theory.

According to Dante's view of authority, a deliberately weighty, loftier style earns the authoritative esteem of others. At first glance, his self-commentary would seem at odds with traditional aims of the commentary-by-another, which seeks to clarify, educate, and impart the moral sense of poetry. There is a discernible, qualified difference between 'comento' and 'quasi comento.' The former, the commentary-by-another, endeavours to avoid assigning significance on any level but the literal one, rigorously reducing even the most allegorical, tropological, and anagogic senses to the letter of its exposition. The 'quasi comento,' however, which is what I understand to be poetic self-commentary in this case, is an extension of the poet's own word. It surrounds the poetry with another veil of significance and demands for itself further interpretation. Poetic self-commentary's inevitably polysemous essence inscribes within itself the promise of revelation.[34]

Dante believes that his deliberately difficult self-commentary, with its higher style, must add a weight of authority and compensate for the lower opinion others may have of him and his work since his exile. Dante felt compelled to convince a wide audience of the seriousness of purpose contained in what he feared would be perceived as lyrics that speak of a mere earthly love: 'Temo la infamia di tanta passione avere seguita, quanto concepe chi legge le sopra nominate canzoni in me avere segnoreggiata; la quale infamia si cessa, per lo presente di me parlare, interamente, lo quale mostra che non passione ma vertù sia stata la movente cagione' ['I fear the disgrace of being thought to have given myself over to a passion so great that it ruled my life, which is how the canzoni mentioned above are understood. This disgrace is entirely removed by what I say of myself here, for this shows that my actions have been ruled not by passion but by virtue'] (1.2.16). In order to attain this wide respect, the self-commentator must look well beyond the choice of the vernacular to consider the register of language in its readily perceivable form, since:

> La maggiore parte delli uomini vivono secondo senso e non secondo ragione, a guisa di pargoli; e questi cotali non conoscono le cose se non semplicemente di fuori, e la loro bontade, la quale a debito fine è ordinata, non veggiono, per ciò che hanno chiusi li occhi della ragione, li quali passano a veder quello. Onde tosto veggiono tutto ciò che ponno, e giudicano secondo la loro veduta.
>
> [The majority of men live according to the sense and not according to reason, like children; as such they do not understand things except simply by their exterior, and they do not perceive the goodness of things, which is

ordained to a proper end, because they keep shut the eyes of reason which penetrate to a vision of it. Therefore, they quickly see all that they are able to, and judge according to their sight.] (1.4.3)

However, Dante emphasizes the necessity of progressing from external appearance, or form, to the central substance or essence of his text:

> E con ciò sia cosa che la vera intenzione mia fosse altra che quella che di fuori mostrano le canzoni predette, per allegorica esposizione quelle intendo mostrare, appresso la litterale istoria ragionata; sì che l'una ragione e l'altra darà sapore a coloro che a questa cena sono convitati.
>
> [Since my true meaning was other than what the previously mentioned canzoni outwardly reveal, I intend to explain these canzoni by means of an allegorical exposition, after having discussed the literal account, so that both arguments will be savored by those who have been invited to this supper.] (1.1.18)[35]

Dante continually strives to point beyond the form of the word to its substance, as evidenced by his procedure of turning the 'fictive words' from what they say into what they mean.[36]

Related to this quest for the *essence*, the true meaning of his poetry, is *absence*, the exile, which necessitates his prose. In fact, exile is the raison d'être of the *Convivio*, for it is the cause of his initial 'excuse':

> Ahi, piaciuto fosse al dispensatore dell'universo che la cagione della mia scusa mai non fosse stata! ché né altri contr'a me avria fallato, né io sofferto avria pena ingiustamente, pena, dico, d'essilio e di povertate.
>
> [Oh if only it had pleased the Dispensator of the universe that the reason for my excuse never existed! For in that case others would not have mistakenly been against me, nor would I have suffered punishment unjustly, the punishment, I say, of exile and poverty.] (1.3.3)

Dante compares himself to a ship without sail or rudder, tossed about by poverty's dry wind to different ports, inlets, and shores. The *Convivio* is a journey at the end of which he hopes to find a safe and praiseworthy port.[37] On one level, Dante is doubtless addressing the citizens of Florence, hoping for an end to his exile and a safe return to the homeland.[38] But on a deeper level, the work represented for Dante's readers a journey with him towards a truth extending beyond the strictly political to describe a broader, metaphysical state of exile from God's essence.

In fact, Dante's reference to the exile of the Intelligences from the heavenly fatherland in his exposition of the second canzone suggests the necessity of this interpretive leap:

> Dico adunque: *Ogni Intelletto di là su la mira*: dove è da sapere che 'di là su' dico, faccendo relazione a Dio che dinanzi è menzionato; e per questo escludo le Intelligenze che sono in essilio della superna patria, le quali filosofare non possono, però che amore in loro è del tutto spento, e a filosofare, come già detto è, è necessario amore.

> [I then say: *Every Intellect there on high gazes on her*. It should be explained here that by the words 'there on high' I indicate a relationship to God, who has already been mentioned; and I thereby exclude the Intelligences who live in exile from their heavenly fatherland, who cannot philosophize, because in them love is entirely extinct, and, as has been explained, love is intrinsic to philosophizing.] (3.13.2)[39]

The high sea is thus equated with the difficult central nexus of his prose discourse, and it is only from the open sea that the poet can begin to fathom the distance between the beautiful form of the poetry and its essential truth. While the poems' form has long been present, Dante states, their essence has been absent to his readers, and his own continued absence from Florence, and the stigma attached to it, makes the search for the essence particularly urgent.

Perhaps Dante's beloved Florence embodies the very deficiency of place that blocks Dante's path to higher learning. According to Dante, there are two reasons, apart from physical impediments and moral depravity, why man is unable to pursue wisdom. The first owes to the unavoidable constraint of family and civic responsibilities, the second is precisely the aforementioned deficiency of place:

> Di fuori dall'uomo possono essere similemente due cagioni intese, l'una delle quali è induttrice di necessitade, l'altra di pigrizia. La prima è la cura familiare e civile, la quale convenevolmente a sé tiene delli uomini lo maggior numero, sì che in ozio di speculazione esser non possono. L'altra è lo difetto del luogo dove la persona è nata e nutrita, che tal ora sarà da ogni studio non solamente privato, ma da gente studiosa lontano.

[Likewise two causes external to man can be specified, one resulting in unavoidable constraint, the other in laziness. The first is family and civic responsibilities, which quite properly absorb the energies of the majority of men, with the result that they cannot find the leisure required for cultivating the mind. The other is a deficiency in the place where a person is born and raised: this is sometimes such that it not only lacks any institute of higher learning, but is even remote from the company of learned people.] (1.1.4)

In other words, the exile, which abruptly altered Dante's familial duties and deprived him of his civic ones, allowed for the *speculazione* that is the *Convivio*. In citing the deficiency of place, apart from alluding in the most literal sense to the obstacle to learning posed by a city without a university, Dante also seems to invoke a certain virtue founded outside of the city. The place of exile paradoxically becomes the place of presence in its metaphysical connotations.

This hermeneutic dynamic in Dante's prose might be expressed in another way as a move between paraphrasis and periphrasis. Both procedures aim to expose the meaning of a text by means of another form of expression. Paraphrasis, beyond indicating close relation or substitution, implies being 'almost' like the paralleled text, or in some way constituting a 'faulty' representation of it or as somehow subsidiary or accessory to the original text. Periphrasis, on the other hand, involves a necessarily longer or more circuitous process of arriving at the ultimate significance of the message. Dante's paraphrastic self-commentary can only attempt to arrive at the core truth of the poetic word by an exilic periphrasis. In this way, the passage is a journey, as well as the textual representation of meaning.

It should come as no surprise, then, that Dante, in the context of the poet's reputation in exile, raises up the reputation of the prophet, who is inevitably less honoured in his own country: 'E questo è quello per che ciascuno profeta è meno onorato nella sua patria' ['And this is [the reason] why each prophet is less honoured in his own country'] (1.4.11). The vatic role depends on a word whose necessary non-presence may point to the essence of an ineffable Other. The prose self-commentary identified with and necessitated by the poet's exile allows Dante to circumnavigate, and thereby attempt to *circumscribe*, the essence which remains unknowable. Both poet and prophet must leave the fatherland in order to glean the perspective of the mystery beyond, and thus to intuit its true message.

The *Convivio* turns out to be less of an aberration among Dante's works than readers might assume at first glance. It is not a philosophical detour from the path towards God that will require countless readings of the *Comedy* in a palinodic key. Instead, it is an important, integral step in Dante's lifelong poetic development.[40] What is more, it is precisely in the conceptualization of the self-commentary that Dante comes to bridge the autobiographical setting of early love lyrics and the *Divine Comedy*.

The relationship between the Incarnate Word and the human poetic act in their ontological functionality as vehicles to God has already been demonstrated in the context of the *Vita Nuova* and the *Divine Comedy*.[41] Its role in the *Convivio*, however, has yet to be understood. The primary metaphor of Dante's text is announced within its title. Dante presents his book as a banquet at which, out of fraternal generosity, he will serve the bread of philosophical and theological wisdom. While the metaphor of the meal certainly refers to philosophical wisdom in the Aristotelian context,[42] it also has important Christian theological and liturgical resonances, invoking the Last Supper and the eucharistic offering.[43]

In the fourteen proposed courses of Dante's banquet, his canzoni provide the meat while the bread is his self-commentary, necessary, Dante asserts, if the philosophical poems are to be properly digested. He thus proposes to divide his food in order that he may satisfy many people, and in particular, the crowds of the non-Latin literate: 'Questo sarà quello pane orzato del quale si satolleranno migliaia, e a me ne soverchieranno le sporte piene' ['This [commentary] will be that fine barley bread by which thousands will be amply satisfied, while for me there will be basketsful left over to enjoy'] (1.13.12).[44] The barley bread by which thousands shall be satiated and the bounty of overflowing baskets allude, of course, to the narration of the multiplication of the fish and loaves in the Gospel (John 6:1–13, in particular 6:11–13): 'And Jesus took the loaves: and when he had given thanks, he distributed to them that were set down. In like manner also of the fishes, as much as they would. And when they were filled, he said to his disciples: Gather up the fragments that remain, lest they be lost. They gathered up therefore, and filled twelve baskets with the fragments of the five barley loaves, which remained over and above to them that had eaten.'[45]

Dante's description mirrors that of the sacred text. For example, Dante emphasizes barley as the bread's distinguishing ingredient ['panibus hordiaceis'] and the fact that a vast number of men ['viri numero quasi quinque milia'] (John 6: 10) were satiated and still the disciples were able to fill twelve baskets with the food that was left ['impleverunt duodecim cophinos fragmentorum']. Christ subsequently makes explicit the association between the bread, Himself, and the spiritual food that provides eternal sustenance: 'For the bread of God is that which cometh down from heaven, and giveth life to the world. They said therefore unto him: Lord, give us always this bread. And Jesus said to them: I am the bread of life: he that cometh to me shall not hunger: and he that believeth in me shall never thirst' (John 6:33–35).

The metaphor of bread is perhaps the most overt of a series of allusions in the *Convivio* to the Gospel narratives.[46] Dante's assertion that prophets do not receive honour in their own countries is a rearticulation of Christ's own words (John 4:44).[47] In another example, Dante exhorts his readers to judge according to right reason, instead of by their senses and by their perception of the mere exterior form of things just as Christ said, 'Judge not according to the appearance, but judge just judgment' (John 7:24). Moreover, Dante, in addition to citing Boethius and St Augustine as justification for speaking about himself, evidently refers to a Christological model as well: 'The Pharisees therefore said to him Thou givest testimony of thyself: thy testimony is not true. Jesus answered, and said to them: Although I give testimony of myself, my testimony is true' (John 8:13–14).

The 'hard' or difficult quality of Dante's words also seems to deliberately echo that of Christ's words: 'These things he said, teaching in the synagogue, in Capharnaum. Many therefore of his disciples, hearing it said: This saying is hard [Durus est hic sermo], and who can hear it?' (John 6:60–61). This is, in fact, a turning point in the Gospel narrative, for it is here that the followers of Christ split among themselves. Jesus pronounces hard words concerning the significance of flesh and blood, death and eternal life, and incomprehensible words versus belief in the spirit of the Word, after which 'many of his disciples went back and walked no more with Him' (John 6:67). The explanation could be contrasted with Christ's speaking in parables. While the parable is intended to reveal some aspect of God's teleological mission in the person and message of His Son, Jesus recognizes that the parables conceal His meaning at the same time that they are the means of delivering it. The parable of the sower in Mark 4:1–20 can serve as a representative example. This parable is a particularly important one, without which, Jesus implies, his hearers cannot understand the others.[48]

After Jesus had spoken of the diverse ends of the sowers' seeds and He was alone with His disciples, the twelve asked Him what the parable meant. He responded to their question saying, 'To you is given to know the mystery of the kingdom of God: but to them that are without, all things are done in parables: That seeing they may see and not perceive; and hearing they may hear, and not understand: lest at any time they should be converted and their sins should be forgiven them' (Mark 4:11–12). While the disciples yearn for greater clarification, their very act of the tending towards, and tending of, the Word places these few within the realm of promise of the ultimate clarity of the mystery. Jesus' speech, in this context, does not seem as much purposefully exclusionary as it does incomprehensible to those who do not enter into its mode of essential (of the spirit) purpose and do not ponder the enunciation as such (in its form or flesh).[49]

From this consideration of the 'durezza' or 'fortezza' of Christ's words comes the most compelling evidence yet for Dante's conceptualization of his 'quasi comento' in terms that somehow go beyond those presented by the *accessus ad auctores* tradition, strictly speaking. Christ's words are difficult to understand because they concern the mysterious nature of God. Anything Christ says, and actually everything He is, becomes a sort of (that is, a 'quasi-') commentary on God's Truth. Furthermore, given the Trinitarian consubstantiality of God's nature, the Word could perhaps be rightly said to be a sort of *self-commentary*.

Having said this, one can see that Dante's own self-commentary is intended to provide a human reflection of the same revelation of Truth, naturally aware of its inevitable failure in human expression. Dante's role as receiver-dispensator parallels that of Christ, who receives the message from God the Father and distributes it to mankind.[50] The objective of Dante's 'quasi comento,' the unveiling of essential Truth, means that his language too must be difficult. The poet notes this necessary difficulty in the context of explaining the unity of body and soul. This is yet another example of Dante's preoccupation with the relationship between form and essence, which he sees as an act of production:

> Non si maravigli alcuno, s'io parlo sì che par forte ad intendere; ché a me medesimo pare maraviglia, come cotale produzione si può pur conchiudere e collo intelletto vedere. Non è cosa da manifestare a lingua, lingua, dico

veramente, volgare. Per che io voglio dire come l'Apostolo: 'O altezza delle divizie e della scienza di Dio, come sono incomprensibili li [tuoi] giudicii e investigabili le [tue] vie!'

[No one should wonder if what I am saying here seems hard to understand, for I myself find it a wonder, how one can actually comprehend and perceive by the intellect how it is brought into being. This is not something that can be clearly put into language, that language, I say, which is truly vernacular. Thus I wish to say, like the Apostle: 'How high is the wisdom and knowledge of God! How unfathomable are your judgments, how inscrutable your ways!'] (4.21.6)[51]

The lofty ambitions of Dante's project to mediate the divulgation of his poetic essence – and His Poetic Essence – are necessarily doomed to failure.[52] However, a reader sensitive to the possibility of such a scope in the *Convivio* has the impression that at least until the project was truncated, this fusion of poetry and 'quasi comento' was the form Dante believed could come closest to embodying such a plenary Sense.

While it may seem something of a stretch to infer so much on the basis of a single-word qualifier like 'quasi' before 'comento,' Dante himself reiterates his unusual use of the term 'quasi.' At one point he identifies himself with those who possess knowledge and are 'quasi fonte vivo' [like a living fountain] by whose waters the natural thirst of wisdom is quenched: 'coloro che sanno porgono de la loro buona ricchezza a li veri poveri, e sono quasi fonte vivo, della cui acqua si refrigera la naturale sete [del sapere] che di sopra è nominata. E io adunque' ['Those who possess knowledge always give generously from their true wealth to those who really are poor, and they are like a living fountain whose waters slake the natural thirst spoken of above. And so I'] (1.1.9–10). Dante alludes to Aristotle's *Metaphysics*, which he paraphrases in the opening line of the *Convivio* ('Just as the Philosopher in the beginning of his First Philosophy says, all men naturally desire to know').[53] He also makes reference to the living fountain throughout the work, especially in his references to form and essence.

Dante's living fountain corresponds to the Gospel words that proclaim Christ as living water and a fountain of the water welling up for eternal life.[54] Christ's encounter with the Samaritan woman at the well is a biblical dramatization of an addressee who is unable to go beyond the letter of Jesus' words. 'Jesus answered, and said to her: If thou didst know the gift of God, and who he is that saith to thee, Give me to drink;

thou perhaps wouldst have asked of him, and he would have given thee living water ... But the water that I will give him, shall become in him a fountain of water, springing up into life everlasting' (John 4:10–14). The poet's suggestion that the Logos is the metaphor for his self-commentary, marked by that qualifier 'quasi,' finds a parallel in his words 'quasi fonte vivo,' since both imply the similitude 'like Christ.' The qualifier serves to approximate Dante's words to those of Christ: Dante's words are like that Fountain of Living Water, which quenches the thirst for wisdom. Dante's weighty use of 'quasi' approximates his self-commentary to the Gospel narration of the Revelation, and indicates the potential of poetry with self-commentary that is itself poetic in its polysemous essence to draw us nearer to the sacred Truth beneath the veils.

At the same time, however, 'quasi' marks a radical difference and deficiency with respect to God's gift to man in the form of His Son with the intent of revealing His own message.[55] Dante's use of 'quasi' represents an awareness of the divergence between the form and essence of his project, a divergence that does not exist in Scripture. At the point at which Dante realizes the full import of these considerations in the *Convivio* and creates a new conceptualization of a possible fusion of form and essence, his polysemous journey in the *Comedy*, replete with incidents of poetic and prophetic doubt, could not but capture his full attention.[56]

2

'Only the ploughshare aided by many clever talents cleaves the soil of poetry':

Boccaccio's Earthly Vision of the Text and the Requisites for Its Interpretation

In his numerous and varied works, Giovanni Boccaccio testifies to a remarkably broad scope of commentative and exegetical strategies. These include, but are certainly not limited to, forms of proems and conclusions by the author, glosses, rubrics, expositions of works by others, interpretive tangents by the narrative's protagonists, and narratorial frames that effectively comment on embedded texts. A plethora of recent critical studies has addressed some aspects of Boccaccio's emphasis on the text's undeniable call for commentary and understanding.[1] In this chapter I concentrate once again on poetic self-commentary, especially as Boccaccio presents it in his *Teseida delle nozze d'Emilia* (The Book of Theseus, 1339–1341). This particular text highlights differences in the self-commentative procedure between Boccaccio and his professed master, Dante. Examining the two self-commentative strategies together proves to be an effective way of delineating the development of the mixed genre during this period, especially in regard to the issues of form, testimony, and exile on which I have concentrated up to this point.[2] The *Teseida* illustrates Boccaccio's most important contributions to the modulation of the self-interpretive mode, that is, his realization of the potential of the margins and the valorization of these liminal spaces of the text.[3]

Were it not for Dante's challenge in the *De vulgari eloquentia* [On the Eloquent Vernacular, 1303–4] that 'Arma vero nullum latium adhuc invenio poetasse' ['[He has thus found] no Italian who has written poetry on deed of arms,' 2.2.8], Boccaccio's *Teseida* might not have been conceived at all. Boccaccio's response to the challenge is confirmed in the *Teseida*'s envoy: 'ma tu, o libro, primo a lor cantare / di Marte fai gli affanni sostenuti, / nel volgar lazio più mai non veduti' ['But you, my book, are the first to bid them sing in the vernacular of Latium what has never been seen thus before: the toils endured for Mars'] (12.84).[4] In accepting Dante's challenge, Boccaccio inherits the debates concerning language that the champion of the eloquent vernacular had earlier to confront.

The *Teseida* is primarily an epic poem, and narrates in octaves the attempts of two Theban princes, Arcita and Palemone, to win the hand of Emilia, the Amazon beauty. The same story serves as the primary source for Geoffrey Chaucer's 'Knight's Tale.' But Boccaccio's work presents a cluster of interpretive difficulties, in part due to the confluence of various modes of writing contained in the text. There are at least four distinct literary forms in the work: the epic poem – in the strictest sense – written in octaves, the sonnets, the prose proem (also referred to as the prefatory letter to Fiammetta), and the self-glosses. Together these strata constitute what one scholar termed the 'failed martial epic' among the minor works written in the vernacular by Boccaccio.[5] Alberto Limentani also perceived Boccaccio as incapable of renouncing the 'lyrical and autobiographical modes ... and prolonged elegiac and amorous notes' that characterized his work.[6] In point of fact, Boccaccio strives to inscribe within the world of *epos* that of *eros*.

Even the most cursory reading of the *Teseida* reveals how commingled the themes of love and war are, from the Amazons' massacre of their husbands to their remarriage with Theseus and his men to the skirmishes between Arcita and Palemone to win the hand of their beloved Emilia. However, this love-war contamination is visible beyond the thematic level, presenting itself on the formal level as well. The envoy of the *Teseida*, a last prayer to the muses followed by their response, provides an apt example. The two sixteen-line poems announce themselves specifically as 'sonnets.' This definition locates them under the category of love lyric par excellence. Reinforcing this categorization is the addition of an extra couplet – in *rima baciata*, literally 'kissing rhyme' – to the sonnet's conventional fourteen lines. In terms of the poems' content, however, the sonnets speak primarily of the *Teseida* as a martial epic. In the sixteen lines of each lyric poem it is possible to see, in fact, a perfect pair of eight-line 'octaves,' that is to say, the poetic form appropriated for poems about war. Form and content could indicate a necessary, reciprocal implication of love and war on the formal and textual levels of the work and the innovative way in which Boccaccio attempts to transform the epic genre while remaining within it.

Boccaccio's linguistic choices reflect a new attitude towards Latin and provide one of the motivations for the inclusion of the poet's self-glosses. Unlike Dante's *Vita Nuova* or *Convivio*, in which both the prose and poetry are written in the first person, Boccaccio creates a striking contrast by juxtaposing the first-person epic narration with a self-commentary whose voice is mostly in the third person. Boccaccio probably sought to imitate works by the classical *auctoritates*, without openly revealing that he himself had written the marginal notes. In fact, the *Teseida*'s prose commentary was not attributed to Boccaccio until Giuseppe Vandelli's 1929 study.[7]

Critics of Boccaccio's *Teseida* have considered the model for his glossing procedure to be classical examples of the scholastic *accessus ad auctores*, stating that the glosses bring literary status to the vernacular work:

> This Italian epic was studiously equipped with apparatus of a kind which accompanied its Latin models in manuscript (e.g. the *scholia* on the *Thebaid*, the *Aeneid* and that highly popular Medieval Latin facsimile of a classical epic, Walter of Châtillon's *Alexandreis*), an apparatus calculated to dispose the discerning reader in favour of the poem and underline for his benefit the superlative literary criteria in accordance with which it had to be judged and esteemed. Here, techniques of exposition traditionally used in interpreting 'ancient' authorities are being used to indicate and announce the literary authority of a 'modern' work.[8]

This is no doubt one motivation behind the self-commentary, but it is unlikely to be the only one. The proem's emblematic phrase, 'solo il bomere aiutato da molti ingegni fende la terra' ['only the ploughshare aided by many clever talents cleaves the soil [of poetry]'] anticipates Boccaccio's rustic, earthly vision of the poetic text. It also embodies an uneasy allusion to an allegorical – that is, a typically moralizing – level of the text's message. In short, the intercourse between poem and self-commentative prose reflects and illuminates the tensions within the *Teseida*'s narrative.

The narrative poem's self-commentative frame consists not only of the glosses, but also of the dedicatory epistle to Fiammetta and the sonnets. Already in the proem there are important clues about the declared motivation of the work that call for careful critical consideration. As it did for Dante's *libello*, Memory provides the initial impetus for Boccaccio's work:

> Come che a memoria tornandomi le felicità trapassate, nella miseria vedendomi dov'io sono, mi sieno di grave dolore manifesta cagione, non m'è per tanto discaro il riducere spesso nella faticata mente, o crudel donna, la piacevole imagine della vostra intera bellezza.
>
> [Although departed joys which return to my memory in my present unhappiness are the unmistakable cause of heavy sorrow, it does not on that account displease me, O cruel lady, to revive in my weary soul from time to time the charming picture of your perfect loveliness.][9]

Boccaccio signals from his very first words the divergence of past and present experience within the same self that gives rise to the complicated narrative-interpretive product that follows. The 'glorious Lady' who appeared to Dante's mind stands in contrast to the 'cruel Lady' of Boccaccio's exhausted mind. While Dante's lady inspired the conversionary experience that opened his 'new life,' Boccaccio's lady provides the impetus for his epic psychomachia.

In addition to recalling the *incipit* of the *Vita Nuova*, this mention of memory reminds us of Francesca da Rimini's words to Dante the pilgrim in *Inferno* 5. Thus Fiammetta enters into a role akin to that of Dante the pilgrim, setting out on a journey of love education. Moreover, the work's first words immediately alert the reader to the fact that the narrator, like Francesca, offers a tale of lust and bloodshed. He may draw the reader's sympathies but is ultimately unreliable.

Boccaccio's proemial writer states that in his youth he fell subject to the beauty of the 'figure' (*figura*) which he contemplated 'with his whole soul' in his mind, and which seemed to him more celestial than human:

> E che essa quello che io considero sia, il suo effetto ne porge argomento chiarissimo, però che ella, con gli occhi della mia mente mirata, nel mezzo delle mie pene ingannando non so con che ascosa soavità l'afflitto core, li fa quasi le sue continue amaritudini obliare.
>
> [And its effect on me is the clearest proof that what I believe is true, because when the eyes of my mind behold it, a hidden sweetness, I know not how, beguiles my tormented heart, almost making it oblivious of its unremitting pains.]

The clarity emphasized in the *argomento chiarissimo* brought on by the contemplation of his 'little flame' (Fiammetta) tricks the narrator's afflicted heart with a hidden suavity, and he hears a most humble thought, 'Questa è quella Fiammetta, la luce de' cui belli occhi prima i nostri accese, e già fece contenti con gli atti suoi gran parte de' nostri ferventi disii' ['This is that little Flame, the light of whose beautiful eyes once enkindled our own and formerly brought a great measure of happiness to our burning desires by its power'].

This voice does not prompt confession, repentance, and conversion as Dante's lady did. The vision of Dante's beloved caused him to feel the effects of the 'signs of the old flame' ['segni de l'antica fiamma'].[10] In the *Teseida* narrator's mind, Fiammetta conjures the earthly satisfactions of love's former pleasures. Although much time has passed since then, Love, who knows the writer's sighs well, can testify to the state in which he remains, victim of her disdain. The personification or deification of Love as witness to the author's feelings should be familiar from the examination in the previous chapter of self-commentary in Dante's works.

To testify to his words of love, Boccaccio's proemial writer goes on to offer Fiammetta the *Teseida* story, which he claims to have translated into the vernacular and set to verse so that it could be more delightful. At this point the writer feels compelled to prove that he composed the work specifically for her ['che ella da me per voi sia compilata, due cose fra l'altre il manifestano']. He cites two proofs, which I will quote in full, as they form the central nexus of this examination of Boccaccio's epic. The first one reads:

> ... che ciò che sotto il nome dell'uno de' due amanti e della giovane amata si conta essere stato, ricordandovi bene, e io a voi di me e voi a me di voi, se non mentiste, potreste conoscere essere stato detto e fatto il parte: quale de' due si sia non discuopro, ché so che ve ne avvedrete. Se forse alcune cose soperchie vi fossero, il volere bene coprire ciò che non è onesto manifestare da noi due infuori e il volere la storia seguire ne son cagioni; e oltre a ciò dovete sapere che solo il bomere aiutato da molti ingegni fende la terra. Potrete adunque e qual fosse innanzi e quale sia stata poi la vita mia che più non mi voleste per vostro, discernere.
>
> [... that, if you remember well, you will be able to recognize in what is related of one of the lovers and of the young lady who is loved, things said and done by me to you and by you to me, if you were not false. Which of

the two it is, I will not reveal because I know that you will discern it. If perhaps there should be [superfluous things], (my translation), the reasons are my desire to conceal what it is not proper to reveal to anyone other than ourselves and my wish to adhere to the story; and besides that you ought to know that only the ploughshare which is assisted by many devices cleaves the earth. Consequently, you will be able to realize what my life was before and what it has been since you no longer wished me to be yours.]

The second reason marshalled to prove Fiammetta to be the true muse of his work is described by the proemial writer as follows:

il non avere cessata né storia né favola né chiuso parlare in altra guisa, con ciò sia cosa che le donne sì come poco intelligenti ne sogliano essere schife, ma però che per intelletto e notizia delle cose predette voi dalla turba dell'altre separata conosco, libero mi concessi il porle a mio piacere.

[The other thing is that I have omitted neither history, nor fable, nor figurative speech, which ladies who are not very intelligent usually dislike, but because I know that you are unlike most of them in intellect and in knowledge of these matters, I allowed myself to set them forth freely at my pleasure.]

The proem closes with a brief summary of the work, a form of *captatio benevolentia* in which the writer requests that Fiammetta assess his *picciolo libretto*[11] not against her greatness, but with respect to his own limitations.

Perhaps the most striking feature of the proemial writer's explanation for composing the *Teseida* and its self-gloss is his open declaration that the work has more than one level of meaning. It offers the ancient story of Emilia's love, but parallels, like other works by Boccaccio, a love between the narrator and his lady, to whom he addresses the work.[12] There is also a certain tension between truth and lies. For Boccaccio, the truth does not find its expression in how it is concretized on the literal level, but rather resides in an allusively invoked wider field of significance that requires a certain measure of discernment. Boccaccio overturns the trustworthiness of a testimony based on personal experience. The truth may not be present in the lady's testimony, since she can lie ['se non mentiste']. Instead, poetry is the surprising, rightful place of truth. This conforms to opinions expressed throughout

Boccaccio's writing career, as he consistently interrogated the nature of poetry and defended it on the basis of its duty to guard the truth under the veils of supposed fictions. Most explicitly, in his *Genealogy of the Gentile Gods*, in a passage cited in this study's Introduction, Boccaccio vociferously insists that poets are not liars. On the contrary, they deserve commendation for their efforts to guard the sacred, essential meaning behind the poetic words: 'Surely it is not one of the poet's various functions to rip up and lay bare the meaning which lies hidden in his inventions. Rather where matters truly solemn and memorable are too much exposed, it is his office by every effort to protect as well as he can and remove them from the gaze of the irreverent, that they cheapen not by too common familiarity. So when he discharges his duty and does it ingeniously, the poet earns commendation, not anathema' (14.12).

Involved in thus decorously dressing the truth, according to Boccaccio, are 'superfluous things.' For Dante poetry had an almost Pauline mission of expressing the truth openly, although that truth was so sacred that it was difficult for its hearers to understand (see chapter 1). According to Dante's poetic expression, there were no superfluous things except the glosses themselves, which under certain circumstances would be useless or superfluous in clarifying the lyric significance (see *Vita Nuova* 7.14 [14.14]).

Dante's *fedele d'Amore* was a sort of Kermodian insider, as I have shown, and stood in stark contrast to Boccaccio's lady. Ironically, Boccaccio's *fedele d'amore,* Fiammetta, lacks this fidelity. The proem asserts that the writer remains tireless in the faithful service of his lady, although she turns against him and refuses to be his love ['che più non mi voleste per vostro']. The author of the *Teseida* effectively turns the Dantean concept of the faithful disciple of Love on its head. Boccaccio's lady is not the faithful insider for whom his gloss would be superfluous, but rather the very outsider who evidently necessitates it. However, she will understand his work without further clarification in the glosses, which paradoxically aim to veil that which the work fails to manifest ['Se forse alcune cose soperchie vi fossero, il volere bene coprire ciò che non è onesto manifestare da noi due infuori [n'è] cagion[e]'].

This evident and purposeful conflict in the self-commentary's motivation continues in the glosses themselves. In the lengthy note to Book Seven (30), consisting primarily of the description of the house of Mars, the self-glossator asserts that there are various things he wishes to point out about the author's treatment of the god of war's dwelling:

Dice similemente: ogni altare di Marte luminoso etc.: quali siano gli altri ornamenti assai chiaro apparisce. Nondimeno so che assai più cose e meglio sopra questa materia si potrebbono dire; lasciole a coloro che con più diletto partitamente le vorranno ancora raguardare e scrivere, perciò che a me basta, scrivendo questo ad instanzia di donne, averne detto quello che qui appare.

[He says, likewise: 'Every altar was luminous, etc.' What the other ornaments might be appears clear. Nonetheless, I know that many other things could be said on this matter and said better. I leave them to those who still want to examine and write about them with more delight and in detail, since for me it is enough to have said what it seems to me I should, as I write this at the instance of ladies.][13]

Boccaccio's language certainly recalls Dantean phrases, such as: 'con ciò sia cosa che per la sua ragionata cagione assai sia manifesto' (*Vita Nuova* 7.13 [14.13]), or 'Forse ancora per più sottile persona si vederebbe più sottile ragione in ciò; ma questa è quella che io ne veggio, e che più mi piace' (*Vita Nuova* 19.6–7 [29.3–4]). However, it is also evident that Boccaccio moves from Dante's emphasis on 'more subtle reasoning' to 'more delight' as the impetus for further exposition. The glossator implies that to say more would be superfluous, since his gloss is written 'at the request of ladies.' Moreover, the glossator's use of the plural 'donne' here casts some doubt on the insistence with which the proem's writer tries to prove that the poem was written exclusively for Fiammetta.

Boccaccio's narrator alludes to a certain distinction between the *fedeli d'amore* and those who are not the faithful of love: 'Qual quella notte fosse all'amadore / qui non si dice; quelli il può sapere, / che già trafitto da soverchio amore / alcuna volta fu, se mai piacere / ne ricevette dopo lungo ardore' ['What that night was for the lovers is not to be said here. He who has once been pierced by excessive love already will know, if ever he found joy after long desire'] (12.76). This instance of the superfluous nature of further elaboration arises in the twelfth book (76), among the stanzas following a rubric primarily concerned with the lascivious side of the double Venus: 'Come Palemone dormì con Emilia' ['How Palemone slept with Emilia'].

All indications appear to point to a precarious realization concerning the narrator's voice: it is a paradox in itself. In much the same way that the man from Crete can state that all Cretans are liars, Boccaccio's espouser of the truth of poetry falls under the aegis of the false judgment of the 'voluttuosi.' These pleasure seekers follow the 'vita voluttuosa nella quale si possono dire tutti coloro li quali, dopo lungo amare, o con arte o con ingegno o con ispesa pervenuti sono alli loro piaceri e in quegli perseverando dimorano' ['voluptuous life in which all those can be said to dwell who, after loving for a long time, have attained to their delights either by art or by cleverness or by expense, and then persevere therein'] (7.50n). Boccaccio clearly indicates the link between the lascivious lover and the narrator as Arcita and Palemone admire Emilia's beauty and fall in love with her, demonstrating all the outward signs of Dante's sufferers for Love. The narrator explains:

> E da' sospiri già a lagrimare
> eran venuti, e se non fosse stato
> che 'l loro amor non volean palesare,
> sovente avrian per angoscia gridato.
> E così sa Amore adoperare
> a cui più per servigio è obligato:
> colui il sa che tal volta fu preso
> da lui e da cota' dolori offeso.
>
> [Now from sighing they advanced to weeping,
> and if it were not for the fact
> that they did not want to reveal their love,
> they would have frequently cried out in their anguish.
> This is how Love treats
> those to whom He is most obliged for service.
> Whoever has been captured by Him at some time
> and afflicted with similar pangs knows this.] (3.35)

The seventh line of this stanza is glossed as follows: '*colui il sa etc.*: che sono io' ['Whoever knows this, etc.: I am that man']. Here Boccaccio borrows again from Dante's use of the periphrasis in the *Vita Nuova*. The words are those of the god of Love in Dante's case: 'E di ciò chiama testimonio *colui che lo sa*, e come tu prieghi lui che li le dica; *ed io, che sono quelli*' (12.7, my emphasis). This is a formula for establishing the authority of speech. In Dante's text, 'colui che lo sa' ['he who knows'] is the god of Love who tells the protagonist Dante that he can cite him in his canzone to testify to the constancy of his love for the beloved Beatrice. The formula is a derivation of that which appears in the Gospel narration of Christ's authority to testify for Himself, which as we have seen reappears in the *Convivio*. In Boccaccio's text, however, ultimate authority rests in the self-glossator. Moreover, this authority has its basis in past experience of the afflictions of love.

The proemial writer's reminder to Fiammetta, 'dovete sapere che solo il bomere aiutato da molti ingegni fende la terra,' is thus indeed emblematic of the self-interpretive procedure of the *Teseida*. There is a certain proverbial quality to the enunciation of this phrase in the context of the proemial writer's two-pronged argument. Nowhere else in the proem is there another harvest metaphor, and indeed the reader would be hard-pressed to find references to plowing elsewhere in the *Teseida*. The phrase truly stands out and demands particular attention. To be understood at all, in fact, the words must be read according to their underlying meanings rather than merely their literal sense. The phrase probably refers indirectly to the famous Veronese riddle:

Se pareba boves, alba pratalia araba,
albo versorio teneba, negro semen seminaba.

[He pushed the oxen forward, white fields he ploughed,
a white plough he held; a black seed he sowed.][14]

The riddle hinges on the identification of plowing with writing; oxen with the fingers; the plow itself with the stylus; and the soil with parchment.[15] Boccaccio draws from the phrase not only its decidedly rustic and scribal connotations, but also its erotic implications, since like most implements for cutting or furrowing, plows symbolize the fecundation by the male of the passive, female earth, the fruit of which is, by extension, the harvest.

Allusions to Dante's self-commentary in the *Vita Nuova* predominate in the *Teseida*'s proem, but there is no lack of references to Dante's more mature prosimetrum. In fact, Boccaccio's division of 'storia,' 'favola,' and 'chiuso parlare in altra guisa' roughly corresponds to Dante's allegorical distinctions of the historical, tropological, and anagogical levels of significance. But by the time the reader reaches the epic's sonnet envoy, it is clear that the *Convivio* is also being taken to task very pointedly in the foregrounding of the banquet metaphor:

O sacre Muse, le quali io adoro
e con digiuni onoro e vigilando,
di voi la grazia in tal guisa cercando
qual l'acquistaron palidi coloro

a' quai poi deste il grazioso alloro
in sul fonte castalio poetando,
i versi lor sovente esaminando
col vostro canto sottile e sonoro,
io ho ricolte della vostra mensa
alcune miche da quella cadute,
e come seppi qui l'ho compilate;
le quai vi priego che voi le portiate
liete alla donna in cui la mia salute
vive, ma ella forse nol si pensa,
e con lei insieme il nome date e 'l canto
e 'l corso ad esse, se ne le cal tanto.

[O sacred Muses, whom I venerate
and honor with fasts and vigils,
as I seek your favour in the way
those pale ones acquired it to whom
you gave the graceful laurel
for the poetry they wrote
near the Castalian fount,
while you frequently tested their verses
with your subtle and sonorous song,
I have gathered some crumbs fallen from your table
and, as you know, I have assembled them here.
I pray you to bear them
joyfully to the lady in whom my salvation lives,
but perhaps she gives this no thought,
and along with her, bestow their name and their place
and their course upon them, for they concern her greatly.]

Like the *Convivio*'s self-commentator, Boccaccio confirms that he gathers the crumbs that have fallen from the banquet table and humbly prepares to serve them to another. However, this table is neither that of the angels nor that of the philosophers, but rather a very different one belonging to the Muses.

The difference between the view of hidden meaning in the poetic text and the task of the self-commentary appears to hinge on a divergence in the conceptualization of the essence of the text. Dante linked the source of his work to the table of the angels, and as in the model of Christ's parables, the difficulties in his text were said to arise from the reader's ability to read but not understand the deeper significance. For Boccaccio, the poetry is a truly human *poiesis*, something put together from what has been found under the table of the Muses, as well as a putting together of the many 'ingegni' ['talents'] of the poetic tradition that has preceded him.

By extension, the interpretive quest for textual meaning imposed on Boccaccio's readers is the arduous task of cultivating the field that stretches before them, of harvesting a significance ostensibly declared as seeded by the author. Boccaccio does not engage in an exilic discourse along the lines of Dante's quest for textual meaning by means of a peri- and paraphrastic pilgrimage of the sacred space of the poetic Word. In some sense for Boccaccio, the reader has already attained the divine dwelling places, those of Mars and Venus, which dominate the central discourse of his poetic and interpretive project. Boccaccio brings the transcendent down to earth through self-commentative procedures that take biblical exegesis as a model, not the Gospel itself, as Dante had done.[16]

With Boccaccio, the glosses are the locus for poetry's playing out of its relationship with the other, not so much the Christian Other as the mythological inheritance, the classical models of textual interpretation, and the clash of cultures distant in time. Boccaccio's denial of ultimate transcendence presents itself in his continual positing of the distance he must maintain from pagan antiquity while remaining dependent on a demonstration of his poetic continuity in the tradition. The repetition of such qualifying phrases in the notes as 'gli antichi dicevano che' ['the ancients used to say that'], 'sì come li poeti fingendo scrivono' ['according to the fictions that the poets write'], and so forth, has the effect of ideologically separating Boccaccio from his primarily Virgilian, Statian, and Ovidian sources, as well as implicitly suggesting a poetic continuity.

By writing self-glosses Boccaccio indicates, of course, that there are further levels to the poem's significance. However, Boccaccio makes an important point by presenting a textual interpreter, Fiammetta, who reads beyond the letter of his self-commentary. Janet Levarie Smarr, in *Boccaccio and Fiammetta: The Narrator as Lover* argued convincingly that Fiammetta also stands for us as readers.[17] Fiammetta comprehends the significances that the author purposefully hides and that the glossator does not clarify. But she also understands differently than the narrator. On the level of the narration, for instance, the reader sees that Palemone, who once adored Earthly Venus in her temple, has abandoned his lustful intentions by the end of the work. He prays to Jove, Hymen, and Juno that they bless his marriage with Emilia, marriage being the seal of Divine Love.[18] By the end of the story, the narrator has not undergone the same conversion. He still prays in his sonnet envoy to the Muses, whom he had just described (12.84) by emphasizing their nakedness in the presence of men. His intent in sending Fiammetta his book, as he has admitted all along, is to win her favours.

In Fiammetta's reading of the work, her one instance of direct speech comes in the final sonnet, 'Ahi, quante d'amor forze in costor foro!' ['Ah, how many were the forces of Love within them!']. Like Dante the pilgrim in *Inferno* 5, to whose words she alludes here (vv. 112–114), Fiammetta feels compassion and seemingly almost gives in to her interlocutor's words, which are still marked by lust. Fiammetta acknowledges by her exclamation her awareness that the book she receives could be a Gallehault between her and the author, just as the tale of Lancelot and Guinevere was for Paolo and Francesca.[19] The Muses describe her, through wordplay on her name, as enflamed by love, which the reader is left to interpret as a divine love. This possibility finds ulterior confirmation in the designation of the poet as prophet ['o vate']. The title Fiammetta gives the work emphasizes the honest ends of heavenly love by referring to Emilia's nuptials. Moreover, by concluding with a reference to the same canto warning against lust in Dante's *Comedy*, she critically underlines the static quality of the narrator's pose, since he opened the *Teseida* by taking Francesca's words as his own.

Fiammetta thus demonstrates that she is a remarkably keen interpreter of the *Teseida*, one not tied to the prescribed underlying significance of the poems found in the glosses. Boccaccio implies that like Fiammetta, we as readers are also called to redoubled interpretive effort; that is, the self-commentary is not a 'manipulation' with a strictly 'functional and pragmatic character.'[20] Examples, like his ideal reader's reaction to his work, show that Boccaccio's self-commentary is not intent on 'packaging, framing, and embalming the poem' in its assumed function of attempting 'to fix and stabilize [the poetry's] meaning forever' either.[21] Instead, Boccaccio pointedly celebrates the polysemous understandings of his work and calls on his readers, with their differing intellectual gifts, to continue harvesting the poetic interpretive ground he has planted: 'Certissima cosa è che come gli *ingegni* degli uomini sono diversi, così esser convengono le maniere del dare la dottrina' ['It is a most certain thing that as the intellects of men are different, so too ought to be the ways of instructing them'].²² One of the most intriguing ways of teaching turns out to be, as Boccaccio shows, not telling, but indicating where the gaps in understanding remain.

Summarizing the examination of poetic self-commentary in the late Middle Ages as presented in chapters 1 and 2, it is apparent that the authorial projects in Dante's prosimetra and Boccaccio's self-glossed poem represent two very different approaches to autohermeneutics. However, formally and ideologically, they are both intent in their own ways on promoting vernacular poetry and poetics. Certain tensions in poetic self-commentary tend to recur. One is the dichotomy presence-absence, which manifests itself in the theme of exile, for example. There is a concern for highlighting what is said as opposed to what the poetic self-commentator glosses over. All self-commentaries, furthermore, must come to terms, to greater or lesser extents, either explicitly or by implication, with the role of the self-commentator as opposed to the outside commentator. Variations on questions of authority and testimonial proof also arise with regular frequency and will continue to do so in the works of Renaissance self-commentators, who are influenced by Dante's and Boccaccio's examples. This pair, in particular, breaks the commentative mold of textual clarification for pedagogical or morally instructive aid. Their prose begins to push the bounds of all definitions of the poetic text.

Dante and Boccaccio provide founding examples of poetic self-commentary in Italian. If we were to consider the third literary crown of early Italian vernacular literature, however, we would have yet another take on poetic self-commentary. Francesco Petrarca's self-glosses largely amount to a denial of the mixed genre as a formal representation of poetic expression. Petrarca penned notes in the margins of his vernacular *canzoniere*, *Rerum vulgarium fragmenta*, the most famous example of vernacular lyric poetry served by Latin self-commentary. Yet it is clear that Petrarca did not view these notes as an integral part of the lyric work. The manuscript in which these marginal annotations appear, *Vaticano latino* 3196, was probably a working draft of his poetry. The Latin marginalia are primarily chronotopical remarks, specifying the location and time of day that events suggested in the lyrics took place. The glosses also serve as reminders of which poems were copied, when, and by whom.²³ There is no evidence to suggest that Petrarca, like Dante and Boccaccio, intended that self-glosses be circulated or published with his verse.²⁴ It would also be difficult to argue that the essence of these glosses generally found poetic expression in the lyrics. While the poetic self-commentator views the integral presentation of poetry and accompanying prose as a formal poetic statement, Petrarca seemingly intended nothing of the sort.

It is difficult to explain exactly why Petrarca differs from the two most important poetic self-commentators of this time. A possible explanation might lie in the fragmented nature of Petrarca's poetics. While the prose of the poetic self-commentary adds a quality of otherness to the verse, lending to the work a fragmentary form, a form that appears pieced together, poetic self-commentary actually tends towards a totalizing view of the text. It seeks to circumscribe within itself a unity in difference, to encompass contending voices within its scope. Dante finds his primary model for this, as I have suggested, in the biblical Word: prophetic and poetic, absolutely true and infinitely interpretable, paradoxically the most simple and the most complex, and both the tangible form of the incarnate and the sign that ever points beyond itself. Boccaccio found a secular, scholastic model for what he perceived as a necessarily totalizing procedure in his endeavour to found authority for the vernacular and the new. Petrarca resisted this unifying strain. His poems are precisely *rerum fragmenta*. One could say, along with Robert M. Durling, that Petrarca is forever calling attention to 'the psychologically relative, even suspect, origin of individual poems and thus of writing itself.'[25] While self-commentary might seem at first glance an egoistic act, it actually avoids solipsism by consciously invoking the need for interpretation by another. One should keep in mind, however, that Petrarca's decision not to provide an integral, circulating self-commentary was actually more conventional. Dante and Boccaccio, in contrast, produced a radically innovative mode of poetic self-commentary.

While the poetic self-commentaries of Dante and Boccaccio instituted the most important exemplifications of this literary manifestation in the Middle Ages, other instances of works in the same mixed genre exist. It is worthwhile to consider these briefly with a view to understanding the broader historical context. The vast majority of single-author *prosimetra* of this time could be seen as didactic treatises in verse with marginal self-glosses. Among the medieval examples are the epic poem *L'acerba* by Cecco d'Ascoli (*c.* 1269–1327) and two of the works by Francesco da Barberino (1264–1348). Cecco d'Ascoli left his encyclopedic poem unfinished when he died at the stake. Composed in Italian *sesta rima*, the poem details all matter of astrological, alchemical, and naturalistic topics. It also includes what is now generally considered the poet's own widely circulated Latin annotations,[26] which serve in part to criticize what he calls the 'false science' of Dante's *Divine Comedy*.[27] Cecco d'Ascoli's self-interpretive procedure has yet to receive the attention it deserves, but the author of *L'acerba* apparently anticipated Boccaccio's mode of self-gloss by referring to himself in the third person. The presentation and tone of the annotations, however, seem more readily to anticipate a self-commentator such as Girolamo Benivieni or Tommaso Campanella. Like Benivieni, Cecco d'Ascoli repeated the first word or words of the phrase of poetry he is explicating in the marginal gloss, following a traditionally scholastic procedure. The gloss itself tries to explicate a largely microcosmic/macrocosmic vision of humanity and the world inhabited. I take *L'acerba*'s first gloss, as it appeared in the 1501 edition (2r) as a representative case:

> Oltre non sigue più. Qui dicie che oltre al primo cielo, zoè el nono, la nostra luce, cioè il nostro intelletto, non pò intendere per via di natura; dico, oltra quella superficie sopra la quale Dio forma l'anima ragionevole, la quale divide noi dagli angioli bruti per habito di ragione; el quale habito la creatura humana non pò sempre per termini di ragione chostregniare né vedere.

> [Beyond it does not go. Here he says that beyond the first heaven, that is the ninth, our light, that is our intellect, cannot understand by means of nature; I say, beyond that surface over which God forms the rational soul, which divides us from the bad angels by habit of reason; this reason the human creature cannot always follow nor see in terms of reason.]

Benivieni, within the larger tradition of metaphysical thought of his own time, was also preoccupied with relating the heavenly spheres to degrees of human capacity for thought and understanding and with distinctions among the natures of animals, men, angels, and God.[28] Cecco's style of self-gloss, however, would more readily seem to prefigure that of Campanella. Cecco concludes his *Commentarî* with the sentence: 'Qui me legit intelligat, et benedicat Dominum qui mihi tribuit intellectum [Let the one who reads me understand and give praise to God who bestowed on me understanding].[29] This type of self-commentative formula – 'Qui [me] legit intelligat' ['Let the one who reads me understand'] – is one that Campanella used repeatedly in the commentary on his philosophical poems.[30]

Francesco da Barberino provides two other examples of didactic self-glosses, the voluminous *Documenti d'Amore* [Documents of Love] (1314) and the *Reggimento e costume di donna* [Guidance and Habits of Women] (1318–1320). The *Documenti* consists of vernacular lyrics illustrated by compendious Latin prose periphrases and commentaries.[31] The *Reggimento* is a twenty-part treatise concerning the upbringing of girls, written entirely in the vernacular in a free alteration of prose and verse.[32] These writings, primarily concerned with issues of medieval science and education, follow the Latin tradition of didactic prosimetra, which includes, among others, Bernardus Silvestris's *De mundi universitate*, and Alan de Lille's *De planctu naturae*.[33] However, they fall outside the scope of the current study, since they cannot aid in our understanding of the *poetic* force behind self-commentaries.

Part Two

Poetic Self-Commentary Reborn in Quattrocento Florence

3

'Know Thyself':
Self-knowledge and New Life in Lorenzo de' Medici's *Commentary on My Sonnets*

Hic situs est Phaethon, currus auriga paterni;
quem si non tenuit, magnis tamen excidit ausis.
– Phaeton's epitaph (Ovid, *Metamorphoseon* 2. 327–8)

Here Phaeton lies; his daring drove the boy to drive his father's chariot; he tried and failed. But in his fall he gained the death of one supremely brave.[1]

Lorenzo de' Medici the Magnificent (1449–1492) experiments in various ways to determine how best to present his poetry to a reading public. He juxtaposes some of his lyrics with the poetry of certain Stilnovisti and of Dante and Petrarca in his *Raccolta aragonese* (1474–75).[2] The diffusion of his *Canzoniere* might also suggest that Lorenzo had joined in the burgeoning vogue of Petrarchism. In this work he carefully ordered more than two hundred of his lyric poems, while excluding some of his most vibrant lauds and other religious compositions. But giving an organic unity to the *Canzoniere* does not seem to have been Lorenzo's objective. Instead, he determined that his collected sonnets must ultimately take a prosimetrical form, and the unfinished *Comento de' miei sonetti* (Commentary on My Sonnets) occupied the Magnificent's attention for significant periods throughout his lifetime.[3] This chapter explores why Lorenzo chooses this specific self-commentative form to order his sonnets on love, and even more to the point, what this form could uniquely offer to Lorenzo's poetic expression.

Two highly influential critical perspectives currently dominate the way readers come to appreciate Lorenzo's *Comento*. The first assumes that Lorenzo's prose is a commentary, in the sense of commentary-by-another. According to this view, Lorenzo's self-commentary represents an exegetical apparatus written at the service of the reader for explanation and clarification of the poetry. Moreover, Lorenzo's prose must be regarded as the most authoritative or correct interpretation possible of the sonnets, since the poet himself wrote it. Angelo Lipari, whose book nevertheless remains a fundamental reference for any study of the *Comento*, confidently asserts: 'We shall all, then, agree with [Lorenzo] that a commentary on his verses was not only useful, but necessary, especially for us moderns, and, smiling perhaps at our own shortcomings, we shall agree with him that the only true expounder (if not the sole judge) of a work is the author himself.'[4] This argument has the distinct advantage of echoing precisely Lorenzo's own words: 'nessuno il può fare con più chiara expressione del vero senso che io medesimo' ['No one can [comment on my poetry] with a clearer expression of its true sense than I myself'].[5] At the same time, this critical view offers the seemingly perfect text in which to prove the ultimate superiority of an authorial intention-oriented approach to poetry. Lorenzo's own words should contain the clearest expression of the one, true meaning of his verse, without the 'confusione che nasce della varietà de' comenti, nelli quali el più delle volte si segue più tosto la natura propria che la intenzione vera di chi ha scritto' ['confusion which breeds from the variety of comments that, most of the time, follow their own agendas rather than the true intention of the one who has written'] (32–3). However, regardless of our perceived shortcomings as moderns, it would be a grave disservice to Lorenzo to assume that there is nothing more to his verse than the indications he managed to leave in the prose, as I hope to show.

The second critical perspective is largely biographical, primarily concerned with understanding Lorenzo's life from indications gleaned from his literary works. This is the enduring focus of much Italian research, manifested in such preoccupations as the identification of the unnamed ladies in the *Comento* or the placement of the work within a chronology of Lorenzo's other works or lifetime achievements.[6] But variations on the biographical theme arise in American critical studies as well, including the introduction to the most recent English translation of the work by James Wyatt Cook. The title imposed on the *Comento*, *The Autobiography of Lorenzo de' Medici The Magnificent*, proclaims an understanding of the work as a self-written record of a lifetime.[7] To suggest that we can ignore cultural and historical contexts in the interpretation of literary texts would be utterly unsustainable. But I do not believe that it is possible to accept unquestioningly attempts to prove historical facts on the basis of passages from literary texts. Ultimately, the approach of these critics does not deal with the essentially *poetic* message of this *poetic* work.[8]

It remains to be seen why Lorenzo literarily redeploys his sonnets together with a prose interpretation, which he sometimes refers to as a 'paraphrase.'[9] Lorenzo dedicates the bulk of the *Comento*'s proem to the explanation and justification of this unusual procedure. In doing so, he creates a proem that is not unlike Dante's first book of the *Convivio*. He begins by addressing anticipated criticisms of his self-commentary and cites three possible objections that nearly cause him to abandon the *Comento* altogether. First, he does not wish to incur accusations of presumption. He fears that others may think that he is showing an excessively high estimation of himself in commenting on his own works: 'comentando io le cose proprie, così per la troppa extimazione che mostravo fare di me medesimo' ['by commenting myself on my own works, I seemed to risk presumption, ... by showing that I esteemed myself too highly'] (30–1). Furthermore, his self-commentary seems to imply that the poet is usurping the office of another, considered of insufficient intellect to understand the poet's work without some clarification: 'Mi pareva assumere in me quello iudicio che debba essere d'altri, notando in questa parte l'ingegni di coloro alle mani de' quali perverranno li miei versi, come poco sufficienti a poterli intendere' ['I seemed ... to usurp the judgment that ought to belong to others, suggesting in this way that the intellect of those into whose hands my verses fall is inadequate to enable them to understand'] (30–1). Lorenzo does not wish to give occasion to those who would upbraid the poet for wasting his time composing and paraphrasing a text of such frivolous subject matter as 'an amorous passion' (30).[10] Finally, even if his readers find the material worthy, they may ultimately object to the task on a linguistic basis, since the vernacular is commonplace and restricted to a very small geographic region:

> Forse a qualcuno parrà reprensibile, quando bene la materia e subietto fussi per sé assai degno, avendo scritto e fattone menzione in lingua nostra materna e vulgare, la quale, dove si parla et è intesa, e però a questa parte questa opera e fatica nostra pare al tutto vana e come se non fussi fatta.

[It may be reprehensible to someone, perhaps, though the material and subject were themselves very worthy, that writing and uttering them in our mother tongue, which, by being very commonplace where it is spoken and understood, may not seem to avoid some base expression. In those places where our language is unknown, it cannot be understood, and thus in that region this work and our pains will seem all in vain and as if they had not been accomplished.] (30–1)

In responding to the first objection, that of presumption, Lorenzo inverts the assertion to restate it in the opposite terms: 'dico che a me non pare presunzione lo interpetrare le cose mie, ma più presto tòrre fatica ad altri' ['I say that it does not seem to me presumption to interpret my own work, but rather eagerness to free others from the task'] (32–3). Lorenzo goes on to declare that no one could better know and clarify the true meaning of the poetry than the poet himself. This statement differs noticeably from Dante's separation of the roles of self-commentator and the other glossator to avoid the reprehensible action of praising oneself. With an argument that suggests the parodic, Lorenzo states that in providing the self-commentary he should be perceived as avoiding presumption because in doing so he submits to the judgment of others more than he would if he were to present the poems on their own.[11] Thus, Lorenzo continues, the poet can provide the reader with the necessary tools to evaluate more informatively the sonnets in question.[12]

Another innovative departure from previous self-commentative excuses is the Magnificent's defence of his intervention on the basis of a single truth that is not served by the confusion born of disparate interpretations by others. Concern over a variety of interpretations has a long and complex tradition, but was rarely the cause of the heightened anxiety that Lorenzo's remark betrays. For example, William of Conches, in his commentary on Boethius' narration of Orpheus and Eurydice, noted that his interpretation departed significantly from that of Fulgentius: 'Let no one blame my interpretation for that reason, since diverse interpretations are composed insofar as the same matter is considered under diverse aspects. The diversity of expositions is no cause for anxiety, but rather for joy.'[13] It is clear that Lorenzo intuits the risks involved in textual interpretations, be they those of other readers or his own.

In this same argument, Lorenzo brings to bear the well-known theme of the necessary *varietas* of human tasks. Variety was associated with interpretations of the many members of the mystical body of Christ. That is, each human person has a place, purpose, and dignity by virtue of membership in Christ's body, regardless of that person's occupation or earthly station.[14] Lorenzo alludes to this concept, but marks a shift in its understanding: a single occupation does not reflect the richness of human intelligence and the exigencies of this life. The implication is that Lorenzo should not feel limited to expressing himself in either poetry or prose, but may write both. This is apparent in the passage that speaks of public reaction to a lady's death, which draws the reader's attention to the work's prosimetrical form:

> Essendo adunque questa tale così morta, tutti e fiorentini ingegni, come si conveniva in tale publica iattura, diversamente e si dolsono, *chi in versi e chi in prosa*, della acerbità di questa morte, e si sforzorono laudarla, *ciascuno secondo la facultà del suo ingegno*.

> [As she was thus dead, then, all the Florentine wits, as is fitting for such a public loss, variously *mourned, some in verses and some in prose*, for the bitterness of this death, and each one felt compelled to praise her *according to his ability and talent*.] (58–9, my emphasis)

Lorenzo also transforms Dante's argument in favour of working for the good of others to that in favour of working for the good of *oneself* or for others: 'Credo sia officio vero d'ogni uomo operare tutte le cose a benificio degli uomini, *o proprio* o d'altri' ['For I believe it is the true office of every man to carry out all things to men's benefit, either one's own or that of others'].[15]

Moving to the second objection Lorenzo anticipates, that he has wasted time in composing and commenting on the unworthy subject of amorous passion, he excuses himself by saying that, given human imperfection, 'quelle cose essere migliori al mondo nelle quali interviene minore male' ['those things are best into which the least harm obtrudes'] (34–5). Furthermore, he argues, love is man's invitation to worthiness, virtue, and relative goodness. If his readers should still wish to condemn him, however, he defers, not without a measure of irony, to the words of Petrarca: 'spero trovare pietà, non che perdono' ['I hope to find pity, if not pardon'].[16] He further bolsters his plea with an appeal to clemency, given his youth and inexperience. A crucial aspect of Lorenzo's defence is his insistence on the relativity of the human basis for understanding such absolutes as truth, the good, and so forth ('quelle cose essere *migliori* al mondo nelle quali interviene *minore male*'). In this case, Lorenzo advocates an understanding of degrees of human perfection, which is, of course, sustained by his Ficinian conception of the human means of union with the divine. At other times, he will acknowledge his troubling reliance on inexact opinion: 'La oppinion è sempre ansia e inquieta, perché, non si contentando l'animo nostro se non di quello che è vero, e non ne potendo avere la oppinione alcuna certezza, non si quieta, ma giudica le cose più presto per comparazione e *respective*, che secondo el vero' ['Opinion is always anxious and unquiet, because our mind is not contented except by that which is true, and opinion is unable to have either certainty or quiet, but very quickly judges things by comparison and *relatively* rather than according to the truth'] (258–9 my emphasis).

Like Dante, Lorenzo insists on the limited nature of human perspective on perfection and truth, testifying to a shift in the concept of authority from a dependence on the *auctoritas* to an authority based on personal experience. Dante defends his decision to write a self-commentary by calling on the authoritative examples of Boethius and St Augustine, who spoke of themselves in order to provide consolation and moral instruction. But Dante also placed a higher premium on the role of personal experience in attesting truth. His insistence on addressing those who had 'intelligence of love' or who were already among the faithful followers of Love and thus could relate to Dante's words because they appealed to a shared experience, are but two examples of his faith in experience.

Lorenzo mentions Dante as a precursor who spoke of himself without succumbing to presumption. At the same time, Lorenzo gives due credit to the founding of authority in personal experience: 'E se alla confermazione di sì vera sentenzia non fussi abastanza l'auttorità d'uno poeta tanto excellente che fu chiamato "divino" [Homer], la experienzia dell'umane cose ne rende assai abundante testimonianza' ['And if the authority of such an excellent poet who was called "divino" were insufficient to confirm this very true pronouncement, human experience gives abundant witness to it'] (172–3). In fact, the value of individual, subjective knowledge by direct participation is intensified in Lorenzo's thought: he becomes the only one who can know his poetry's true significance and, therefore, have any grounds to judge it.

Lorenzo goes on to state that by his self-commentary he hopes to spare others the task of trying to expound the true sense that is known only to him:

La fatica di questo comento convenirsi massimamente a me, acciò che altro ingegno di più excellenzia che il mio non abbia a consumarsi o mettere tempo in cose sì basse; e se pure la materia è alta e degna, come pare a me, el chiarirla bene e farla piana e intelligibile a ciascuno essere molto utile: e questo, per quello che ho detto di sopra, nessuno il può fare con più chiara expressione del vero senso che io medesimo.

[I say that the effort of this commentary agrees particularly with me, so that another intellect of greater excellence than mine will not have to consume itself wasting time on things so low. And even if the subject is elevated and worthy, as it seems to me, clarifying it well and making it plain and intelligible to each person is very useful. And this, because of what I have said above, no one can do with a clearer expression of its true sense than I myself.] (40–1)

Lorenzo never concedes, however, that this is a work concerning only lowly things. On the contrary, commentaries may provide edification, consolation, or utility, but they ultimately treat theological or philosophical issues: 'E comenti sono riservati per cose teologiche o di filosofia e importanti grandi effetti' ['Commentaries are reserved for matters of theology or philosophy, and for consequential and significant concerns'] (30–1). Lorenzo again explicitly invokes Dante, simultaneously accusing him of wasting his time on such trifling matters as commenting verses on love, and excusing himself, by claiming that he was but following the example of such a lofty poet: 'Né io sono stato il primo che ho comentato versi importanti simili amorosi subietti, perché Dante lui medesimo comentò alcuna delle sue canzone e altri versi' ['Nor have I been the first to comment on verses treating of similar amorous subjects, because Dante himself commented upon some of his canzoni and other poems'] (40–3).

Lorenzo then responds to the third objection, concerning the writing of the work in the vernacular. Here he argues that the Italian language's 'common'[17] quality only adds to its dignity, for the closer a language comes to being universal, the closer it approaches the perfection of the *Sommo Bene*. His other arguments are familiar from Dante's treatment of the subject in the *De vulgari eloquentia*, and include the advantage of a language well-suited to express the concepts of the mind which is also sweet and harmonious in its expression. Lorenzo further emphasizes that the expression of all things subtle, grave, and necessary to human life make any language worthy. Furthermore, no more proof is necessary to comprehend the dignity of the Italian language than to consider the works of Florentines like Dante, Petrarca, and Boccaccio.[18] The final lines of the proem excuse the prolixity of Lorenzo's lengthy preparation with a gesture of *captatio benevolentiae* that states that the proem had to make up in its ornamentation for the 'inezzia [dei] versi' ['the inconsequentiality of these verses of mine'].

Lorenzo is, after Dante, the next poet to take up so consciously the practice and, to a somewhat lesser extent, the theory of prosimetrical poetic self-commentary. Not only does Lorenzo borrow from the *Convivio* in order to anticipate criticisms of the procedure and to articulate the motivational basis for his own self-commentary, he also looks to the *Vita Nuova* even more insistently as a model for his 'Argumento' and the 'Nuovo Argumento.' But Dante is not Lorenzo's only point of reference. Ovid ranks among a number of poets expressly cited, and the influence of Petrarca's *Canzoniere* was considerable and unavoidable.[19] Lorenzo also draws on a number of philosophical and poetic arguments made by his contemporaries, including Marsilio Ficino, Giovanni Pico della Mirandola, and Cristoforo Landino. Pico, in a letter frequently cited by scholars of the *Comento*, discusses even more of Lorenzo's mimetic models:

> Quot enim ibi ex Aristotele, *auditu* scilicet *physico*, ex libris *de anima, de moribus, de caelo,* ex *problematis,* quot ex Platonis *Prothagora,* ex *Republica,* ex *Legibus,* ex *Symposio,* quae omnia, quamquam alias apud illos legi, lego tamen apud te ut nova, ut meliora, et in nescio quam a te faciem transformata, ut tua videantur esse et non illorum, et legens discere mihi aliquid videar.
>
> [How many maxims of Aristotle, from the *Physico,* the *De anima,* the *De moribus,* the *De caelo,* the *Problematis;* how many from Plato's *Protagoras, Republica, De legibus,* and *Symposio,* all things that I had read before in those authors, but that in you seem to me to be new, better, transfigured in such a way that they now appear to be yours and not theirs, and when I read them it seems to me I learn new things!][20]

Many scholarly volumes attest to the modes in which Lorenzo adopted the literary and philosophic traditions that preceded him. In concentrating on why Lorenzo chooses to reinscribe his youthful love lyrics in a mixed form that is obviously intended to recall the *Vita Nuova* specifically, I argue that the way in which he can allude to, and in Pico's word, 'transfigure' Dante's example, offers Lorenzo the best opportunity of communicating his poetic message concerning love, wisdom, death, and the possibility of transcendence.[21]

Lorenzo's woefully under-studied, enigmatic *sonettiere* exemplifies one man's search for felicity along the 'dark and difficult way of perfection,' which is opened to the poet by the death of one lady and rendered somewhat less dark and difficult through the mediation of another's love. His *argumento*, which comprises the first four sonnets and their exposition, is central in both its formal and thematic considerations. It follows the proem and precedes the *nuovo argumento*, while treating the issue that death is not an end in itself, but the beginning of a new life.

Taking his cues from Aristotle's assertion in the *Physics* (1.9) that lack is the originating principle of created things and Ficino's insistence that love is a death to all less perfect things, Lorenzo marks the creation of his *Comento* with the death of an unnamed Florentine lady. Scholars have been able to identify this first lady as Simonetta Cattaneo Vespucci, Giuliano de' Medici's mistress and Botticelli's artistic model for his Primavera. Critics have conjectured that Lorenzo thought of Simonetta's role in the *Comento* as similar to the one that Giovanna played in the *Vita nuova*. She was the one who would come first [prima verrà] before the real lady of the poet's heart.[22] Lorenzo insists that opening a work with death is not inappropriate: 'Il principio della vera vita è la morte della vita non vera; né per questo pare posto sanza qualche buono respetto la morte per principio de' versi nostri' ['the principle of the [true] life is the death of the life that is [untrue]. Because of this, employing death as the beginning of our verses seems not without some merit'] (56–7). The lady's passing stirred a universal outpouring of grief, according to the poet, whose own emotion took the form of the first sonnet, 'O chiara stella, che coi raggi tuoi' ['O brilliant star, which with your rays']. From the concerns raised in this poem develop the rest of the 'Argumento's metaphorical elaborations of stars, light, the sunflower, and so forth, which must be the subject of closer analysis.

> O chiara stella, che coi raggi tuoi
>   togli alle tue vicine stelle il lume,
>   perché splendi assai più che 'l tuo costume?
>   Perché con Phebo ancor contender vuoi?
> Forse i belli occhi, quali ha tolti a noi
>   Morte crudel, che omai troppo presume,

accolti hai in te: adorna del lor nume,
  il suo bel carro a Phebo chieder puoi.
O questo o nuova stella che tu sia,
  che di splendor novello adorni il cielo,
  chiamata essaudi, o nume, i voti nostri:
leva dello splendor tuo tanto via,
  che agli occhi, che han d'eterno pianto zelo,
  sanza altra offensïon lieta ti mostri.

[O brilliant star, which with your rays make fade
  The light of all your neighboring stars, why now
  Do you shine brighter than your custom is?
  Why do you wish with Phoebus to contend?
Those lovely eyes, perhaps, which cruel Death,
  Who until now presumes too much, has reft from us
  You've welcomed to yourself: decked with their glory,
  From Phoebus his fair car you can demand.
If this, or if a new star you've become,
  Which with fresh glory so adorns the heavens,
  When called upon, o saint, please grant our prayers:
Abate your splendour, so to eyes that yearn
  To weep eternally for you, without more harm
  You, joyful, can reveal yourself to us.] (58–9)

Here Lorenzo sets before the reader the underlying conflict: the lady's physical death is the *inmediate* beginning of a new life, and the illumination of this significance brings with it all the perils of the radiance of unconcealed truth. The 'chiara stella' is so bright, in fact, that the narrator begs the lady to dim somewhat her light. This focus on the blinding potential of truth calls to mind the Old Testament account of Moses' revelation to the people of God's will, which Pico della Mirandola also relates in his *Heptaplus*, dedicated to Lorenzo:

Ille quidem in montis sublimitate, montis utique illius in quo et Dominus saepe discipulos alloquebatur, divini solis lumine collustratus tota facie mirum in modum splendescebat; sed quia lucem ferre non poterat populus oculis caecutientibus et noctuinis, velata, facie illis verba faciebat.

[However, Moses, at the top of the mountain, like that mountain on which the Lord often spoke to his Disciples, was so illumined by the rays of the divine sun that his entire face shone in a miraculous manner; but because the people with their blinded and darkened eyes could not sustain the light, he addressed them with his face veiled.]²³

The whole of the *Comento*'s *argumento*, in fact, highlights a particular interest in what is veiled or revealed. The author's focus on this issue shows itself, even prior to the first sonnet, in the narration of the funeral procession of the Florentine woman. Her beauty in death outshines what it had been in life, as the mourners could attest, since she was carried 'scoperta' ['uncovered']. This event, in the midst of deprivation, sorrow, and abundant tears, appears to signal the 'scoperta' ['discovery'] that death might not actually be what it seems. Quoting Petrarca, Lorenzo declares: "Morte bella parea nel suo bel volto" ["Death seemed lovely in her lovely face'] (58–9). Lorenzo, in fact, valorizes appearance nearly as much as Dante emphasized the essence, as such statements as the following can attest: 'Pure è assai agli amanti gustare una felicità che paia alloro propria, perché il contento umano consiste più tosto nel parere che nell'essere' ['Very much to lovers' taste, however, is one felicity that seems to them their own, for human happiness consists more in seeming rather than in being'] (178–9).

All of these issues come together in a consideration of Lorenzo's view of rhetoric, and more precisely, of his self-commentary as a rhetorical project. He acknowledges that telling the truth of poetry is as difficult as understanding it: 'È impossibile che altri che io lo possi intendere, perché, quando bene l'avessi ad alcuno narrato, così era impossibile a lui lo intenderlo come a me referirne il vero' ['It is impossible that anyone other than I could understand, because, until I had clearly recounted these things to someone, understanding them would have been as impossible for him as referring to the truth about them for me'] (42–3). Moreover, Lorenzo is aware that he lacks the force of words, as well as faith among his audience, to impose his view: 'Io vorrei avere o tal forza di parole o tanta fede apresso degli uomini, che potessi bene exprimere e fare credere la excellenzia della donna mia, perché a llei sarebbe onore e io fuggirei qualche pericolo d'essere stimato poco veritiero' ['I should like to have either such a power of language or such great faith [among] men, that I could well express and make people believe in the excellence of my lady, because it would do her honour and I would flee some danger of being esteemed untruthful'] (108–9).²⁴ It is not by chance that at this point Lorenzo turns back to talk again of the paradox of life and the death that is the true life.

By inverting his reader's expectations and through the use of paradox, Lorenzo offers the first attempts at understanding and spiritual progression.[25] However, it is through *literary* example that he exhorts the way of *truth*. In Virgil and Dante, for instance, *katabasis* narratives, which insist on a descent or passing through death before the possibility of ascent, demonstrate that one arrives at perfection by this [circuitous] way ['mostrare che alla perfezzione si va per questa via'] (56). Likewise, Orpheus' failed attempt to bring Eurydice back among the living is itself an exercise in perception: '*si può interpetrare* Orfeo non essere veramente morto' ['One *could interpret* Orpheus as not being truly dead'] (56, my emphasis).

I have said that a moral allegory of the potentially harmful radiance of truth in Lorenzo's text is possible if one calls to mind such passages of the Bible as the one that Pico points out concerning Moses. However, the first sonnet also should remind the reader of the myth of Apollo's son Phaeton. While the lady can presume to demand from Phoebus his radiant chariot, Phaeton shows himself by his death to be too presumptuous in rashly requesting to drive Apollo's 'bel carro' across the heavens. Underlying Lorenzo's project is the tension between that desired light of harmony and reason that shines forth from a new life subsequent to a self-knowing death, and that falsely presumptive light evoked in the oblique allusion to Phaeton's fate. In Lorenzo's exposition is the glimpse of an awareness of the risks of presumption, which in Phaeton's case lead to both his own destruction and that of the world at large, to which he is supposed to bring an illuminating, but not annihilating, force.

Lorenzo acknowledges the source for the Phaeton myth in Ovid, who framed the story in terms of doubt, secrecy, and the search for truth. The motivation for the rash youth's fatal escapade was the desire to know himself by confirming the identity of his father:

Ille refert 'O lux inmensi publica mundi,
Phoebe pater, si das huius mihi nominis usum,
Nec falsa Clymene culpam sub imagine celat,
Pignera da, genitor, er quae tua vera propago
Credar, et hunc animis errorem detrahe nostris.'

[The boy replied: 'O you, the common light
of this vast world, o Phoebus, who are my
own father – if you say I have the right

to use that word, and if it is no lie,
a false guise that Clymene used to hide
her shame – remove my doubt, give me some proof,
o Father, that I am your son in truth!'] (2.35–9)

Phaeton sought the 'signature of what [he was],'[26] stripped of the fictions under which his mother Clymene may have hidden some unacknowledged sin. He desired a certain proof beyond potentially deceptive words. Apollo rightly prophesied that Phaeton's self-knowledge would also be his death. He pleaded with his son not to be the author of his own death, continuing, 'Adspice vultus / Ecce meos: utinamque oculos in pectora posses / Inserere et patrias intus deprendere curas!' ['Look at my face! And would you could inspect / my heart and learn what cares a father bears!'] (2.92–4).[27] Apollo further begged his son not to dare assume the rightful task of another[28] for which he was not fit and to be content in safely watching him give light to the world (2.149). But Phaeton rejected this reasoning. Only when it was too late did the youth regret his overly curious presumption:

Ut vero summo despexit ab aethere terras
Infelix Phaethon penitus penitusque patentis,
Palluit et subito genua intremuere timore,
Suntque oculis tenebrae per tantum lumen obortae.
Et iam mallet equos numquam tetigisse paternos,
Iam cognosse genus piget, et valuisse rogando,
Iam Meropis dici cupiens ita fertur.

[Sad Phaeton looked down from heaven's heights
at earth, which lay so far, so far below.
He paled; his knees were seized by sudden fright;
and there, within the overwhelming light,
a veil of darkness fell upon his eyes.
Would he had never touched his father's steeds! –
so he repents. Would he had not received
proof of his origins, would that his plea
had been refused. If only he had been
a son of Merops!] (2.178–84)

Phaeton was overly dazzled by the blazing light of the sun, just as Lorenzo's narrator is dazzled before the bright star of the first sonnet.

There is an unusual shift in emphasis between this sonnet and the second one, 'Quando il sol giù dall'orizzonte scende' ['When, from the far horizon, sinks the sun']. As we have seen, in the first sonnet, the brilliancy of the star could contend with that of the sun. In the second sonnet, however, the focus shifts to the poet's compassion on seeing the plight of Clytie, lover of the sun:

> Quando il sol giù dall'orizzonte scende,
>   rimiro Clyzia pallida nel vólto,
>   e piango la sua sorte, che li ha tolto
>   la vista di colui che ad altri splende.
> Poi, quando di novella fiamma accende
>   l'erbe, le piante e' fior' Phebo, a noi vòlto,
>   l'altro orizzonte allor ringrazio molto
>   e la begnigna Aurora che gliel rende.
> Ma, lasso, io non so già qual nuova Aurora
>   renda al mondo il suo Sole! Ah, dura sorte,
>   che noi vestir d'eterna notte volse!
> O Clyzia, indarno speri vederlo ora!
>   Tien' li occhi fissi, infin li chiugga morte,
>   all'orizzonte extremo che tel tolse.

> [When, from the far horizon, sinks the sun,
>   I gaze again on Clytie's pallid face,
>   And I lament the fate that snatched away
>   From her the sight of one who elsewhere shines.
> When with new flame, then, Phoebus, back with us,
>   Sets grass and plants and flowers all alight,
>   The alternate horizon much I thank,
>   And thank kind Dawn who gives him back again.
> But, woe! I know not what new Dawn can give
>   The world its sun again! Ah, cruel fate,
>   Which wished to clothe us in eternal night!
> O Clytie, vain your hope to see him now:
>   Until death close your eyes, fix them upon
>   The far horizon that took him away.] (60–1)

In Ovid's account, Clytie was jealous of Apollo's love for Leocothoe. And when Leocothoe's father learned from gossiping Clytie of his daughter's relationship with Apollo, Leocothoe could only protest that Apollo raped her (4.238–9). Leocothoe's resulting death at her father's hand was, significantly, Apollo's saddest sight after Phaeton's fiery fall: 'Nil illo fertur volucrum moderator equorum/ Post Phaethonteos vidisse dolentius ignes' ['And nothing that the one who guides swift steeds / had ever suffered since the fiery death / of Phaeton had brought him deeper grief'] (4.245–6). Apollo subsequently avoided Clytie, causing what Ovid noted as her transformation into the flower that bears her name.

In Lorenzo's verse, the narrator compares himself to the sunflower of Ovidian myth whose face perennially turns to gaze on the beloved, except that his new sun will never rise again. Now Clytie, and likewise the poet, can only fix until death their gaze on the horizon beneath which the sun has departed (2.12–14). In Lorenzo's commentary, the emphasis falls on the desire to see something whose sight is necessarily and forever forbidden: 'Questa sorte di Clyzia, diversa e alterna, mi fece dipoi pensare quanto era più dura e iniqua sorte quella di colui che desidera assai vedere la cosa, il vedere della quale necessariamente gli è interdetto, non per una notte, ma per sempre' ['This fate of Clytie, strange and different, made me then think how much harder and how unjust was that fate for one who very much desired to see something whose sight was necessarily forbidden him, not for one night, but forever'] (62–5). Moreover, the harshest fate belongs to one who awaits with great desire that which can never come to pass ['durissima sorte è quella di colui che con assai desiderio aspetta quello che non può avere'] (64–5). There follows a brief exposition of the meaning of 'horizon': '"Orizzonte" non vuole dire altro che l'ultimo termine, di là dal quale gli occhi umani non possono vedere' ['"horizon" means nothing more than the ultimate terminus, beyond which human eyes cannot see'] (64–5). The definition of horizon is further allegorized by the statement: 'E però convenientemente possiamo chiamare la morte quell'orizzonte che ne tolse la vista degli occhi suoi' ['And therefore we can fitly call death that horizon that took from us the sight of her eye'] (64–5). By steps Lorenzo's narrator arrives at the motto of Apollo's temple, 'Nosce te ipsum' ['know thyself'], thus reiterating a point he made in reference to a different myth of Apollo in the preceding sonnet, that death is the necessary consequence of the full knowledge of oneself.

Clytie's introduction into Lorenzo's 'Argumento' presents at least two problems for which satisfactory explanations remain elusive. First, there is certainly something audacious about presenting Clytie as the ideal example of knowing oneself:

> E chi considera questo in altri, può facilmente conoscere questa condizione e necessità in sé medesimo, servando quello sapientissimo detto che nel tempio d'Appolline era scritto, 'Nosce te ipsum,' perseverando in questo pensiero infino che la morte venga; la quale renderà il Sole suo a questo nuovo Clyzia, come l'Aurora lo rende a Clyzia già convertita in fiore, dell'anima di costei, molto più bella che quella la quale era prima visibile agli occhi: perché la luce degli occhi umani è come ombra respetto alla luce dell'anima. E cosi come la morte di colei è stata orizzonte all'occaso del sole degli occhi suoi, così la morte di questo nuovo Clyzia sarà l'orizzonte orientale che renderà a llui il suo Sole, come l'Aurora lo rende a Clyzia già conversa in fiore.

> [And whoever considers this in others can easily understand this condition and necessity in himself, if he observes that very wise saying, written in the temple of Apollo, to 'know thyself,' and perseveres in this thought until death comes. Death will render his Sun to this new Clytie, just as the Dawn restores it to that Clytie already converted to a flower, of her soul, which is much more beautiful than the one that was first visible to the eyes, since the light of human eyes is like a shadow compared to the light of the soul. And just as her death was the horizon of the setting of the sun of her eyes, so the death of this new Clytie will be the eastern horizon that will render to him his Sun, like the Dawn rendered it to Clytie already converted into a flower] (64, my translation).

Ovid's Clytie, for it is to this version that Lorenzo explicitly refers,[29] certainly did not posses the virtues of a beautiful soul, according to the Neoplatonists, and the poem may have an as-yet-unexplored ironic tone.

Second, in reassessing the significance of the Clytie narration for Lorenzo, one must keep in mind that the understanding of Ovid's story is effected by its narrative frame. In Book Four, Clytie's story was one of a number of narratives, including those of Pyramus and Thisbe, and Salmacis and Hermaphroditus, which King Minyas's daughters told while they weaved, thereby defying the Bacchic festival customs of drunkenness and revelry. They placed their faith in Minerva, chaste goddess of wisdom (4.38). Ovid's framing strategy for the presentation of the Clytie story necessarily influences the reader's ultimate impression of it. For not keeping holy Bacchus' feast day, the girls were punished by being overcome by a house fire in the twilight and transformed into bat-like creatures that haunt building attics:

> Quod tu nec tenebras nec posses dicere lucem,
> Sed cum luce tamen dubiae confinia nocti:
> Tecta repente quati pinquesque ardere videntur
> Lampades et rutilis conlucere ignibus aedes
> Falsaque saevarum simulacra ululare ferarum.
> Fumida iamdumum latitant per tecta sorores,
> Diversaeque locis ignes ac lumina vitant,
> Dumque petunt latebras, parvos membrana per artus
> Porrigitur, tenuique includunt bracchia pinna.
> Nec qua perdiderint veterem ratione figuram,
> Scire sinunt tenebrae. Non illas pluma levavit.
> Sustinuere tamen se perlucentibus alis.
> Conataeque locqui minimam pro corpore vocem
> Emittunt peraguntque leves stridore querellas.
> Tectaque, non silvas celebrant lucemque perosae
> Nocte volant seroque tenent a vespere nomen.

> [Indeed, the hour had come when it is hard
> to say that it's still day or it is dark,
> when an uncertain light trespasses on
> the boundary of night. And suddenly,
> the walls began to tremble and the lamps –
> oil-fed – to flare up, and the palace seemed
> ablaze with ruddy flames, while phantom beasts
> were roaring. Now the sisters rush to seek
> some hidden corner, any place to keep
> the flashing flames away; but smoke invades
> the halls. And as the sisters try to hide,
> their limbs – grown smaller now – are covered by
> a membrane, just as thin wings cloak their arms.
> Within the dark, they cannot see just how
> they've lost their former shape. Though they can show
> no feathered plumage, their transparent wings
> sustain them; and when they attempt to speak,
> the sounds they utter fit their shriveled shapes;

and each to each, they grieve in thin, thin squeaks.
They do not haunt the houses, but the woods;
since they detest the day, they fly by night.
It is from twilight that their name derives,
for bats are often called the Vesperites.] (4.400–15)

The play of light and shadow in this passage, as well as the insistence on wisdom, divine worship, death, and transformed life brings an ominous undercurrent of significance to Ovid's version of Clytie, as well as to Lorenzo's.

It should by now be evident from my considerations of Phaeton, Clytie, and the motto 'know thyself' that the Apollonian figure lies at the heart of Lorenzo's poetics. Indeed, the much-exploited pun on Lorenzo's own name indicates as much. Lorenzo is the one who bears the laurel wreath, the sign of Apollo's love for the elusive Daphne. Their love was one that transcended her 'death,' the metamorphosis into the laurel tree. Here again Ovid's treatment of the Apollo myth was the one of primary concern to Lorenzo, and it is worthwhile to review briefly the Daphne episode.[30]

Ovid's version of the love story emerges out of the *discors concordia* (1.433) at the very dawn of the world, when the sun was newly wakened, and great Python, the serpent of temptation that lurks in the darkest recesses of the human heart, was subdued by bright Apollo's murderous arrow. The attack greatly angered Cupid, the god of earthly love, who vowed revenge by piercing Apollo's heart with an arrow of love and that of beloved Daphne with one of hate. In so doing Cupid proved that his arrows were superior to Apollo's, to the same degree that immortality is greater than death. Cupid's arrows wrought the desired effect, and Phoebus burned for the chaste maiden, comparing her, as Lorenzo does in 'O chiara stella,' to the stars ['Videt igne micantes / Sideribus similes oculos, videt oscula, quae non / Est vidisse satis'] (1.498–500). The god, in trying to convince the fleeing girl to halt, also stated that medicine was his invention. Lorenzo also likely encourages another well-known pun on his name, deriving it from this context since 'medici' are physicians.[31] Daphne's prayers were answered and she became laurel, 'praecordia libro' (1.549). Her midsection or heart was the bark, but also the book. 'Te coma, te citharae, te nostrae, laure, pharetrae' (1.559): she was hair/foliage/sunbeams, lyre, and quiver, which Apollo took as his own seals.

All of this is vitally important because Lorenzo takes up the central conflict between Apollo and Amor in Ovid to mark the difference between the guiding principles of his self-commentative procedure and that of Dante. Lorenzo's self-commentary is, as I have said, also a commentary, a commentary on Dante's poetic project. Imitation is, in fact, an important, rarified form of commentary, since it is through the interpretation of Renaissance literary mimetic works that readers can explore vast realms of aesthetics and poetics, as well as the spiritual dimensions of the text, which the strictest *explications du texte* would never quite be able to contain. One cannot help but wonder if it were precisely the greatness of Landino's commentaries on Dante, and their simultaneous disengagement from other aspects of Dante's works central to Lorenzo's literary interests, which might have motivated Lorenzo to attempt the *Comento* in the first place. Moreover, while explicit allusions, similarities in form, theme, and so forth, mark Lorenzo's emulation of Dante, it is in his own 'divisions,' in Lorenzo's delineations, dialogue, and difference with respect to the Dantean model, that the heart of the commentary burns, and is, in the end, consumed.

Dante insisted on the role of Amore in the *Vita Nuova*. From the moment Dante first set eyes on Beatrice, he explained, 'Love ruled my soul' ['Amore segnoreggiò la mia anima']. As the *libello* unfolded, Love appeared to his disciple various times, guiding and counselling him. The turning point came in chapter 12, as we have seen, after Beatrice denied Dante her 'saluto,' leaving him devastated. Dante implored Love to come to the aid of his faithful one. Love then visited Dante in a dream and addressed him very obscurely, saying, 'Ego tanquam centrum circuli, cui simili modo se habent circumferente partes; tu autem non sic' ['I am like the centre of a circle, equidistant from all points on the circumference; you, however, are not']. But Amore refused to explain his meaning further presumably because he knew that it would become clear to his disciple in time. Dante followed Love in not clarifying his own meaning at such points as when he refused to divide his poems because their significance was clear to any other faithful devotee of Love. The importance of time in the full comprehension of Love's significance seemed also to rule the understanding of Dante's first sonnet, 'A ciascun'alma presa e gentil core.' The poet had received many interpretations of the dream, none of which was the true one. However, *now*, he said, the poem is 'very clear even to the simplest ones' ['manifestissimo a li più semplici'].

As if the reader were not sufficiently challenged by the radical role Dante ascribed to Love, he went on to say: 'E chi volesse sottilmente considerare, quella Beatrice chiamarebbe Amore, per molta simiglianza che ha meco' ['Anyone of subtle discernment would call Beatrice Love, because she so greatly resembles me'] (24.5).[32] Dante then dedicated the entire subsequent chapter to the exploration of what he meant by Love, explaining in Scholastic terms that it was but an accident in a substance; nevertheless, poetic licence, including the whole of the Latins' trove of images and rhetorical colouring, must be at his disposal in order to relate to us his new life.

From this close association between the lady, the accident, and the poet's lord, we have already begun to see Lorenzo's shift with respect to the lady, the *chiara stella* of the first sonnet, who makes her appearance in the second as the sun, the Apollo, whom the poet-as-Clytie follows in its path across the heavens.[33] At this point the reader must turn back to Lorenzo's proem, in order to see that he constructs his *Comento* on the Dantean model from the very start, and that any possible conclusions to be drawn about Lorenzo's self-commentary must take into account his circular form of narration and circumscription of literary allusion.

Memory guided the development of Dante's little book. Indeed, the *Vita Nuova* asserted itself as the transcription of the poet's Book of Memory. Lorenzo's *incipit* posits both a recognizable, if tenuous, similarity, and a critical difference: 'Assai sono stato dubbioso e sospeso se dovevo fare la presente interpetrazione e comento delli miei sonetti' ['I have been very doubtful and uncertain about whether or not I ought to prepare the present interpretation of and commentary upon my sonnets'] (30–1). The opening words, which employ a formulaic *captatio* used at least from the time of Statius,[34] provide a particularly appropriate and poetically complex opening chord for Lorenzo's self-commentary: doubt. That dubious hesitation implicitly acknowledges an awareness of the unusual nature of the project and anticipates the objections the writer will shortly raise. Like Dante's invocation of Memory, doubt signals the temporal disjunction in the composition of poetry and commentary. The writer effectively reinterprets his poetry by inscribing it within a subsequent prose narration. The discrepancy between an assumed truth of the past and a new and somehow conflicting view of the present prompts such an uncertainty. It becomes the point of departure of Lorenzo's quest for self-knowledge, which the self-commentary comes to represent.[35]

Regular reminders of the function of memory spring out of Lorenzo's proem and argument. For example, Orpheus's memory of the old life, the fact that in turning back to Eurydice he was not entirely dead to it, destroyed the object of his quest and blocked his spiritual reascension. Moreover, Lorenzo must flee his own sad memory in his last 'song' before embarking on the 'Nuovo Argumento' and his new life:

> In qual parte andrò io, ch'io non ti truovi,
> *trista memoria*? In quale obscuro speco
> fuggirò io, che sempre non sia meco
> *trista memoria*, che al mio mal sol giovi?
>
> [Where shall I go where I won't find you, *sad memory*?
> To what dark cavern shall I flee
> where you won't still be there with me,
> *sad memory*, you who only aid my troubles?] (70, the translation and italics are mine)

Death brings the *inmediate* birth of a possible mystic-poetic ascension for both Dante and Lorenzo. With Dante, the deaths of one of Beatrice's friends, and then of her father, foreshadowed the blessed lady's own passing, which signaled Dante's first steps of recognition and praise on his itinerary to God. But it was only with Dante's turning away from the 'pietosa donna's' comforting glances that he could overcome the point of Orpheus's failure and hope to fulfil his pilgrimage.

For Lorenzo, death is likewise a central metaphor, but the unfinished nature of the *Comento* makes it difficult to speculate what death might signify in the 'Nuovo Argumento.' Why, for instance, are the words of the prophet Jeremiah ['Quomodo sedet sola civitas plena populo! facta est quasi vidua domina gentium'], which Dante cited to announce Beatrice's death, the last allusion Lorenzo makes before his *Comento* mysteriously breaks off? However, Lorenzo treats the Florentine lady's death in the *Argumento* almost as a 'pietosa donna.' The first lady does not become the object of unceasing praise that moves in one direction from the poet to the lady. Rather, she marks the essential passage from a sort of simulacrum to the love of the second lady in the 'Nuovo argumento,' and this shift emphasizes the gracious nature of participation in a reciprocal love relationship.

The difference in perspective between the two poetic self-commentators underlies many aspects of the ways they portray love, death, and spiritual progression. However, this difference is most evident in the perspective paradigm mentioned by both authors: the relationship between the point and the circumference of the circle. In the *Vita Nuova*, Love spoke in Latin the words I have already cited, and which placed him at the centre of the circle (where the lover was not), equidistant from all points of the circumference. Thus, for Dante there was an absolute point from which Love radiated outward, seeing and ordering everything else. Lorenzo phrases his response in such a way that the issues of love and language come together in a declaration of perspective from the point of view of a relative, circumferential point seeking the circle's centre: 'avendo in genere dimostrato la perfezzione d'essa [vernacular language], giudico molto conveniente *ristringersi al particulare e venire dalla generalità a qualche proprietà, quasi come dalla circumferenzia al centro*' ['having demonstrated its perfection in general, I consider it very fitting to limit myself to particulars and to come from generality to certain properties, almost as from the circumference to the centre'] (50–1, my emphasis).

The context in which these words appear is Lorenzo's argument for the worthiness of the vernacular. It is in some way an implicit critique of Dante's wording of Love's 'explication' in Latin, discarding the vision that departed from an absolute point to forward one that attempts to seek the point by necessary circumnavigation. Significantly, this reasoning leads to Lorenzo's assertion of the superiority of the sonnet form, which runs counter to Dante's preference for the canzone.[36] While Lorenzo is careful to stress repeatedly that he has in mind Latin poetry, it is perhaps difficult to ignore his suggestion that sonnets should attract greater admiration than canzoni if they avoid obscurity and harshness or difficulty of style:

> Le canzone ancora, per avere più larghi spazii dove possino vagare, non reputo tanto difficile stile quanto quello del sonetto; e questo si può assai facilmente provare con la experienzia, perché chi ha composto sonetti e s'è ristretto a qualche certa e subtile materia, con grande difficultà ha fuggito la obscurità e durezza dello stile.

> [The canzone, moreover, by having wider spaces in which to wander, is not considered as difficult in style as the sonnet. And this one can very easily demonstrate from experience, because whoever has composed sonnets and been restricted to some certain and subtle material, has with great difficulty escaped obscurity and harshness of style.] (52–3)

Lorenzo evidently wishes to call to mind the obscure and difficult style that Dante himself defended in his *Convivio*, which consisted, furthermore, exclusively of commented canzoni.

Summarizing, in his unfinished *Comento* Lorenzo is particularly concerned with the continual process of coming to know oneself. Implicit in such a quest is a careful examination of what is veiled as opposed to what is revealed, a dialectic grounded not only in the thematic motifs of Lorenzo's verse, but also in his formal juxtaposition of poetry and prose. The relationship between the poetic message and the representation of its form in the *Comento* is vitally significant, especially since Lorenzo links the Delphic injunction, know thyself, to the task of self-commentary. He insists that the poet is the only one who can know the true significance of the poetry and, thus, to comment on it. Lorenzo's quest leads him to write another 'new life' and in commenting on his own sonnets, Lorenzo implicitly writes a commentary on Dante. The reader finds that Dante's *Vita Nuova*, precisely because it served as an evident model of the *Comento*'s form, came to highlight the fundamental differentiation in the authors' poetic projects. Lorenzo marks the composition of a *new* 'new life' through a work that is simultaneously commentary and self-commentary; indeed it is commentary *because* it is self-commentary.

Study of Lorenzo's *Comento* has become all but lifeless in recent years, discouraged by variations on the assumption that his self-commentary is the authoritatively definitive word on his poetry. But as the Neoplatonic and Christian philosopher-poet himself would have asserted, recalling the examples of Ulysses, Aeneas, Dante, and others, death is but the beginning of a move towards the true, new life. In the end, the reader is left with many questions concerning Lorenzo's self-commentary. No less than the poems from which it purports to elicit the truth, poetic self-commentary requires the keenest interpretive efforts. But let me leave Lorenzo with one final self-commentative passage, which might have been among the final words of the *Comento* that he wrote before his death:

> Concluderemo per questo il verso vulgare essere molto difficile, e, tra gli altri versi, lo stile del sonetto difficillimo, e per questo degno d'essere in prezzo quanto alcuno degli altri stili vulgari. Né per questo voglio inferire li miei sonetti essere di quella perfezzione che ho detto convenirsi a tal modo di stile; ma, come dice Ovidio di Phetonte, per al presente mi basta

avere tentato quello stile che appresso e vulgari è più excellente, e se non ho potuto aggiungere alla perfezzione *sua* o conducere questo curro solare, almanco mi sia in luogo di laude lo ardire d'avere tentato questa via, ancora che con qualche mio mancamento le forze mi sieno mancate a tanta impressa.

[From this we conclude vernacular verse to be very difficult, and, among the other genres, the style of the sonnet the most difficult, and therefore worthy of being as highly regarded as any of the vernacular styles. I do not wish to infer from this that my sonnets are of that perfection that I have said belongs to such a stylistic genre; but, as Ovid said of Phaeton, for the present it is enough to have attempted that one that is the most excellent among the vernacular styles, and if I have not been able to achieve his ... perfection or to drive this solar chariot, at least I may deserve a place of merit for having attempted this way, even if among my failings I lack the strength for such a great enterprise.] (52–3, my emphasis)

The English translation of the third person singular pronoun 'sua' has proven problematic. Cook suggests that it refers to Phaeton: 'if I have not been able to achieve his [Phaeton's] perfection.' But this makes little sense, since Phaeton showed himself to be anything but perfect. I think the passage refers on one level to the most difficult style of the sonnet when it is written on 'certain and subtle matters' that find expression in a rhyme scheme without the rhyme dictating the material. On another level, however, would seem to loom the solar chariot of the task of poetic self-commentary itself: though Lorenzo may not have succeeded, he should at least receive praise for attempting the difficult enterprise of self-interpretation. Moreover, although he did not attain Dante's perceived perfection in writing certain and subtle canzoni (or canzoni and sonnets in the case of the *Vita Nuova*), his only hope of coming close to that perfection rested in the composition of a strict *sonettiere*.

In the end, Lorenzo's commentary is also a critique of Dante's failure to know himself in Phaeton's flight. In the *Divina Commedia*, for instance, Dante portrayed the risks he ran in his project, most explicitly in *Inferno* 27, when on Geryon's back he felt the fear that Phaeton must have experienced at the reins of Apollo's chariot,[37] and in the rhetorical enterprise that led to Ulysses' 'folle volo' ['mad flight'] in *Inferno* 26.[38] However, in Dante's confident flight and transgression of all bounds, which is the *Commedia* itself, Dante seemed to attract criticism from Lorenzo for not truly acknowledging those risks as his own. By means of a self-commentary that emphasizes the role of wisdom (and specifically self-knowledge) under the aegis of Apollo, as opposed to Dante's faithfulness to Amore, Lorenzo can point out the weaknesses and strengths of Dante's project and of his own. Dante's lack of self-knowledge can permit him to complete his journey, while Lorenzo's project shipwrecks at the point of Jeremiah's prophecy, that is, the point at which Dante must go beyond seeing Beatrice as a muse of mere earthly love.

The daring quality implicit in this chapter's epigraph is also the audacity of the commentator, as Lorenzo would have discussed with members of his intellectual circle, such as Landino. In reference to his commentary on Virgil, for instance, Landino defended himself against critics who insisted that he did not follow closely enough the author's intention: 'If they wish to slander me, let them speak of my *rashness*' (my emphasis). Could it be that Lorenzo's 'commentary' on Dante wished daringly to approach that sphere of understanding that exceeds both of them?

Thus, paradoxically, it is precisely Lorenzo's failure that is his success. He acknowledges the risks that his poetic project squarely addresses and emblematizes in the figure of Phaeton. Behind the paradox of this failure/success, is *gnothi seauton*, the self-knowledge that is both death and new life, the self-commentary that is both letter and spirit. Only because Lorenzo 'fails' in his task of poetic self-commentary does he acquire the capacity to point out the *inmediate* life potential of the poetic project.

4

'Distorted in contrary senses': Girolamo Benivieni's Self-Commentative Reformation

In the shadows of the Magnificent's limelight was a rigorous self-commentator of a much different sort, the poet Girolamo Benivieni. Not only did Benivieni append a self-exegetical apparatus to his youthful love poems, he also repeated the procedure for his eclogues and wrote a Christian canzone with his own self-commentary in response to an earlier Platonic canzone of his on which Pico della Mirandola had expounded. In Benivieni's case, however, self-commentary turns out to embody a very different intent and function than those previously considered. In this chapter I examine Benivieni's notable emphasis on *re-forming* his lyrics and on his literalizing procedure of repentance and recantation.

Since Benivieni is significantly less well-known than other self-commentators of this study, and his self-commentary is in many ways more explicitly linked to the events of his life,[1] I will begin by providing a brief biographical account. Girolamo Benivieni was born in 1453 to what would be a particularly distinguished family. His siblings included older brother Antonio Benivieni, innovative surgeon and author of important medical manuals, and younger brother Domenico, the theologian at the University of Pisa widely known as 'Lo Scotino.' By his teenage years, Girolamo had employed his quick wit, musical talent, and poetic flair to win Lorenzo de' Medici's favour. His viola concerts and lyric improvisations earned him the nickname 'l'altro Orfeo,'[2] and his early poetry, imbued with stilnovistic and Petrarchan influences, began to circulate before 1472. Benivieni reveled in the ostentatious pomp and cultural vivacity associated with the Medici circle and Florentine Neoplatonic Academy, and around 1489 he published his poetry under the title *Canzone e Sonetti di Girolamo Benivieni fiorentino: Come, dove, quando e di cui prima se inamorò, et quale fructo ne seguitasse* [Songs and Sonnets by the Florentine Girolamo Benivieni: How, Where, When, and With Whom He First Fell in Love, and What Good Came of It]. These compositions praising earthly love are the ones the poet would particularly come to regret, and in reparation for which he would write the poetic self-commentary that is the focal point of this investigation, the *Commento di Hieronymo Benivieni sopra a più sue canzone et sonetti dello Amore et della Belleza Divina* [Commentary by Girolamo Benivieni on Some of His Songs and Sonnets on Love and Divine Beauty] (1500).[3]

Benivieni's childhood and youth, according to his biographers, passed happily and uneventfully, with the exception of a grave illness the poet contracted in 1470. This illness caused Benivieni to abandon a regular course of study. Nonetheless, he was able to learn Greek and Hebrew, among other subjects. His health remained delicate for the duration of his life, influencing some of his crucial decisions, including that never to marry, nor to enter a religious order.

Perhaps the two greatest influences in Benivieni's life were his dearest friend Giovanni Pico della Mirandola, who would subsequently write a commentary on his 'Canzona dell'Amor celeste e divino' ['Song of Celestial and Divine Love'], and the fiery Dominican preacher Girolamo Savonarola. The years between 1492 and 1494 were particularly turbulent and mournful ones for Benivieni, who lost Lorenzo de' Medici in 1492, and Pico in 1494, on the same day Charles VIII marched on Florence. Collectively these events apparently pushed Benivieni close to suicide, thoughts of which were seldom far from the sickly and melancholic poet's mind. They probably influenced Benivieni's closer adhesion to Savonarola's *piagnone* movement, characterized as it was by extreme austerity in penance. The poet was one of the first intellectuals whom Savonarola converted. Benivieni wrote various songs sung during the greatest of the Savonarolan processions and the famous Burning of the Vanities in 1496–7. He also translated into the vernacular Savonarola's treatise *De Simplicitate Christianae Vitae* [On the Simplicity of the Christian Life] and into Latin some of Savonarola's vernacular works. Benivieni signed the failed petition to Pope Alexander VI to free Savonarola from excommunication. (The Ferrarese preacher was eventually hanged and burned as a heretic in 1498).

Expecting death at any moment, the sickly Benivieni instead lived nearly another half century. His was a relatively quiet, private life of study and pious works of charity. In 1524 he refused an attractive offer to tutor Giovanni delle Bande Nere. He participated in the Florentine government only as member of the Duecento in 1532. The project that most occupied his attention was the erection of a mausoleum at San Marco in honour of Pico, a tomb he would share after his own death in 1542.

Benivieni's profound spiritual metanoia in his thirties corresponds with a crucial turning point in his poetic production. He turned away from the Neoplatonic and metaphysical syncretism of the Florentine Academy and a stilnovistic-Petrarchan poetic manner towards a poetic production charged with patristic piety and an ethical-didactic intent.[4] By means of revisions to the poems and the addition of a self-interpretive prose apparatus, Benivieni sought to reform his earlier lyrics,[5] which celebrate his love for a number of women.[6] The Florentine calls for spiritual and civic reform impelled Benivieni to make changes in both his personal life and his poetic production.

The *Commento* consists in part of a reissue of his collection of youthful lyrics, as I have noted, but to these, which he does not hesitate to change, Benivieni added a number of new poems, as well as a moralizing self-commentary intended to elucidate the allegorical significance of all the compositions.[7] It is the most ostensibly prescriptive self-commentary considered in this study. On the surface, at least, Benivieni's self-commentary strikes the reader as very straightforward. His project more closely approximates the procedure of the standard outside commentary, especially a Christian reinterpretation of a pagan text, such as the *Ovide moralisé*.[8] It delimits the sphere of possible significance of the poetic text, presenting a reading of the work which, in seeking to be unambiguous, becomes inevitably partial. In fact, Benivieni borrowed significant sections of his self-commentary, nearly word for word, from Pico's commentary on a canzone by Benivieni.[9] Much of the self-commentary recalls the scholastic procedure of the *divisio textus*, in which each poem receives an 'expositione summaria' [a summary or general exposition], that declares the work's intention. Benivieni candidly announced:

> El fine e lo obiecto della quale [della 'opera presente'], perché altro non è che figuratamente descrivere lo ascenso, la ruina e la revocatione della anima humana in el suo fine, che è epso Dio, congrua allo ordine nostro e

consequente cosa mi parve dare a ciaschuno de e' tre premessi concepti la sua parte.

[The aim and objective of [the present work] is none other than to figuratively describe the ascension, fall, and recalling of the human soul to its end, that is God. In keeping with our order, it seemed an appropriate thing to me to give to each of these three abovementioned concepts its place.] (Canzone 1.1.1)

Following the general exposition is a so-called particular exposition, that is, a line-by-line dissection of the poems in which the glossator transcribes the first words of the pertinent excerpt and expounds on the moralizing significance, as for example: 'Le amate luce: epsa divina belleza' ['The beloved lights: that divine beauty'] and 'Del suo sole: di epsa divina belleza' ['Of its sun: of its divine beauty,' sonnet 1.15].[10] It is also not unusual for the gloss to be of highly dubious necessity as far as its content is concerned, for example, 'Amor: o amore' ('Love: or love,' canzone 1.2.4). In addition, Benivieni tends to repeat certain definitions over and over again. The repetition becomes, if not monotonous, suspiciously superfluous, and the effect could not have been lost on his early audience.

Benivieni typically does not divide his poems, as Dante did in his *Vita Nuova*, limiting himself to a definition of the poem's form, most often sonnet, canzona, sestina, or sometimes 'cantilena,' a term probably meant to designate a more humble or less serious song. Benivieni's prose apparatus addresses a surprising variety of topics. He includes autobiographical material, philosophical disputation, and an eyewitness account of Florentine processions and the Burning of the Vanities in his often lengthy 'digressions.'[11] This prose is interspersed among the poems within the body of the work. Benivieni uses the margins of the text exclusively for selective attributions of his biblical, patristic, and literary or philosophical sources, and for catch phrases of the material presented in each section, presumably for ease of reference within the work, which consists of 150 numbered folios.[12]

Like the poetic self-commentators before him, Benivieni is especially concerned with justifying his project. This is the foremost issue of the *Commento*'s proem, dedicated to Pico's nephew, Giovanfrancesco Pico. Benivieni relies in particular on four works to introduce his *Commento*: Dante's *Vita Nuova*, *Convivio*, and *Divina Commedia*, and Lorenzo de' Medici's *Comento*. Benivieni's literary allusions help him to justify the work's form and to avoid accusations of presumption for writing commentary on his own poetry. They also enable Benivieni to define his project largely in opposition to his literary precedents. It is in this way that Benivieni's counter-imitative procedure should come to light.[13]

In language that accentuates Benivieni's heavy debt to Dante, the *Commento* presents the footsteps of a journey ['inditio [di un] nuovo cammino'] (8). It opens with a didactic metaphor. Benivieni wishes to teach his readers the correct path so that they may avoid the errors he committed. The didactic metaphor matches his pedagogic intent:

> Intendendo maximamente che se mai di questa nostra già deplorata fatica altra utilità non risultassi che questa una, non gli sarebbe forse in tutto denegata. Et etiam senza la copia di epsi amorosi miei versi non si potrieno remuovere dalla delectatione di quello con manco pericolo o leggeranno le cose nostre qualunque epse si sieno, o forse ad exemplo e imitatione di quelle lasciato el subiecto e male per e più usurpata materia dello amore lascivo, si extenderanno ad comporre e loro versi di questo nostro amore.
>
> [Most of all, the intention is this: perhaps our already deplored efforts would not be entirely useless if their utility were none other than this: that is, that many who are dedicated to that poetic exercise, whom without a copy of my amorous verses could not be deterred from delighting in them, with less risk either they will read our things as they are, or perhaps by example and imitation of them, once the subject and evil usurpation of the material on lascivious love is left behind, will go on to compose their own verses on our [divine] love.] (Canzone 1.1.1)

Like the protagonist in the first canto of the *Divine Comedy*, the Renaissance poet-commentator finds at about the midpoint in the journey of his life that he has lost his spiritual way. Benivieni confesses that the 'lonza' ['leopard'], which is the first beast that Dante the pilgrim encounters, is the one that hinders his own progress.[14] Moreover, Benivieni, who on another occasion wrote a well-known commentary on Dante's *Inferno*,[15] adopts the same metaphor as his Florentine predecessor to describe his feelings of gratitude as he sets out to recount the difficulties of the journey he has made: that is, the metaphor of the shipwreck survivor. In fact, the whole of the *Commento* testifies to Benivieni's survival of that 'pelago' of the Proem to which I will turn shortly.[16]

Like Dante's masterpiece, the *Commento* moves from the soul's narrow escape from the whirlpool of damnation to the arrival at the heavenly Jerusalem in a hundred cantos (or in the case of Benivieni, in a hundred canzoni and sonnets).[17] As the opening pages of Benivieni's *Commento* unfold, it becomes evident that two other episodes in Dante's *Inferno* serve as important points of reference for this project. Benivieni alludes to these Dantean episodes in passages such as the following:

> Non sono certo, *non sono desideroso di accrescere con la expositione del nostro amore e de le incomparabile sue excellentie e virtù la cagione de' miei troppo pure per insino a qui nutriti dolori*. Ma sì bene di satisfare in qualche modo a el debito e a le legge comune de la amicitia nostra, e di excusare parimente la infirmità del animo mio, da la quale come in primo *a Dio piacque che io in qualche modo resurgessi*, apersi subito li occhi de la mente e conobbi che nessuna cosa si fa in terra senza cagione.

> [I am certainly not eager to augment with an exposition of our love and of [Pico's] incomparable capacities and virtues the cause of my pains, which have been up until now already too well-nourished. But in order to satisfy in some way the debt and the common law of our friendship, and likewise to excuse my soul's infirmity, *from which God willed that I in some way be resurrected*, I opened the eyes of my mind and understood that nothing happens on earth without a reason.] (Proem, my emphasis)

Arguably the most famous scenes of the *Divine Comedy*, the encounter with Francesca da Rimini among the lustful souls of *Inferno* 5, and that with the fraudulent counsellor Ulysses in *Inferno* 26, are particularly appropriate allusions at the outset of Benivieni's work. Benivieni's stated primary objective is the reform of earthly love, especially as it is represented by his self-described lascivious love lyrics. But he must also come to terms with the same risk of madness and impious daring, he perceives in Dante's association between Ulysses' fate and Dante's own poetic 'mad flight.'

It is as if the whole of Benivieni's *Commento* is the reckoning of the 'first root of love' by one who 'weeps and tells.' The allusion is, of course, to Dante's dialogue with Francesca da Rimini:

> 'Nessun maggior dolore
> che ricordarsi del tempo felice
> ne la miseria; e ciò sa 'l tuo dottore.
> Ma s'a conoscer la prima radice

del nostro amor tu hai cotanto affetto,
dirò come colui che piange e dice.'

['There is no greater sorrow than to recall, in wretchedness, the happy time; and this your teacher knows. But if you have such great desire to know the first root of our love, I will tell as one who weeps and tells.'] (*Inferno* 5.118–26)

But unlike Francesca's account, which is peppered with allusions to erotic lyric traditions and with sensuously suggestive details that help to explain her impenitent eternal damnation, Benivieni's words seem more remorseful. There is almost a confessional tone in his desire to 'excuse the infirmity of [his] soul':

E quali [alcuni altri nostri precedenti versi] insino dallo ardore della mia adolescentia temerariamente decantiti furono, credo per diabolica suggestione, non solamente raccolti ma (che peggio è) in varie e publice copie disseminati. Della emendatione del quale errore conoscendo io essere e a Dio e a qualunche altro debiotre, né altrimenti satisfare potendo, publicamente hora in me la sua colpa reconosco, e per questo a la infinita bonità e clementia di Dio supplice recorrendo el priego che a lui piaccia aprire gli occhi della mente a tutti quelli e quali in simile vanità si dilectano.

[(Some of our previous lyrics) were composed temerariously from the ardor of my adolescence (I believe from a diabolic impetus), not only to gather them together, but worse, to disseminate them in various public copies. For the emendation of such an error, I recognize that I am in debt to God and to others, and I could not in any other way satisfy this penance than by publicly begging the infinite goodness and clemency of God now. So I pray that it be pleasing to Him to open the mind's eyes of those who in similar vanities take delight.] (Canzone 1.1.1)

The second allusion is by contrast to another of Dante's most recognizable characters of the *Inferno*, Ulysses, whose fraudulent counsel leads his men to ruin when their ship is wrecked 'come altrui piacque' ('as Another willed,' 26.141).[18] Benivieni's own ship, as he himself makes clear, is the explication of his poems: 'Appena mi ero da el porto de la mia quiete ad questo effecto partito, e ad le prime onde d'uno tanto pelago commesso, che ecco subito come a Dio piacque fu per corporale morte alli occhi nostri subtracto epso mio bene Iohanni Pico predecto' ['As soon as I had set off from the port of my quiet to this effect [to bring about this self-commentary], and committed myself to the first waves of such a sea, in an instant, as God willed, my dear aforementioned Giovanni Pico was by bodily death taken from before our eyes'] (Proem).[19] 'As God willed' returns again in this passage, effectively uniting Pico's death with Benivieni's own resurrection.

Benivieni's proem narrates the genesis and consequence of a spiritual conversion. It is at Pico's death that Benivieni is resurrected by God's grace. The sickly, older Benivieni, who by his own account should have preceded Pico to the grave, finds himself left to mourn the young count and to contemplate the mysteries of Divine Providence. This sad event provokes in the poet a profound change and the resolution that in the life left to him he must serve God before all, then 'per lui' [by God, for God ...] his own health and salvation, and finally, 'ad utilità de' miei proximi deservissi' ['he must serve the utility of [his] neighbours'].[20] The poet-commentator also calls his reader's attention to the conversion, which he contrasts against the perversion of those who distort without manifest violence ['senza manifesta violenza distorcere'] the pure concepts of his verse.

Encouraged and finally convinced by Pico to undertake the self-commentary, Benivieni takes the boat of his project out of port. The account of Pico's physical death and Benivieni's spiritual and poetic one continues to parallel the Ulysses account: '"Noi ci allegrammo, e tosto tornò in pianto; / ché de la nova terra un turbo nacque / e percosse del legno il primo canto"' ['"We rejoiced, but soon our joy was turned to grief, for from the new land a whirlwind rose and struck the forepart [*canto*] of the ship"'] (*Inferno* 26.136–8). While Pico's untimely passing is blamed for stifling Benivieni's initial intent to compose the *Commento*, it is in actuality precisely that which provides the impetus and the aspired true life to his endeavour.

In order to accomplish the association with the impious daring of Ulysses, however, Benivieni chooses to make use of Lorenzo de' Medici's *Comento*. Although the only other self-commentary that Benivieni explicitly acknowledges in his *Commento* is Dante's *Convivio*,[21] it is clear that Benivieni has read Lorenzo's work with minute attention.[22] A number of Lorenzo's concepts find rearticulation in Benivieni's project; indeed, significant passages from the Magnificent's *Comento* recur nearly word-for-word in Benivieni's self-commentary. Nowhere more than the proem are the similarities and crucial differences between the self-commentaries more evident.

As discussed in the previous chapter, Lorenzo opens his work with an acknowledgment of doubt ('Assai sono stato dubbioso e sospeso se dovevo fare la presente interpetrazione e comento delli miei sonetti'). The doubt incurred by memory in Lorenzo's work is an oblique allusion to Dante's Book of Memory, which consists of the remnants of the words remaining in Dante's intellect, or at the very least, their meanings. Lorenzo's self-commentary departs from the occasion of a lady's death to speak of the new life made possible by another lady's love. It thus provides a paradigm for Benivieni's project, but one which he must alter in order that it can rightly serve divine love. Benivieni's acknowledgment of his own doubts about writing a self-commentary on his poems ('fui sempre dubio in questa parte e sospeso') explicitly recalls Lorenzo's words. However, the two poets hesitate for very different reasons. Lorenzo is confident of the viability of his poetry but feels a need to defend the self-commentative prose on the basis of authority, function, and language. Benivieni admits to having greater doubts about his poetry and privileges the self-commentary as a necessary defence of the verse.

Like Lorenzo, Benivieni also chooses death as the occasion for his self-commentary. However, Benivieni realizes his *Commento* not at the death of a lady, but at the passing of his dearest friend Pico. Love, both in Plato and in Christ, serves as the instigation of the reform of his so-called spurious lyrics in celebration of a youthful, worldly love of a woman.[23] The love object is a point of marked contrast between the two Florentine contemporaries. Lorenzo readily admits that the love object and inspiration of his *Comento* can hardly be considered 'quella perfezione d'amore che si chiama "sommo bene"' ['that perfection of love that is called "the highest good"'] (36–7). In the earliest version of Benivieni's *canzoniere* there is a notable affinity to Lorenzo's project in terms of the source of poetic inspiration. In fact, the love object of at least one of Benivieni's early lyrics is none other than Simonetta Cattaneo Vespucci, whose death is the purported focus of the first four sonnets in Lorenzo's *Comento*.[24] However, Benivieni draws a sharp line of differentiation between his later work and that of his more famous contemporary, making it clear from the very title of his self-commentary that he dedicates it to *divine* beauty and love.

Like Lorenzo and Dante before him, Benivieni recognizes that the new life that love heralds brings with it a death to worldly concerns. In Benivieni's work, this death/new life finds its most explicit articulation in terms of a Christian spiritual fall and redemption. He feels impelled to love God through the love of His creatures not as an end in itself, but as a means to the End. Through beauty, in the form of a very attractive lady, man tends towards love: 'vede spiritualmente e contempla epsa divina belleza in forma d'una spetiosissima donna' ['He spiritually sees and contemplates that divine beauty in the form of a most attractive lady']. By a disordered attachment to the creature rather than an ordered one to the Creator, the soul loses its own form, excellence, and dignity ['gli è tolta la propria sua forma, excellentia e dignità']. According to the condition of the soul's poorly ordained desires, it is transformed into various and monstrous figures. The worst of these, according to Benivieni, is lust, which causes the true, rational soul to go astray and to appear, after the transformation, as a filthy leopard:

> E perché in fra tutti e vitii humani nessuno al mio parere è, che più la anima nostra deforma, che el vitio della luxuria, intendendo per luxuria ogni lascivia et effrenata voluptà sensuale, di qui è che io dico, come mentre che la anima già da Dio separata lungo le onde fugacissime de' sensuali dilecti segue e' vestigii di questa umbratile e transitoria belleza humana, di vera anima rationale si converte subito spiritualmente e transforma in una immonda Lonza, certa imagine et expressa figura della carnale concupiscentia.

> [And among all human vices none, in my opinion, deforms our souls more than the vice of lust, by which I mean every lascivious and unrestrained sensual voluptuousness. Thus I say that while the soul already separated from God pursues the traces of this shadowy and transitory human beauty along the fleeting waves of sensual delights, the true rational soul is immediately converted in spirit, and transforms itself into a filthy *lonza*, sure image and explicit figure of carnal concupiscence.][25]

The result is a soul *deformed* by its vanity.

In avoiding the *pelago* and successfully crossing the living and abundant waters of sacred letters, the soul can recognize the deformed figure of itself. This true and horrifying recognition contrasts with the merely Narcissistic reflection of oneself, without true knowledge, in the surface of water. From true recognition, according to Benivieni, results the necessary repentance and conversion to divine wisdom. The penitent can then set a new course along the holy waters of moral discipline, which will lead to the fountainhead of Divine Grace. Immersed three times in this fount, in correspondence to the baptismal rite, the soul is reborn ['la sua pristina figura resumme'] and passes into the circle of Christ's eternity ['el circulo della sua eternità'].

This conversion depends upon certain complex notions that have their roots in stilnovistic theories of love and a nobilizing self-education through love. Given that Benivieni and Pico claim they share one soul between them, when one dies the other is also largely deprived of life: 'che se gli è che in due corpi una alma viva/ Da Amor nutriti, advien che se l'un more/ L'altro in gran parte di sua vita priva' (sonnet 3.5). Benivieni takes this concept one step further by suggesting that at Pico's physical death, Benivieni comes to another sort of death, which can open the way for his spiritual conversion. With significant consequences, Benivieni modifies the role of the stilnovistic Lady. Typically, 'ingentilimento' caused by the lady's eyes is the first step of the philosopher-lover's self-making. On an allegorical level of Lady Philosophy, for example, this 'ingentilimento' is the lover's intellectual education. The second step in the adept's ascension proceeds from 'her beautiful hand,' which is the 'reformatione.' This step tends to imply on an allegorical level the making of something with a new form, by putting what had been only a sort of reading into action. However, it also alludes to that same inheritance to which Lorenzo's prose on sonnet 30 refers:

> Quando Amore prima fece la via agli occhi della donna mia per la quale entrorono al cuore, allora quella gentilissima mano entrò drieto agli occhi nel petto e ne trasse il cuore mio ... e in luogo del mio cuore pose quello della donna mia ... Amore non è altro che una transformazione dello amante nella cosa amata, e, quando è reciproco, di necessità ne nasce la medesima transformazione in quello che prima ama, che diventa poi amato, per modo che meravigliosamente vivono gli amanti l'uno nell'altro; ché altro non vuole interire questa commutazione di cuori.

> [Love first made the way for the eyes of my lady by which they entered my heart, and then that most gentle hand entered my breast after the eyes did, and drew my heart forth from it ... and in place of my heart he put that of my lady ... And considering truly, Love is nothing other than a transformation of the lover into the beloved, and when it is reciprocal, of necessity the same transformation takes place in the lover who first loves, and who

then becomes the beloved through that means by which lovers miraculously live in one another – for this exchange of hearts would not otherwise occur.] (216–17)

Benivieni emphasizes precisely the 'immedesimazione' of the lover in the beloved. To love is to become the very thing that one loves. It is an intimacy that abolishes all distance between the self and the object. For this reason, especially in certain strains of Augustinian thought, love is held as a form of authentic wisdom.[26]

Love brings with it a death to the concerns of this world and a new life in the divine Spirit. Benivieni ends his proem by asking his dedicatee to bear this thought in mind and determine if his reformed verses on love are still 'di vita non indegni, che e' vivino in virtù del loro amore: "Per cui chi viver vuol già mai non muore"' ['not unworthy of life, that they live in virtue of their love "For which he who wants to live never dies"']. Earthly things, in contrast, unworthily continue living in the temporal realm, only to be denied ultimately eternal life: 'Che muoino per cagione del loro errore./ Per cui chi viver vuol, per sempre muore' ['That they die because of their error, since he who wishes to live dies forever']. The crucial difference between Benivieni and his predecessors rests not in the abstract agreement concerning the conversion to a new life in the divine Spirit, but rather, how the poet may best express such a conversion.

Opening poetry by means of prose has already been an object of study. In chapter 1 I suggested that in the *Vita Nuova* Dante departs from the narrow sense of traditional medieval exegesis of providing the key to the initially closed and inaccessible significance of the text. By his self-commentary, Dante implicitly asserts that poetic texts may be opened in ways that the reader may least expect, and may actually find counterintuitive. Benivieni, on the other hand, tends to ressurrect a more typical, although not more conservative, approach to the poetic text's interpretation. He sets out to expound in the clearest possible terms a single, authorized version of authorial intent in the poetry, denying the original impetus for the 1489 publication in praise of the love of an earthly woman. The commentary radically resemanticizes the text upon which it depends. Thus, Benivieni's plea for an opening of the text at the outset of his *Commento* announces a Christianizing rereading of a work yet in need of purification: 'Siami lecito priego Benignissimo Dio aprire in qualche modo e depurare le tenebre delli amorosi miei versi acciochè infra le ombre di quelli nudo in tutto apparisca "Quel primo e vero amore/ Vero el cui foco in cielo/ Arde"' ['I pray to the most benign God that I be allowed to open in some way and purify the darkness of my amorous verses so that from within their shadows can appear entirely nude "That first and true love, True whose fire burns in heaven"'] (Canzone 1.1.1).

A prominent symbol for Benivieni's reform of poetry, in particular, is that of the veil or of the appropriate dressing of poetry.[27] After gathering together his poetry on divine love, Benivieni begins to doubt if the verses should be 'presented in public so naked, that is without an exposition' ['se così nudi, cioè senza alcuna altra expositione in publico si monstrassino'] (1). Without the expository words to shield the verse compositions, Benivieni asserts that they would be too much exposed to the perversity of certain bestial men. In language that recalls certain traits of Renaissance hermetic thought, the veil implicitly serves to separate this poetry on divine love from eyes that would peer on it with a view to the delights of earthly love. But it also separates the reformed poetry from its original version of love. The veil may hide as well as reveal. Given that Benivieni emphasizes the motion of placing the veil over his poetry, he effectively draws attention to the way in which self-commentary can cover over meaning. He can hide the work's secret significance as much as he can reveal it in the self-gloss.

The act of veiling may not solely protect the poetry, however. It may also protect the reader. Like a screen against a potentially blinding light, the veil of self-commentary filters the poems' radiant ardour of the Divine, which must be apprehended in steps. This metaphor, in fact, defines sonnet 1.9 ('Se el cieco e debil sol, che in questa obscura,' ['if the blind and weak sun, that in this darkness']), for example. Only partially concealing, however, the self-commentative veil of love also flirts with readers, teasing them to pursue an ever less impeded vision or knowledge, a conceit expressed in such poems as sonnet 1.19 ('Signor mio dolce ovunche gli occhi gira,' ['My sweet Lord wherever He turns His eyes']). Here the essence of God figures in the human soul in the form of 'creature sensibili, come uno vestigio e subobscura similitudine' ['perceptible creatures, like a vestige and shadowy similitude']. Showcasing his Augustinian inheritance, Benivieni states that the soul does not rest in such a vision; instead, its desire in seeing the shadow increases at the thought of knowing the true form.[28]

While his language presents poetic self-commentary as something that dresses up or disguises poetry originally written in praise of earthly love, Benivieni seems to insist on the veil as indicative of the pure nature of the poems' essential truth, as a natural extension of the verse, rather than a mask of contrast. In a work that also wishes to present itself as a public repudiation of past sin – the publishing of lascivious lyrics – and as a gesture of penance and reparation, the *Commento*'s clothing metaphor obliquely recalls a biblical source such as 2 Corinthians 5:1–6:

> For we know, if our earthly house of this habitation be dissolved that we have a building of God, a house not made with hands, eternal in heaven. For in this also we groan, desiring to be found clothed, not naked. For we also who are in this tabernacle, do groan, being burdened; because we would not be unclothed, but clothed upon, that which is mortal may be swallowed up by life. Now he that maketh us for this very thing is God, who hath given us the pledge of the Spirit. Therefore having always confidence, knowing that while we are in the body we are absent from the Lord, for we walk by faith, and not by sight.

Benivieni's discussion of the essence of God being represented to the human soul in the form of 'perceptible creatures, like a vestige and shadowy similitude,' also refers to the Neoplatonic notion of the human soul's exile from its heavenly homeland. According to this notion, the human soul originally inhabited the heavenly realm, contemplating the harmonious beauty of God's mind and creation. Impelled by desire, the soul falls to earth and takes the form of a human body, no longer clearly recalling its divine origin. Traces and shadowy similitudes of God's essence help the soul to remember itself and to return to Him.[29]

It is on this very notion that Benivieni bases his *Commento*, making the link explicit in the opening pages of the third and final part of the work. Benivieni finds the corresponding biblical truth in Exodus 14–16, the account of the Israelites' deliverance by Moses out of Egypt. In his tropological exposition, Benivieni notes that he must cross the Red Sea and the desert of solitude and sin in order to reach the Promised Land – God, heaven, and by extension, the correct understanding and contemplation of Love:

> Poiché dinanzi alla faccia dello impetuoso exercito di Pharaone fuggendo habbiamo passato el mare rosso e superata la solitudine del deserto,

> tempo è horamai che per virtù di quello primo et infinito bene, dal quale noi siamo suti per insino ad questo luogo condocti, ultimamente tentiamo di entrare in quella terra sanctissima, nella quale noi insino dal principio di questo nostro amoroso cammino promettemo di introducere l'anima peregrina.
>
> [Since, fleeing before the face of the Pharaoh's impetuous army, we have passed the Red Sea and crossed the solitude of the desert, it is now time, by virtue of that first and infinite Good by Whom we have been led to this point, for us to finally try to enter that most holy land in which we have promised from the beginning of our loving journey to introduce the pilgrim soul.] (*Incipit* of the third part)

The reader of the self-commentary similarly flees Pharaoh's impetuous army, as if fleeing hurried and incorrect readings of the work in terms of pagan love.[30]

It is necessary to pause at this point to consider at greater length what Benivieni intends in using such terms as 'form,' 'reform,' and 'transform.' Form and reform have very different meanings depending on their contexts. For the Christian, form can signify something akin to 'in the image and likeness of God,' and reform can mean 'conversion,' which can only be effected with the help of God's grace. For the Platonist, on the other hand, form is above all educational formation, and reform can have varying connotations of 'restoration,' the 'undoing of a previous change,' 'rejuvenation,' and so forth.[31]

Benivieni evidently tries to bring together the Christian and Platonic resonances. For the author, form as a verb indicates first and foremost the sense of making and creating (and by substantive extension the thing made or created). It represents both a human and divine capacity, precisely because God 'formed man in His image' ['Et quivi per la conformità e unione della anima amante ad epso suo sposo amato recevere l'ultima sua forma e absoluta perfectione e virtù'] (sonnet 1.16). The yet-imperfect human soul's desire for the divine Form increases the more it nourishes itself on the shadow of the beloved, true Form (sonnet 1.19). In short, the human soul is formed by nature, deformed by sin, and reformed by grace (sonnet 3.11).

Benivieni implicitly associates this form, the make-up of the soul in nature, with the author's composition of the verse, thus bringing together a number of issues I have treated in the preceding pages:

Benché el fine e la intentione primaria di epsi amorosi versi non sia altro che revocare l'anima nostra dallo affecto inordinato delle creature allo amore del suo creatore, e che loro in tale modo e con tale purità faccino questo, che nè anchora per se soli, cioè senza questa nostra presente expositione tirare ad alcuno pravo senso se non malignamente si possino, che io non so però se epsi per questo sono così in tutto da ogni colpa alieni. Imperochè quando mai in loro alcuno peccato non fussi (il che rispecto alla mia imperfectione giudico essere quasi impossibile) negare per questo non possono, che e' sono versi, e consequentemente che in loro è qualche cosa, in ella quale non così schiettamente apparisce epsa nuda e per se.

[The end and primary intention of these love lyrics is none other than to recall our soul from the excessive affection for creatures to the love of its creator. They [the lyrics] do so in such a way and with such purity that even alone, that is without this (our present exposition) could anyone maliciously draw from them any depraved sense. However, I do not know if they are because of this completely cleared of every fault. Therefore even if there were in them no sin (which I should consider almost impossible given my imperfection) they could not deny it because they are verses. Consequently, there is something in them that which does not appear so unabashedly nude.]

The guiding principle of Benivieni's *Commento* emerges in this move from poetry's form to its reform. In this sense, the work is very much a product of its time, inbued as it is with strains of civic reform (witness the Burning of the Vanities), and with a personal metanoia linked to the spirit of the *piagnone* movement, which itself anticipates the imminent Protestant reform initiatives.[32]

Benivieni stands in stark contrast to the proponents of Protestant Reformational thought, however. The Reformation of history, as an *historical event* happened at a single point in time. Benivieni, on the other hand, suggests that reform concerns the human soul, as well as the world soul, and as such represents an ongoing process. His philosophical, Neoplatonic heritage, which Luther and his followers largely reject, proves to be Benivieni's distinctive theology. This has significant implications for the way in which Benivieni expresses his own personal reform, or conversion, in the *Commento*.

For Benivieni, reform cannot and must not be represented as a temporally and narratorily orderable event in the course of a life. His expression of conversion departs from Dante's *Vita Nuova* and Lorenzo's *nuova vita* primarily in that Benivieni's *Commento* is not a book of memory. Benivieni does not foreground in the 1500 edition his subjective experience of his youthful love story. He does not arrange his poems in any discernible order (other than their numbering of 100 poems in three parts: 25–25–50). The glosses intervene unpredictably and randomly within the body of the text, expounding some terms and concepts and foregoing others. On the one hand, Benivieni's glosses of common or obvious terms may impart a sense of monotony, but they also suggest a different view of existence than one presented in a remembered and sequentially ordered narrative. Instead, in Benivieni's example, the reforming hand intrudes upon the representation of a quotidian existence to bring sudden and surprising graces. The pedagogical appropriation of the form constitutes a re-experiencing more than a re-membering of conversion. It embodies a mysterious mode of exploration and an unpredictable procedure of coming to knowledge that rejects the strictly logical or temporally sequential mode.

The prosimetrical accounts of Dante and Lorenzo appear to order grace by means of an artificially imposed narrative. Benivieni's move away from a narratorily reordered account of his conversion to one that seems to come closer to enacting the motions of the divine hand brings with it a risk of presumption that the poet fully recognizes. He expresses the high stakes of his moral quandary in one of the most moving passages of the *Commento*:

> Se o revocare o altrimenti che con la expositione e publica copia delle altre cose nostre havessimo in alcuno modo potuto supprimere, non mi era hora necessario affaticare un'altra volta la inepta e ad questa mia nuova impresa per sè poco sufficiente penna. La quale perché sempre in elli orecchi della mia mente risuona, 'Peccatori autem dixit deus, quare tu enarras iustitias meas e assummis testamentum meum per os tuum?' trema certo in fra le immunde mie mani e vacilla.

> [If we had been able to revoke or to suppress our things, in some other way than with their exposition and public circulation it would not be necessary for my inept and insufficient pen to undertake again now this new endeavour. Since in my mind echoes 'Peccatori autem dixit deus, quare tu enarras iustitias meas e assummis testamentum meum per os tuum?' ['But to the sinner God hath said: Why dost thou declare my justices, and take my covenant in thy mouth?'] my pen certainly trembles in my lowly hands and falters.] (canzone 1.1.1)

Benivieni's pen probably trembles in his hand at the thought of the wider context of this Psalm (49:16). Benivieni, who in his work rails against hypocritical worship and the dangers of false conversion, finds himself confronted by the condemning words of the sacred text, 'Tu vero odisti disciplinam. Et proiecisti sermones meos retrorsum ... Os tuum abundavit malitia. Et lingua tua concinnabat dolos' ['Seeing thou hast hated discipline: and hast cast my words behind thee ... Thy mouth hath abounded with evil, and thy tongue framed deceits'] (Psalm 49 [50]:17–19). Benivieni accuses himself on precisely these points on a number of occasions, and suggests that the askesis of his self-commentative writing aims to address his previous lack of discipline.

I wish to suggest that Benivieni's reform differs from other approaches to poetic self-commentary in that the others seem to be interested not in reformations but rather *transformations* of their poetry. What results in the more *poetic* self-commentaries (of Dante and Lorenzo, for example) is a vision that exceeds the mere quantitative formulation of the poetry-plus-prose apparatus. The essence of Dante's and Lorenzo's transformations rests in the dialogue with the Other. By yoking reform to human will (to the intention of the poet/author) Benivieni, on the other hand, effectively denies the possibility of the Other's power to transform his lyrics. By destroying the spheres of possible significance, by seeking to render all ambiguity in a system of fixed (in this case, moralized) meaning, Benivieni closes down the poetry. The poetry's veil becomes in the end its shroud. No longer does the poetry contain the risk of radical misunderstanding that sparks the dynamism necessary to animate it.

At the point at which the verse form can offer nothing more substantial than its exegesis, the self-commentary has failed, but in the worst possible way. If Lorenzo, precisely because of his 'failure,' succeeds in pointing out the *inmediate* life potential of his poetic project, Benivieni's success in scrupulously carrying out his self-commentative project fails to transform his work. Reform, even in its etymological sense, points to the central problem. The poet who reforms his lyrics merely revises the original form. However, the one who succeeds in transforming them transfers or carries their form to an entirely new level. It is important to clarify that in using the active voice of the verb 'transform,' I do not wish to attribute a more active role to the poetic self-commentator than necessarily befits him. It might be more accurate to say that self-commentators allow for a transforming potential of their work when they 'open [their] works by means of prose.' The transformation itself does not rest in the hands of the poet, but relies on another (the Other, the reader, etc.). In this sense, the notion of *scriba Dei* is one way, but not necessarily the only way, of understanding this transformative quality.

If what I have just suggested is true, the implications are great and far exceed the immediate context of Benivieni's self-commentary. I have implied that a poet who becomes dissatisfied with prior compositions cannot realistically retract the offending works by recalling and burning all copies, as Benivieni initially wished to do, nor will the most conscientious and methodologically straightforward approaches to redefining the poetry be of much use. After all, Benivieni's exegetical procedure of reading an exact correspondence to a newly imposed moral intent, for instance, succeeds in reforming the lyrics only on the level of exegete. One can imagine, moreover, that self-critical remarks made by the poets in separate works, or other sorts of plain, palinodic revisionism, would likewise not supplant the regrettable work. Indeed, such remarks may even have the opposite of the intended effect; that is, they may actually excite the reader to go back and peruse the original cause for scandal or shame.

Dante, for instance, seems to apprehend intuitively a lesson that Benivieni, despite his numerous reworkings of texts, never quite grasps. Only in the *poetic* transformation of his early lyrics in the *Vita Nuova* can Dante move beyond the confines of the *Stilnovo*. Likewise, it is only in another poetic work, which in turn far outshines the *Vita Nuova* and the *Convivio* (i.e., the *Divine Comedy*) that Dante can atone for his deviations (be they 'screen ladies,' Lady Philosophy, etc.) from his path of True Love. It is significant in this respect that Dante does not turn to look back at the petrifying potential of the Medusa in *Inferno* 9, and so can proceed beyond this emblem of his stony rhymes.[33] On the other hand, Benivieni's return to dress his lascivious poems with an exegetical self-gloss marks him as an inherently tragic *new Orpheus*. By looking back on his earthly love, he fails to win for his poetry the much sought-after new life.

Nevertheless, Benivieni's reform of the sort of poetic self-commentary form I have examined in Dante and Lorenzo is not without its important positive contributions. The lessons concerning the potential for the representation of divine time and the formal aperture to a dialogue with the Other in the self-gloss form are not lost on subsequent authors, most notably Tommaso Campanella. But before I turn to Campanella, and to Giordano Bruno, I shall pause for a brief reflection on Marsilio Ficino's *De Amore* [On Love] and Pico's commentary on it, to highlight another way in which we can think about Lorenzo's and Benivieni's self-commentative contributions.

The *De Amore* was a particularly popular and influential work, and much of its popularity may be attributable to the aura of esotericism that surrounded it. Its emphasis on Platonic *topoi* (the question of love's nature, the banquet setting, etc.) and on its non-discursive form encouraged the widely held assumption among Renaissance contemporaries that the work contained hidden meanings. In fact, Ficino admits in a letter that different readers will understand different levels of his text.[34] The less adept will focus on the so-called fiction of the banquet and follow closely the literal explanation of the apparatus. His ideal readers, who could look beyond this level to grasp the underlying significance of his work, would view the text, as Pico did, as a treatise on human and divine love: 'The fictions and the multiple authorities, the confusing aspects of the method of the work, are deliberate strategies of the technique of esotericism, the desire to write a work which says different things to different groups of people.'[35]

Benivieni alludes to the custom of reading other significances into texts, especially Florentine philosophical or poetic texts on love, from the very first words of his *Commento* proem.[36] Because of this fear of having his pure concepts distorted, he endeavours to write an exposition that will open in order to remedy ['aprire per rimedio'] the dark significances of the poetry and show beyond any shadow of doubt what love is and what its scope and subject matter are. He goes on to admit in the commentary to the first canzone that in the past he hid divine concepts beneath the veils of poetic fictions, a way of writing that he now regrets and abjures:

> Et veramente se io havessi così in prima conosciuto come hora per divina gratia conosco con quanta poca utilità di altri e con quanto pericolo di se medesimo tenti qualunche a me simile, cioè poco o per doctrina o per exemplo e auctorità di vita approvato di mettere in versi e sotto poetici figmenti licentiosamente nascondere le cose divine, non piangerei hora certo el damno e la vanità delle mie preterite vigilie.

> [And truly, if I had known then as I know by divine grace now with how little utility to others and with such great risk to oneself that others like myself attempt, though hardly worthy either by wisdom or by example and authority of life, to put into verse and to hide divine concepts licen-

tiously beneath poetic fictions, I would certainly not be weeping over the damning effects and the vanity of my previous efforts.]

However, it is likely that especially on this count Benivieni and Lorenzo have very different viewpoints. Lorenzo, instead, probably wilfully composed his *Comento* with an intent much closer to Ficino's in the *De Amore* than Benivieni's in his *Commento*. I believe, as I have tried to show, that the primary purpose for Lorenzo's self-commentary did not actually lie in what he said about his poetry. This was probably an *exoteric* aspect of his work meant to satisfy his less perceptive reading audience. The underlying *esoteric* meaning likely concerned a lesson in the fall from stilnovistic love in the first four canzoni and the redemptive power of a different kind of love in the second part. But it would have been a lesson whose meaning was intricately tied to an understanding of many of the forms of intellectual currency at the time, including Platonic love, the Italian poetic heritage, and a profound understanding of classical mythology. Encouraged by Pico's way of reading Ficino and by similar interpretive methods employed by Renaissance Florentine academics, I have presented an initial attempt at understanding poetic self-commentary as a kind of literary-philosophical decodification of other, less self-evident meanings.[37] It is in this hermeneutic direction that further studies of poetic self-commentaries must point.

Part Three

Poetic Self-Commentary at the
End of the Renaissance

5

'It is neither formed nor form':
Reading Beyond the Lines of Bruno's Dialogic Self-Commentary, the *Heroic Frenzies*

> A proposito di questo voglio seguitar quel che poco avanti ti dicevo, che non bisogna affatigarsi per provare quel che tanto manifestamente si vede: cioè che nessuna cosa è pura e schetta.
> – Giordano Bruno, *Eroici furori* (1.2)

> [A propos of this poem I would like to return to what I was saying a little while ago. It is not necessary to tire one's self out proving what is so evident: that nothing is pure and unmixed.]

Consistent with his belief that everything is in All, the form of Bruno's works also frequently combines poetry, prose, ideograms or other emblems or illustrations, and tables or lists. In other words, Bruno was a rigorous experimenter of literary and philosophical mixed forms and mixed genres.[1] In this chapter I consider the work that adheres most closely to the poetic/self-commentative form and intent of the epistemological current I have been tracing thus far, that is, his *Eroici furori* [The Heroic Frenzies].[2]

Bruno's work presents a series of ten dialogues, divided into two parts of five dialogues each, in which the interlocutors examine, among other things, the relationship between the various kinds of love and the mode of acquiring wisdom. For the most part, Bruno forgoes contextualizing the dialogues. There is no specified setting for the exchanges, and the reader must rely on extratextual research to identify the historical counterparts to the literary figures.[3] Unlike the vast majority of Renaissance dialogues, the *Heroic Frenzies* lacks a narrative frame and development, and instead focuses closely on expounding the poems (most of which are sonnets) intercalated in the dialogue. While Bruno writes most of these compositions himself, four are composed by Luigi Tansillo (1510–1568), a poet and emblem writer and older contemporary of Bruno. Tansillo appears in the first five dialogues as himself, although his role consists in enunciating the author's (that is, Bruno's) perspective.

Bruno actually wrote and published the *Eroici furori* in 1585 in England with the typographer John Charlewood, despite the fact that the title page reads: 'Parigi, appresso Antonio Baio.'[4] He dedicated the work to Sir Philip Sidney, as he did the *Spaccio de la bestia trionfante* [Expulsion of the Triumphant Beast]. While the so-called English Petrarch was already well-known for his collection of sonnets, *Astrophel and Stella*, whose influence on Elizabethan lyric was undeniably great, Bruno's dedication of the *Heroic Frenzies* to Sidney may have been prompted more by his admiration for Sidney's *Apologie for Poesie*, written in 1580 and published posthumously in 1585, than for the collection of sonnets. In the *Apologie*, Sidney touches on a number of the cardinal points of Bruno's poetics that later reappear in the *Eroici furori*, including the notions that only the poet is unfettered by the rules or physical realities to which other writers are subject, and that heroic poetry is 'the best and most accomplished kinde of Poetry' since it 'teacheth and mooveth to the most high and excellent truth.'[5] Also of interest for Bruno might have been Sidney's discussion of the poetic origin and nature of philosophical dialogues (3–4) and the authority of the poet to create his own world:

> So then the best of the Historian is subiect to the Poet; for whatsoever action, or faction, whatsoever counsell, pollicy, or warre strategem the Historian is bound to recite, that may the Poet (if he list) with his imitation make his own; beautifying it both for further teaching, and more delighting, as it pleaseth him: having all, from *Dante*, his heaven to hys hell, under the authoritie of his penne (22, emphasis in the original).

Bruno's debt to Dante's *Vita Nuova* and *Convivio* is apparent both on the formal and thematic levels of the work. The *Heroic Frenzies* evidences the *Vita Nuova*'s concerns for the physical and psychological effects of love upon the lover. It considers in particular the centrality of the lover's praise of the love object, as well as the stilnovo's ethos of the lover-poet striving to be worthy of that object, which in Bruno's work is not a lady, but the divine principle.⁶ In their focus on the immediate concern of the self-commentary, these two authors appear to think in very similar terms. We might consider the instances in which they suggest that the self-commentary is unnecessary. Dante insists in his *Vita Nuova*, as I have shown, that to a sector of his intended audience his meaning is already clear and does not require his exposition, while for another (in this case, those who are not among the faithful of Love) his meaning would remain obscure even with a commentary (7.14). Bruno echoes Dante's discourse in almost the same exact terms:

> Dove l'amore non è un basso, ignobile ed indegno motore, ma un eroico signor e duce de lui; la sorte non è altro che la disposizion fatale ed ordine d'accidenti, alli quali è suggetto per il suo destino; l'oggetto è la cosa amabile ed il correlativo de l'amante; la gelosia è chiaro che sia un zelo de l'amante circa la cosa amata, *il quale non bisogna donarlo a intendere a chi ha gustato amore, ed in vano ne forzaremo dechiararlo ad altri*.

> [Here love is not a base, ignoble, and unworthy mover, but a heroic lord and his guide. Fate is nothing else than the fatal disposition and order of mishaps to which he is subjected by his destiny. The object is the lovable thing and the correlative of the lover, and it is clear that jealousy is the zeal of the lover concerning the thing loved; *it is not necessary to explain this to him who has tasted love, and in vain shall we strain ourselves to explain it to others*.] (1.1, my italics)

In its intellectualization of love, however, the *Heroic Frenzies* more closely approximates Dante's treatment of love in the *Convivio*. It also shares certain interests with Benivieni's *Commento:* Bruno and Benivieni both insist that although their works may appear to treat earthly love, their true significance lies in what they say about divine love. They also concern themselves much less with the narrative of love's development.

Nonetheless, the work that the *Heroic Frenzies* most insistently and explicitly invokes as a model for its treatment of love is the biblical Song of Songs. In fact, Bruno states, he would have liked to title his work the *Cantica*, after the *Canticum canticorum:*

> Avevo pensato prima di donar a questo libro un titolo simile a quello di Salomone, il quale sotto la scorza d'amori ed affetti ordinarii contiene similmente divini ed eroici furori, come interpretano gli mistici e cabalisti dottori; volevo, per dirla, chiamarlo Cantica.

[I thought at first of giving to this book a title similar to the book of Solomon, which under the guise of lovers and ordinary passions contains similarly divine and heroic frenzies as the mystics and cabbalistic doctors interpret; I wished, in fact, to call it *Canticle*.] (Argomento)[7]

Bruno gives two reasons why in the end he did not adopt such a title for his collection of poems on heroic love. Both closely relate to previous self-commentators' proemial excuses. First, Bruno fears others will accuse him of excessive pride in profaning a sacred text by associating it with his natural and physical discourse.[8] Second, even though Bruno's text and the Song of Songs share an underlying concern for the mystery and substance of the soul, they have very different surface appearances. The Old Testament book, Bruno suggests, makes its metaphoric associations evident, while his own work on love risks misleading the reader into thinking that it concerns itself only with the most superficial levels of erotic love made 'heroic' through disdain. In the following passage, in fact, Bruno succeeds in evoking that lower Venus of erotic love without ever mentioning the term. Bruno suggests the *erotico* (erotic) almost anagramically in the terms *eroico* (heroic) and *profetico* (prophetic) with important consequences for his larger discourse on interpretation and philosophy:[9]

> Onde facilmente ognuno potrebbe esser persuaso che la fondamentale e prima intenzion mia sia stata addirizzata da ordinario amore, che m'abbia dettati concetti tali; il quale appresso, per forza de sdegno, s'abbia improntate l'ali e dovenuto eroico, come è possibile di convertir qualsivoglia fola, romanzo, sogno e profetico enigma, e transferirle, in virtù di metafora e pretesto d'allegoria, a significar tutto quello che piace a chi più comodamente è atto a stiracchiar gli sentimenti.

> [Thus anyone could be easily persuaded that my primary and fundamental intention may have been to express an ordinary love, which may have dictated certain conceits to me, and afterwards, because it had been rejected, may have borrowed wings for itself and become heroic; for it is possible to convert any fable, romance, dream, and prophetic enigma, and to employ it by virtue of metaphor and allegorical disguise in such a way as to signify all that pleases him who is skillful at tugging at the sense.] (6)

What leaps immediately to the reader's attention is Bruno's ambivalent estimation of the interpretation of the literary text. On the one hand, it is a necessary action in order to understand Bruno's hidden feeling ['occolto sentimento'] (Argomento). On the other hand, however, certain false interpretations can stretch or twist its content to make of it anything and everything, thus negating the literary work's fundamental ability to signify, that is, to point to a meaningful number of significances. This leads Bruno to declare, in words strongly reminiscent of Lorenzo de' Medici's (*Autobiography*, 32), that no one can better expound the title, order, and mode of his work than he can himself:

> Ma pensi chi vuol quel che gli pare e piace, ch'alfine, o voglia o non, per giustizia la deve ognuno intendere e definire come l'intendo e definisco io, non io come l'intende e definisce lui: perché come gli furori di quel sapiente Ebreo hanno gli proprii modi, ordini e titolo che nessuno ha possuto intendere e potrebbe meglio dechiarar che lui, se fusse presente; cossì questi Cantici hanno il proprio titolo, ordine e modo che nessun può meglio dechiarar ed intendere che io medesimo, quando non sono absente.

> [But think who will as it seems to him and pleases him in the end, willy nilly, if one is to be just, each must understand and define it as I understand and define it, and not I as he would understand it and depict it; for just as the passions of that sage Hebrew have their own proper modes, succession, and names, which no one has been able to understand and could never explain better than he, if he were present, so these canticles of mine have their own names, succession, and modes, which no one can explain better and understand than myself, since I am not absent.] (Argomento)[10]

The ironic tone Bruno displays in this passage and at crucial points throughout the work (especially in other contexts in which the author pokes fun at, and even mocks, the Petrarchan poetic economy of earthly love), highlights the very disparity between the *dechiarar* and the *intendere* that is the object of this excerpt. Bruno's position of absolute authorial precedence in defining the work is further undermined by the qualifiers 'if [Solomon] were present' and 'since I am not absent.' The first qualification plays, in a manner of highly dubious Catholic orthodoxy, on a tenet that was generally held as unquestionable: God is the author of Sacred Scripture; He-who-is-eternally-present inspires human writers to witness to His Word. Moreover, it is not Solomon who can help the faithful reader understand the true meaning of his songs, since their meaning (to paraphrase another Dominican, Thomas Aquinas, in his

Espositio in Psalmos 21.11, for example)[11] is closed and obscured before Christ's Passion, but whose allegorical significance since the Passion is open to us with the interpretive aid of the Holy Spirit.

The second qualifier is also less straightforward than the possible assumptions Bruno intends by 'since I am not absent,' that is, since I am present to answer the doubts of the reader concerning the significance of the work's title, organization, and mode. However, Bruno deviates from the tradition of poetic self-commentary (which is, by his time, fairly well-established, moving from Boethius, through Dante, to Lorenzo de' Medici) by essentially writing himself out of the role of self-commentator. Bruno is not a protagonist in his dialogues; he is only mentioned in them in the third person, and then never by name, but rather as 'the *furioso*' or 'the Nolan.' In writing the commentary on his poems under the guises of the interlocutors of his dialogues, Bruno marks a distance, a space of absence, between his poetry and an absolute definition of its significance. At the same time, Bruno's rhetorical exploitation of the litote 'not absent' for 'present' serves to affirm his presence by denying the contrary of it.

It would seem that Bruno, in writing a lengthy self-commentary on his poetry, is not taking any chances of having the reader misconstrue its meaning. He risks creating the kind of work to which he would most object – one of pedantic monotony – particularly in the detailed and seemingly prescriptive definitions of the significance of the work's 'imprese' [emblems]. In fact, the body of the *Heroic Frenzies* consists in large measure of exegetical interpretations of emblems, *absent* emblems. Unlike the emblems, tables, and illustrations in other works by Bruno, for instance, the central focus of more than half of the *Heroic Frenzies* (from dialogue five of the first part through the five dialogues of part two) is on describing and understanding the significance of these invisible emblems. As the reader might expect, the prose self-commentary serves to describe and present the interpretations of the interlocutors concerning the emblems' significances. However, the poems, accompanied by Latin 'motti' (serving almost as titles for the compositions), also play a crucial role in the commentative function of the emblems. One particularly apt example arises in the fifth dialogue of the first part: 'L'allusione al fatto delle tre dee che si sottoposero al giudicio de Paride, è molto volgare. Ma leggansi le rime che più specificatamente ne facciano capaci de l'intenzione del furioso presente' ['The allusion to the story of the three goddesses who submitted themselves to the judgment of Paris is most familiar. But let us read the verse which will inform us more precisely of the intention of this frenzied one'] (1.5). Referring back to the discussion of Bruno's litote not absent/present, in 'l'intenzione del furioso *presente*' the reader sees Bruno's insistence on his status as being simultaneously present and absent, especially when it comes to filling an interpretive role.

The very fact that the emblems are invisible coincides with the hermeneutic approach Bruno follows in the *Heroic Frenzies*. Just as Bruno in his dialogic approach to the poet's search for the true path of wisdom is never monologic, never arrives at a definitive answer, and never fixes a point of absolute understanding, so the emblem remains graphically undelineated. It is not an object that may be taken in as a whole, but its outlines come slowly into focus in the mind's eye through a process of description and sometimes abrupt comments that illuminate the image for the reader's imagination. Because the emblems are never given a definitive dimensional form, but are merely described by the interlocutors, Bruno succeeds in making his readers believe that he refers to an objective reality, when in actuality he leads them down the path of the subjective imagination, the *furioso*'s creative and learning centre. The reader participates in Bruno's search for true wisdom by inventing in the imagination the figure that he poetically describes.

Bruno's poetic self-commentary differs significantly from other examples of the mixed genre because it is written in dialogue form. Luigi Tansillo is the primary voice of the first five dialogues.[12] I focus on him more than the other interlocutors because of his more pronounced presence and his status as a historical poet within the dialogue, whose role is to illuminate the commentator/self-commentator relationship.[13] Within the fictionalized world of the dialogue Tansillo comments on his own verse (and thus represents a fictionalized poetic self-commentary), as well as on Bruno's poetry (the fictionalized commentary). Of course in reality it is Bruno who writes the poetic self-commentary (the *Heroic Frenzies*) and Bruno who implicitly comments on Tansillo's poetry. Bruno thus sets up a complex network of correspondences, tellingly arranged in chiastic symmetry. Bruno is the actual self-commentator, fictionally commented upon, while Tansillo is the fictional self-commentator, actually commented upon.

It may seem from what I have cited thus far that Bruno believes that his interpretation of the *Heroic Frenzies*' poetry is the only correct one. However, he betrays a certain readiness to acknowledge the limits of self-commentary and to invite other commentators to aid in the opening of poetic significance:

> *Cicada:* Ma questa demostrazione non è troppo aperta e propria. *Tansillo:* Basta che sia la più aperta e propria che lui abbia possunta fare. Se voi la possete far megliore, vi si dà autorità di toglier quella e mettervi quell'altra; perché questa è stata messa solo a fin che l'anima non fusse senza corpo.
>
> [C: But this figuration seems to be obscure and not precise. T: It is sufficient that it is as clear and precise as he was able to make it. If you can find a better one, you are given every authority to remove this one and replace it with one of your own. For this is presented only in order that the idea might not be without some concrete form [or more literally, 'so that the soul should not be without a body'] (1.5)

Just as Dante in his *Vita Nuova* envisioned his poems and divisions as wedded together, two bodies with one soul – such that after Beatrice's death, their inverted order was meant to reflect the widowed state of the poet – so Bruno assigns the corporeal and spiritual natures of the *Heroic Frenzies* to the self-commentary and poetry respectively. Both are absolutely necessary in order to understand by experience heroic *furore*. Bruno continues, 'Conchiudesi dunque, che a chi cerca il vero, bisogna montar sopra la raggione de cose corporee' ['One concludes then, that he who seeks the truth must ascend above the order of corporeal things'] (2.2). From these statements, the reader can infer that Bruno demands renewed interpretive effort. The reader must not rely on the self-commentary alone.

The dialogue form perfectly suits Bruno's penchant for syncretic thought, for his representations of the many and the One, of the *coincidentia oppositorum*, and of his other frequently paradoxical notions. In the prosimetrical form of the work, Bruno brings together the poetry and the prose in a unified text, as a reflection of this thematic unity in wilfully maintained opposition. Likewise, the different voices of the dialogue come together in a unified poetic vision, while maintaining their unique modulations. While the dialogue provides a concrete representation of the poet/self-commentator's fragmented self, the dialogue form can also attempt to transcend the narrow demarcations of a subjective perspective. The dialogue seeks always to encompass the Other (be it another interlocutor, the radically unhuman Divine

Principle or a different mode of expression – i.e., poetry/prose), which it openly acknowledges.

It is significant that Bruno presents his philosophical poetry within the Socratic mode of dialogue. In fact, his dialogues resemble the Platonic models in that in each there is a primary voice of the master (not by chance much like the figure of Socrates), who serves as the mouthpiece of Bruno's position, and a relatively insignificant secondary voice.[14] The exchanges carefully focus on the collaborative paedeutic pursuit of greater wisdom, relegating factors that were given greater relevance in other prosimetrical self-commentaries, such as the context and setting of the poetic interpretations, to the background. The dialogues in the *Heoric Frenzies* take place in a geographically and temporally indeterminate setting. A few of them underline this indeterminacy by closing the exchanges with an agreement to continue to discuss the topic in question as they proceed in true peripatetic fashion to wander elsewhere:[15] 'Andiamone, perché per il camino vedremo di snodar questo intrico, se si può' ['Let us go now so that as we walk we shall find a way to untie this knot, if possible'] (1.5) or 'Bene, ma andiamone discorrendo verso la stanza, perché è notte' ['Good, but let us go now, and discuss it on the way home, for it is getting dark'] (2.1).

Bruno explicitly associates the unending and *errante* quest for divine wisdom with the question of form, and in particular, with the impossibility of establishing a single centre point in an infinite universe. The human intellect is limited to always perceiving its understanding as a measure of the universe and the *ente absoluto* in its finite specificity. Its scope is to progress by degrees towards that which 'does not have any margins or circumscriptions' ['non ha margine e circonscrizione alcuna'] (1.4). In Bruno's words:

> Non è cosa naturale né conveniente che l'infinito sia compreso, né esso può donarsi finito, percioché non sarrebe infinito; ma è conveniente e naturale che l'infinito, per essere infinito, sia infinitamente perseguitato, in quel modo di persecuzione il quale non ha raggion di moto fisico, ma di certo moto metafisico; ed il quale non è da imperfetto al perfetto, ma va circuendo per gli gradi della perfezione, per giongere a quel centro infinito, il quale non è formato né forma.
>
> [It is neither fitting nor natural that the infinite be understood or that it present itself as finite for then it would cease to be infinite; but it is perfectly in accord with nature that the infinite, because of its being

infinite, be pursued without end, in that mode of pursuit which is not physical movement, but a certain metaphysical movement. And this movement is not from the imperfect to the perfect, but it goes circling through the degrees of perfection to reach that infinite centre which is neither form nor formed.] (1.4)

The attempt to explain the relationship between the circle and the centre point in the context of understanding poetic self-commentary is nothing new for this study. In Dante's dream in the *Vita Nuova*, Amor addresses him with obscure words then refuses to explain what he means. It becomes more evident in the course of reading the *Vita Nuova* that for Dante there is an absolute point from which Love radiates outward, seeing and ordering all else. Lorenzo uses the same geometric terms to illustrate his understanding of this issue. In the *Comento*, love and language converge in a declaration of perspective from the point of view of a relative, circumferencial point seeking the circle's centre.

The same analogy animates Bruno's considerations of the process of understanding and the function of poetic self-commentary, his characteristic emphasis on the infinite quality of Perfect Wisdom and the impossibility of approaching it by rationally explicative terms. In fact, immediately following Bruno's discussion of the infinite centre comes the moment of greatest dramatic tension of the entire *Heroic Frenzies*. Cicada presses Tansillo to make his paradoxical reasoning simpler or more logical:

> *Cicada:* Vorrei sapere come circuendo si può arrivare al centro? *Tansillo:* Non posso saperlo. *C:* Perché lo dici? *T:* Perché posso dirlo e lasciarvel considerare. *C:* Se non volete dire che quel che perséguita l'infinito, è come colui che discorrendo per la circonferenza cerca il centro, io non so quel che vogliate dire. *T:* Altro. *C:* Or se non vuoi dechiararti, io non voglio intenderti.

> [*Cicada:* I would like to know how by circling you can arrive at the centre? *Tansillo:* This I cannot imagine. *C:* Then why do you say it? *T:* Because I can say it and leave it for you to consider. *C:* If you don't mean that he who pursues the infinite is like one who, moving along the circumference, seeks the centre, I don't know what you mean. *T:* It is other than that. *C:* Now if you don't wish to explain it, (I cannot understand you).] (1.4)

This self-commentary refers back to the sonnet, 'Abbiate cura, o furiosi, al core' (my emphasis), in which Tansillo insists on its address to those who understand heroic frenzy:

> Ivi l'anima dolente non già per vera discontentezza, ma con affetto di certo amoroso martìre parla come drizzando il suo sermone a gli similmente appassionati: come se non a felice suo grado abbia donato congedo al core, che corre dove non può arrivare, si stende dove non può giongere, e vuol abbracciare quel che non può comprendere; e con ciò perché in vano s'allontane da lei, mai sempre più e più va accendendosi verso l'infinito.
>
> [Here the sorrowing soul not in real discontent, but in the passion of a certain amorous martyrdom, speaks as though addressing its discourse to those who are similarly impassioned. It has dismissed its heart, as it were, against its will, for the heart directs its course toward an impossible goal, extends itself where it cannot reach and would embrace what it cannot grasp; and the more the heart is estranged from the soul, the more does it enkindle itself toward the infinite.] (1.4)

By juxtaposing this passage with the tense exchange between Cicada and Tansillo mentioned above, Bruno seems to portray two very different approaches to understanding poetic significance, to say nothing of divine wisdom. Cicada must fill the role of the pedant or even of the certain rulemakers of poetry ['certi regolisti de poesia'] (1.1) when he demands the kind of straightforward explication (in line with the traditional commentary-by-another) concerning which Bruno elsewhere sputters disdainfully: 'E questo baste, se l'intendi (perché non ho da pedanteggiar sul quarto de la Fisica)' ['and this will suffice – if you have the wherewithal to grasp it, for I have no time to give you a pedantic discourse on the fourth book of the *Physics*'] (1.5).[16] But the most precious significance of the poetry or the divine wisdom remains incomprehensible and inexplicable to those who, like Cicada in this instance, do not make the sort of frenzied leap of interpretive faith that Bruno demands.

There are other occasions in which Cicada importunes Tansillo to be more specific in his explanations. Cicada betrays a certain wariness in making frenzied leaps of interpretation, which, rather than leading to a greater understanding of significance, may result instead in the loss of significance altogether:

Bisogna che questa significazione sia specificata in qualche maniera, se non vogliamo far che sia il motto vicioso in equivocazione, onde possiamo liberamente intendere ch'egli voglia dire, che l'amor suo sia d'uno instante, *idest* d'un atomo di tempo e d'un niente: o che voglia dire che sia, come voi interpretate, sempre.

[This meaning ought to be specified one way or another, if we wish to avoid the motto's being viciously equivocal. Thus we ought to be free to understand him to mean either that his love is the love of one instant, that is, of one atom of time and of no consequence, or on the contrary, as you interpret it, that his love is eternal.] (1.5)

In reply, Tansillo recognizes that a certain literal understanding of his words would make a mockery of everything. He goes on to say that to avoid this kind of unproductive scholasticism, they should not continue along the lines of the mere commentator, but should instead read another sonnet to resolve their dilemma ['E per uscir di scuola, leggasi la stanza'] (1.5). After the reading of 'Un tempo sparge, ed un tempo raccoglie,' Cicada responds, in fact, 'Assai bene ho compreso il senso; e confesso che tutte le cose accordano molto bene. Però mi par tempo di procedere a l'altro' ['I have understood the meaning quite perfectly; and I confess that everything corresponds very well. [Thus] I think it is time to proceed to the next one'] (1.5).

In this way, Bruno also blurs the traditional functions of poetry and ostensibly explicative prose. Here the poetry functions to illuminate, actually to comment on the issue at hand in the prose dialogue.[17] Heroic frenzy, Bruno implies, is not most clearly or fully explained by scientific prose, the logical linearity of the typical philosophical tract, or other expository or simplificatory procedure, but rather by poetry and poetry's dialogue with self-commentary.[18] There is no lack of examples to illustrate this inversion of the traditional roles of poetry and commentary. One instance arises in the first dialogue, when Tansillo is explaining to Cicada how love allows the intellect to open onto and to penetrate the Whole. Cicada responds by stating, 'I'm quite certain the Nolan shows this in another one of his sonnets' (1.1). Cicada then goes on to recite 'Amor, per cui tant'alto il ver discerno' ['Love who shows me so high a truth']. Another example comes in the fifth dialogue of the first part, in which the sonnet 'Venere, dea del terzo ciel, e madre' ('Venus, goddess of the third sphere and mother') is cited as the source that may make the *furioso*'s meaning clear: 'Ma leggansi le rime che più specificamente ne facciano capaci de l'intenzione del furioso presente' ['But let us read the verse which will inform us more precisely of the intention of this frenzied one'] (1.5).

Given Bruno's adherence to the notion of a continuum from poetry, which modulates through prosaic poetry to poetic prose and finally to prose, he would have likely found an aspect of Sidney's *Apologie* particularly stimulating:

> the greatest part of Poets have apparelled their poeticall inventions in that numbrous kinde of writing which is called verse: indeed but apparelled, verse being but an ornament and no cause to Poetry; sith there have beene many most excellent Poets that never versified, and now swarme many versifiers that neede never aunswer to the name of Poets (12).

This allows Sidney to declare the poetic nature of Plato's dialogues:

> And truely, even *Plato*, whosoever well considereth, shall find, that in the body of his work, though the inside and strength were Philosophy, the skinne as it were and beautie depended most of Poetrie: for all standeth upon Dialogues, wherein he faineth many honest Burgesses of Athens to speake of such matters, that, if they had been sette on the racke, they would never have confessed them. Besides, his poetical describing the circumstances of their mettings, as the well ordering of a banquet, the delicacie of a walke, with enterlacing meere tales, as *Giges* Ring, and others, which who knoweth not to be flowers of Poetrie did never walke into Apollo's Garden (4, emphasis is in the original).

Bruno is aware that the frenzied interpretive leap is not one that many readers can or will make, which accords well with the tone of Hermetic secrecy pervading the work. When Cicada remarks, 'Vedo che non può esser facile l'interpretazione' ['I see that this cannot be easy to interpret'], Tansillo answers: 'Tanto il senso è più eccellente, quanto è men volgare: il quale vedrete essere solo, unico e non stiracchiato' ['The meaning is the more excellent as it is the less vulgar, and you will see that it is single, unified, and not strained'] (1.5). But the tone of the work also conforms to a feeling that Dante expressed as early as the *Vita Nuova*, 'I fear having communicated its meaning to too many people already through the divisions made' (10.33 [19.22]). The authors indicate that there will always be a deeper significance available to those few who are willing to make the unusual effort to move beyond easy or generally accepted notions of the meaning of the work.

Like the non-fixity of allegory or of a centre point in the infinite universe, for instance, the indeterminacy present in this timeless wandering of the conversing interlocutors works to Bruno's advantage. The interlocutors' insistence that their dialogues continue while they walk towards home, not necessarily ever reaching it, emphasizes the dialogues' inherent inconclusiveness. The self-commentative allegorical interpretation is marked by this same inability to come to a definitive conclusion. The dialogue form reinforces the process of the exchange of knowledge. For Bruno, true understanding of the Divine Principle does not come as an ultimate revelation, but is rather the result of a never-ending process by which the *furioso*'s mind comprehends, but in the end casts off, its perceived limitations.[19] In other words, the quest of the *furioso* is an epistemological inquiry into one's own mode of thought. Bruno effectively portrays the response to the Socratic dictum to know oneself.

The dialogue furthermore poses a special dilemma in considering what is usually regarded as a temporal split between text and gloss, since it belongs to an atemporal realm. It insists on a future orientation in its unpredictability of point-of-view and of the possible unresolvability of the written debate through the process of one interlocutor trying to convince another of a given interpretation. The dialogue is a space of divergent perspectives in which readers must negotiate for themselves a position to take. Unlike the moral or didactic tract, the dialogue relegates necessity to a realm of possibilities. As one might say with Mikhail Bakhtin, truth is not given in an official version, but unfolds in the play of oppositional positions. Personal investment on the part of the reader in the playing out of dialogue becomes the only means of approaching the truth of the text, one in which the reader does not simply come to perceive through reading, but to know through a kind of experiential participation.

Bruno's valorization of frenzy over moderation or a passive reception of knowledge goes hand in hand with the demand implicit in the work's form that the reader actively participate in the dialogue.

> *Cicada:* Ma che perfezione o satisfazione può trovar l'uomo in quella cognizione la quale non è perfetta? *Tansillo:* Non sarà mai perfetta per quanto l'altissimo oggetto possa esser capito, ma per quanto l'intelletto

nostro possa capire: basta che in questo ed altro stato gli sia presente la divina bellezza per quanto s'estende l'orizonte della vista sua. C: Ma de gli uomini non tutti possono giongere a quello dove può arrivare uno o doi. T: Basta che tutti corrano; assai è ch'ognun faccia il suo possibile; perché l'eroico ingegno si contenta più tosto di cascar o mancar degnamente e nell'alte imprese, dove mostre la dignità del suo ingegno, che riuscir a perfezione in cose men nobili e basse.

[*Cicada:* But what perfection and satisfaction can man find in a cognition which is not perfect?
Tansillo: Cognition can never be perfect to the extent that our intellect has the power to understand this object. It suffices that in this state of ours and in any other our intellect may perceive that divine beauty to the degree that it extends the horizon of its vision. C: But all men cannot reach that point, but only one or two. T: It is enough that all attempt the journey. It is enough that each one do whatever he can; for a heroic mind will prefer falling or missing the mark nobly in a lofty enterprise, whereby he manifests the dignity of his mind, to obtaining perfection in things less noble, if not base.] (1.3)[20]

It is not the *pedante* or the *sapiente* who, by reading and expounding mere facts in strictly logical and artificially simplified terms, attains the highest learning, according to Bruno. Instead, it is the *furioso*'s transgression of rational bounds that can allow the enthusiast to intuit something of that which by nature lies beyond the human means of comprehension. Self-commentary can help us to understand the gap in poetic comprehension by positing those rational bounds while at the same time transgressing them.

6

'Did we not prophesy in Your name?':
Settimontano Squilla as the Apocalyptic Seventh Trumpet in Tommaso Campanella's Vatic Project

> *Non qui dicunt: 'Domine, Domine' et 'Nonne in nomine tuo prophetavimus et miracula fecimus?' sed ab operibus cognoscetis eos. Tutta la dottrina di questo sonetto si truova nel Vangelo.*
>
> Not those who say, 'Lord, Lord' and 'Did we not prophesy and work miracles in your name?' but by their works you will know them. All the doctrine of this sonnet is found in the Gospels.
>
> – Campanella's self-commentary on Poem 43

Tommaso Campanella's *Scelta di alcune poesie filosofiche di Settimontano Squilla cavate da' suo' libri detti 'La Cantica' con l'esposizione* [Selection of Some Philosophical Poems by Settimontano Squilla Taken from his Books Called 'The Canticle' with the Exposition] (1622) represents the final example of the Italian Renaissance poetic self-commentaries. In this work, Campanella struggles to retain a Renaissance interpretative sensibility during a period of changing expectations for commentary as Cartesian rationality and the new sciences emerge. In particular, he emphasizes an appreciation for the great proximity of the poetic and hermeneutic spheres. Only in this particularly intriguing and sophisticated example of the mixed form is Campanella able to express his unusual poetic vision.

The *Scelta* is the work of a remarkable visionary. Son of an illiterate slipper-maker, born in the little town of Stilo, Calabria, Campanella became one of Italy's most original poet-philosophers. The life-path of the Dominican friar was anything but easy, however. By the young age of twenty-one Campanella had already had his first taste of prison, accused, among other things, of harbouring a demon in his pinky fingernail. What ultimately procured for him too much of the Inquisition's attention, however, was his fervent adherence to a Telesian-inspired, sensistic naturalism and to other anti-Aristotelian and hence anti-authoritarian positions.

The action that won for Campanella his longest prison sentence was his leadership of a doomed Calabrian peasant insurrection against both Spanish and Church authorities. The millennialist 1599 plot aimed to establish a communistic theocracy not unlike the Republic of the Solarians Campanella later described in his utopian dialogue, the *Città del sole* [City of the Sun]. Unlike Bruno, Campanella escaped burning at the stake to atone for heresy and sedition by simulating insanity. He set fire to his cell and managed to maintain his raving posture even under a series of bone-wrenching tortures. What sustained him was a deep-seated conviction that God had entrusted him with a special mission of reform and renewal. His wide-ranging compendious volumes, many of which he wrote from prison, contain scientific treatises, theological disquisitions, and books of magic and astrology, poetics and grammar, history and politics, apology and autobiography, metaphysics and prophecy. The *Scelta* represents a synthesis, or better yet a *summa*, of the whole of his thought. For present purposes, I focus on only one aspect of Campanella's vast and ambitious project: how his unique conceptualization of the self-gloss and the selection of his pseudonym create a particularly efficacious, allusive and elusive, vatic voice.

As the title of his self-commentary indicates, Campanella makes his selection of philosophical poems from a much larger corpus referred to as the *Cantica*. This *Cantica* now appears to be lost, although a few isolated examples of poems excluded from the *Scelta* exist. The *Scelta* consists of eighty-nine compositions, mostly sonnets, madrigals, and canzoni, along with a substantial prose commentary written by the poet himself, first published in Germany in 1622.[1] The poetry is notably difficult, given its obscure allusions, weighty philosophical content, and the condensed and sometimes almost impenetrable quality of the verse. The reader would naturally turn to the exegetical glosses for help in understanding the poetry. Here, however, the poor reader finds yet more material that demands interpretation: ciphered references and occasionally long glosses on comparatively easy passages.[2] Campanella also goads the reader with seemingly snide remarks to the effect that the meanings of his poems are self-evident: 'il sonetto è chiaro: desidera attenzione ed osservanza, riconoscimento ed imitazione' ['the sonnet is clear: it deserves attention, observance, recognition, and imitation'] (21n), and 'è chiaro' ['it is clear'] (60n). The prose apparatus Campanella purposefully includes with his poetry evidently does not have the same pedagogical function that a commentary-by-another would have, and must impel the reader to search deeper for the justification of his glosses.

Like Dante in the *Vita Nuova*, Campanella underlines the distinction between the self-commentator's task and that of outside commentators. Campanella states that he explicates only the hidden meanings of the poems or the significances that are unique to himself: 'Come Cristo vinse la morte morendo, è noto tra' teologi, ed io non dichiaro qui se non i sensi occulti e propri dell'autore' ['How Christ conquered death by dying is known among theologians, but I declare here none but the hidden or intrinsic meanings of the author'] (19n). The self-commentary on poem 27 provides another example: 'Le sottigliezze del sonetto noti un altro, ch'io solo dico il senso occulto e nuovo' ['Let another note the subtleties of the sonnet, since I only state the hidden and new meaning']. However, in some instances the self-commentator limits himself to acknowledging other significances without elaborating on them, as in the exposition of poem 28.1: 'Qui ci sono sensi mirabili' ['Here there are wondrous senses'], or the gloss on poem 37: 'Questo sonetto è fatto perché l'intendano pochi; né io voglio dichiararlo ... *Qui legit intelligat*' ['This sonnet is written so that few understand it; nor do I want to explain it ... *Qui legit intelligat*'].

Especially evident in this last remark is the move to protect the hidden sense of the poetry, an action typical of the Hermetic tradition, which greatly influenced the poet.[3] However, *qui legit intelligat* is also a recognizable formula, similar to the Gospel passage on the interpretation of Christ's parables, 'He that hath ears, let him hear.' It is intended to prompt the reader's or listener's interpretive faculties. Demand of such an interpretive effort is usually made for the benefit of one's soul. In particular, Campanella's gloss should remind the reader of the context of Jesus' elaboration on His parable of the sower's seeds to His disciples: 'To you is given to know the mystery of the kingdom of God: but to them that are without, all things are done in parables: That seeing they may see and not perceive; and hearing they may hear, and not understand; lest at any time they should be converted and their sins should be forgiven them (Mark 4: 11–12).[4] While forming one Truth,

God's message says different things to different people. In an analogous way, Campanella aims to write a work that speaks on a number of different levels, with varying significances available to diverse readers. Specifically, he confounds the arrogant lot he sees around him, although he speaks in a way that is recognizably wise in God's eyes:

> Sciolto e legato, accompagnato e solo, gridando cheto, il fiero stuol confondo: folle all'occhio mortal del basso mondo, saggio al Senno divin dell'alto polo.
>
> [Loosed and bound, accompanied and alone, screaming quietly, I confuse the haughty crowd, being mad to mortal eyes of the lowly world, wise to the divine Intellect of the high pole.] (61.1–4)[5]

Campanella describes his ideal of communication in the last line of the same poem, which is also of Dantean derivation, given that the souls of Paradise always understand each other without actually speaking.

It is not my purpose to argue that Campanella was a prophet. However, there are indications that he saw himself in that role. Campanella writes poems expressly titled 'Some Prophetic Sonnets' (poems 50–2). Moreover, he had long yearned for freedom from prison, where he spent a total of more than thirty years, in order to proclaim what he felt was God's urgent message to His people. In his gloss on poem 73.5, Campanella marvels at God's will to free not him, but a prisoner named Bocca: 'e fece suo profeta un altro tristo senza meriti' ['and He made another sinner without merits His prophet']. However, Campanella remained convinced of his own prophetic vocation, since God gave signs to His true prophets: 'Niuno deve predicare novità o cose donde pensa che s'abbia a migliorare la Repubblica, se da Dio visibilmente non è mandato e, come Moise, armato di miracoli e contrassegni, ecc.' ['No one should predict novelties or things that one believes will improve the Republic unless he is sent by God and like Moses, armed with miracles and other marks, etc.'] (80.4n). Campanella openly states his own qualifications, referring to himself in the third person:

> Dice che Dio, avendogli fatto tanti favori di dargli nuove scienze, sette monti in teste prodigiosi, e volontà di fare la scuola del Primo Senno per divino istinto, e 'l cavallo bianco, ch'è l'ordine sacerdotale dominicano, e 'l vincere tanti tormenti e tormentatori, ciò è segno che Dio l'abbia da liberare per qualche gran cosa.

[He says that God, having granted him so many favours by giving him new sciences, seven prodigious mounds on his head, the will to create the School of the First Spirit by divine instinct, the white horse, which is the Dominican order of preachers, and triumph over so many torments and tormentors, these are signs that God is to liberate him for some great thing.] (75.8n)[6]

Campanella persistently asserts that what he presents in his philosophical poems is a true testimony of God's message, and not a poetic exercise or mere invention:

Or, c'han visto i miei sensi,
non più opinante son, ma testimonio,
né sciocche pruove ho de' secreti immensi.

[Now that my senses have seen,
I am a witness, not merely one expressing an opinion,
nor do I have silly proofs of the immense secrets.] (79.4:3–5)

The verses betray a rejection of Aristotelian forms of understanding by means of syllogisms or other so-called silly proofs. Campanella continues in the self-commentary on the same poem, 'Egli ha conosciuto per esperienza esser vero l'altro secolo dopo la morte, ed ebbe molte visioni manifeste al senso esteriore' ['He learned by experience that the other age after death is true, and he had many visions manifesting this to the exterior senses'].

The witnessing function that Campanella proclaims here – and that he shares with other self-commentators discussed in the present study – deserves further attention. On one level, which one might call the legalistic level, witnesses attest to the truth of a past action or another's word, something that is no longer self-evident or empirically demonstrable.[7] This has far-reaching implications for poetic self-commentary, as Dante realized. One acceptable motivation for speaking about oneself is to provide an example that may enable readers to avoid mistakes made by the speaker. In his *Convivio*, Dante stated that, like St Augustine in his *Confessions*, he hoped his personal testimony could direct others along a path of human and divine wisdom. Various biblical contexts also rely on this legalistic witnessing function. John the Baptist's words and the disciples' performing of miracles witnessed to Christ.

On another level, though, the very person may become the testimonial sign of a greater truth. Jesus can claim to be His own witness since He is the Word (John 8:13–14). The believers who witness to Him with their lives are martyrs, as the Greek etymology of witness suggests. Campanella does not hesitate to consider his own martyrdom in the experiences that he has endured, the 'cinquanta prigioni, sette tormenti / ... e dodici anni d'ingiurie e di stenti' ['fifty prisons, seven torments ... and twelve years of insults and suffering'] (73.3:12–14). Ultimately, he declares: 'mirate al mio martoro' ['behold my martyrdom'] (80.12:10). His experience makes him a witness, not someone merely expressing an opinion or writing poetic fictions.

Moreover, Campanella views his own life as the realization of previous prophecies:

Va', amaro lamento,
tratto di salmodia,
ch'è di altri profezia,
ma di me troppo assai vero argomento.

[Go, bitter lament,
taken from a psalm,
which for others is prophecy,
but for me history all too true.] (72.8:1–4)

Of course, mortal beings cannot fully comprehend God's true message. Even for the Apostles the message turns out to be a 'hard saying.' Prophets, as Dante attests in his *Convivio*, are not understood in their homeland. Campanella takes this understanding of the difficult mission of the prophet as consolation for his many trials and tribulations. He employs a particular understanding of poetic self-commentary in order to draw out the richly suggestive potential of this mixed form as a prophetic mode of expression. As the epigraph of this chapter suggests, prophecy cannot consist merely of words ('Nonne in nomine tuo prophetavimus et miracula fecimus?'), but must encompass actions or works that, through the interpretive act, come to be recognized as potentially prophetic.

Some critics have explained Campanella's reticence and resistance to making his meaning clear by saying that he resorts to necessary dissimulation in the face of persecution by the Inquisition. Campanella wrote the *Scelta* in prison, where he was serving a sentence for heresy and sedition consequent to the 1599 uprising.[8] However, the utopia, if it can be called so, of his poems is certainly not the ideal society of the Solarians that he argues for in his *Città del sole*.

In fact, during the twenty years between the composition of the *Città del sole*, completed by 1602, and the publication of the *Scelta*, Campanella experienced a significant philosophic-religious conversion. He transformed his metaphysics of Telesian derivation into a Christ-centred missionary vocation. The vision his poems present, in fact, is the kingdom of heaven to be established on earth after God's final judgment. The concordance of astronomical signs, prophecies, and political and social upheavals led Campanella to believe that the final age, after the ultimate unification of the divine and the human realms, was very proximate. It is a concern that emerges frequently from his poetic compositions, such as the 'Sonetto sopra la congiunzion magna, che sarà l'anno 1603 a' 24 di dicembre' ['Sonnet on the Great Conjunction that Will Occur in the Year 1603 on 24 December']:

> Già sto mirando i primi erranti lumi,
> sopra il settimo e nono centenario
> dopo alcuni anni, insieme in Sagittario
> raccozzarsi, a mutar legge e costumi ...
> Oh, voglia Dio ch' i' arrivi a sì gran sorte,
> di veder lieto quel famoso giorno
> c'ha a scompigliare i figli della morte!

> [Already I see the first wandering lights
> around the seventh and ninth century
> assembling together in Sagittarius in a few years
> to overturn law and customs ...
> May it please God that I make it to such a great event
> to happily see that famous day
> which is to upset the children of death!] (56.1–4 and 12–14)[9]

In his Calabrian eschatological insurrection the poet aimed for radical change in his situation and in society as a whole. However, the vision of the poems appears much more apocalyptic than that of the *Città del sole*. In the poems, the golden age, which Campanella adopts to refer to the edenic first age of man, must return to earth after the final judgment:

> Allor potrete orar con ogni istanza
> che venga il regno, ove il divin volere,

come si fa nelle celesti sfere,
si faccia in terra e frutti ogni speranza.
Ché i poeti vedran l'età ch'avanza
ogn'altra, come l'òr tutte minere;
e 'l secolo innocente, che si chere
ch'Adam perdéo, darà la pia possanza.
Goderanno i filosofi quel stato.

[Then you will pray with great insistence
that the kingdom come, in which the divine will
is done as in the celestial spheres,
on earth, and nourishes every hope.
That poets will see the age that surpasses
every other, as gold all other metals;
and the innocent age, for which we ask
and which Adam lost, pious power will render.
Philosophers will enjoy that state.] (49.1–9)[10]

The verbs in the future tense (*potrete, vedran, darà, goderanno ...*) stress the visionary, prophetic mode of Campanella's poetry. The widespread popularity of Isidore of Seville's *Etymologies* may also serve to emphasize the temporal quality of prophecy as a 'speaking beforehand.' Prophecy properly derives from 'speaking in the place of' God.[11] When Campanella reiterates these same themes in poem 53.9–14, the fact that he shifts the temporal form to the present creates an effect of noticeable proximity or urgency:

Vien l'altissimo Sire in Terrasanta
a tener corte e sacro consistoro,
come ogni salmo, ogni profeta canta.
Ivi spander di grazie il suo tesoro
vuol nel suo regno, proprio seggio e pianta
del divin culto e dell'età dell'oro.

[The most high Lord comes to Terrasanta
to hold court and sacred consistory,
as every psalm, every prophet sings.
There he wishes to extend by grace his treasure
in his kingdom, rightful seat and offspring
of the divine cult and of the golden age.] (53.5–14)

It is evident that these excerpts, while making reference to the mythic golden age of man, also allude to the final age on earth.

Also crucial for any understanding of Campanella's poetry is poem 3, 'Fede naturale del vero sapiente' ['Natural Faith of the True Wiseman'], which begins, 'Io credo in Dio, Possanza, Senno, Amore, / un, vita, verità, bontate, immenso, / primo ente, re degli enti e creatore' ['I believe in God, Power, Intellect, and Love / life, truth, goodness, an / immense first being, king of beings, and creator']. Like the Nicene Creed recited by the Catholic faithful at Mass, Campanella's version of suspect orthodoxy considers in turn the triune nature of God, His eternity and relation to time and history, the nature of sin, and His upcoming judgment. Also in this instance, Campanella's version strikes a more apocalyptic tone than the Creed's ('we look for the resurrection of the dead and the life of the world to come'), as evidenced by the following tercets:

> La santa Chiesa, il Primo Senno avendo
> per maestro, e 'l libro che Dio scrisse, quando
> compose il mondo, i suoi concetti aprendo,
> sette sigilli or or disigillando,
> chiamerà tutto l'universo insieme
> al tempio vivo dove va rotando.

> [The holy Church, having the First Intellect
> as her guide, and the book that God wrote when
> He composed the world, and opening His concepts,
> unsealing now the seven seals
> will call the whole universe together
> revolving towards the living Temple.] (3.94–9)

The revelation of truth that Campanella mentions in his gloss on these lines ('Aspetta la revelazione della verità qual sia la vera legge, quando si farà universal concilio, e una fede e un pastore') is a different Book of Revelations, one whose seventh seal is about to be broken and whose call for just retribution and reward is immensely attractive to the imprisoned poet. I am referring to Christ's second coming as it is announced in Apocalypse 11:15–18:

> And the seventh angel sounded the trumpet: and there were great voices in heaven, saying: The kingdom of this world is become our Lord's and his

Christ's, and he shall reign for ever and ever. Amen. And the four and twenty ancients, who sit on their seats in the sight of God, fell on their faces and adored God, saying: We give thee thanks, O Lord God Almighty, who art, and who wast, and who art to come: because thou hast taken to thee the great power, and thou hast reigned. And the nations were angry and thy wrath is come, and the time of the dead, that they should be judged, and that thou shouldst render reward to thy servants the prophets and the saints, and to them that fear thy name, little and great, and shouldst destroy them who have corrupted the earth.

As unlikely as it may seem, Campanella's choice of pseudonym is related to his insistent allusions in his poetry and self-commentary to the context of biblical eschatology.

In the traditional explanation of the pseudonym, Settimontano refers to the 'sette monti' or seven protrusions supposedly visible on the skull of the poet. Campanella himself suggests this interpretation in the envoy of poem 75: 'Tre canzon, nate a un parto / da questa mia settimontana testa, / al suon dolente di pensosa squilla' ['Three canzoni born in one birth / from this my *Settimontana* head, / to the mournful sound of a thoughtful *squilla*'].[12] On the other hand, *squilla*, an acute ringing sound, as from a horn or bell, recalls the 'little bell' of the poet's last name, Campanella. However, given Campanella's rigorous cultivation of the widest possible field of significances in the words of his poetry, we might add to these considerations a few others. For example, instead of reading Squilla as a noun, it might be possible to view it as a verb (from *squillare*, to ring out shrilly). By *Settimontano*, Campanella may also mean to recall obliquely some fusion of 'settentrionale' (northern) and 'oltremontano' (roughly, beyond the mountains). The Calabrian poet was particularly fascinated by the north, where he insisted on publishing his poems. In this sense, a book whose title is *Scelta d'alcune poesie filosofiche di Settimontano Squilla* might be construed approximately as a selection of philosophical poems that ring out from beyond the Alps. This spatial dislocation is a crucial component in the prophetic discourse. The prophet is the interpreter of divine revelation. The message that he brings refers back to an ineffable truth that belongs to an Other Place far from its actual collocation.

It would be easy to assume that the pseudonym Campanella employs for his *Scelta* might not be so problematic. It seems perfectly reasonable that a writer who passed more than two and a half decades in prison for attempting to realize his suspiciously heretical ideas would choose a fictitious name under which to publish poems that neither contain strictly orthodox concepts nor praise the institutions of power responsible for his detention. In fact, some passages of his work present bitter critiques of the political government guided by false princes ('prìncipi finti contra i veri' 15.14). This sort of subversive opinion in an age of aggressive persecution of heretics encouraged a number of Campanella's commentators to conclude that he chose the pseudonym in order to protect his identity.[13]

However, there must be more to Campanella's choice of a pseudonym. Squilla hardly conceals the last name of the poet. Moreover, in the poems' self-glosses, Campanella cited works he had previously written and published under his actual name, like the *Metafisica*, *Gli aforismi politici*, the *De sensu rerum*, and the *Città del sole*, all of which he attributed to the same author as that of the poems.[14] And in his self-commentary Campanella even helps the reader to identify him by referring to his persecuted and imprisoned status and to his place of birth: 'Son più che venti anni che sempre travagliato esso autore da invidi, con carceri e persecuzioni, per ben far a chi non merita e pe' peccati suoi ancora. Egli è da Stilo, città di Calabria, a cui, ecc.' ['For the past twenty years this author has been tormented by the envious with imprisonments and persecutions for his good deeds to others who did not deserve them, and also for his own sins. He is from Stilo, a city in Calabria'] (36.4).

It is also important to keep in mind that Campanella would have harshly condemned the creation of a fiction, such as a pseudonym, without good reason. Even this aspect of his poetics, the invention of the pseudonym, must have what he calls an 'architectonic' basis. In the fourth chapter of the Italian edition of his ten-chapter treatise on poetics, the *Poetica*, Campanella considers the duty of the poet and concludes that the true poet need not follow Aristotle's exhortations to invent fables, but should instead create a poetic work with ethical ends. The poet, according to Campanella, need not invent pretexts for poetry, 'non bisognarebbe punto finger cose nuove' ['the poet should not invent new things at all']. For Campanella life itself is fantastic and poetry must express it. In order to build such an ideal, he advocates the mixture of the genres of poetry, medicine, law, and religion in order to represent an entirely new sense of poetics based on classics and moderns, but with some profoundly personal intuitions. Thus Campanella distinguishes between 'uomini di felice giudizio, poeti architettonici' ['the men of happy judgment, the architectonic poets'] and 'vili fabricatori e impostori magni' the ['vile fabricators and great imposters'] (*Tutte le opere*, 322).¹⁵ The designation of poet has for Campanella decidedly negative connotations ['quoniam "poëta" graece, "fictor" latine dicitur' (*Tutte le opere*, 968)]. The term describes one who fictionalizes or invents, and not one who tells the truth, a characteristic most prized by the Dominican friar. In referring to himself as an author, Campanella effectively assigns for himself a broader and more authoritative title than that of poet. This ethical end of Campanella's poetry coincides on a more global level with his untiring quest to unite earthly knowledge with divine wisdom. The synthesis in their differences, the truth in the integration of the fields of human knowledge in the natural sciences, in philosophy, and in metaphysics, should lead finally to unification with the Absolute.

In the poems in which Campanella uses the trope of *interpretatio nominis*, he mentions *Squilla* almost exclusively in reference to an apocalyptic context. The last lines of poem 27 and its exposition offer a clear example:

Pur dalla *squilla mia* sento un rimbombo:
– Cedi, bestia impiagata, sorda ed orba,
al saggio Amor dell'anime innocenti.

[From *my ringing* I hear an echo:
'Yield, wounded beast, deaf and blind,
to the wise Love of innocent souls.' (my italics)

Campanella explains in his note, 'Qui si mostra che l'Amor cieco fu deificato nel secolo rio, e che poi peggiorò nell'età nostra tenebrosa; e ora sta per tornar al mondo il vero Amore, savio e puro, secondo ch'e' predice del secolo d'oro futuro, dopo la caduta dell'Anticristo' ['Here is shown how blind Love was deified in the dark century, and how it worsened in our own shadowy age; and now true Love, wise and pure, is about to return to the world, according to what he predicted of the future golden age after the fall of the Antichrist'].¹⁶ As the mouthpiece for such a message, it would seem that the poetic voice seeks to approximate itself to the role of the seventh apocalyptic angel.

The notion that Settimontano Squilla might represent the angel of the seventh trumpet should not seem at all far-fetched if we remember the traditional associations between the angels of the Apocalypse and designated historical figures. The most notable among these is St Francis of Assisi, linked to the apocalyptic angel of the sixth seal. The passage from Revelations 7:2 reads: 'And I saw another angel ascending from the rising of the sun, having the sign of the living God.' Joachim of Flora's prophecies at the beginning of the thirteenth century describe the attributes of this sixth angel.[17] According to tradition, St Francis could be identified with the sixth angel because he possessed the sign of the living God in the miraculous stigmata.

Among the prophetic writers most familiar to Campanella was that 'calavrese abate Giovacchino / di spirito profetico dotato' ['Calabrian abbot Joachim, who was endowed with prophetic spirit'].[18] Joachim presents in his *Liber figurarum* [Book of Figures] – and later elaborates in his *Expositio in Apocalypsim* [Exposition on the Apocalypse] – a division of human history into three epochs corresponding to the three persons of the Trinity. The epoch of the Father began in the time of Adam ending with Christ; that of the Son began at Christ's death and was about to end, according to Joachim of Flora; and the epoch of the Holy Spirit was to come after the death of the Antichrist. Contained in the first two epochs, which correspond to the periods of the Old and New Testament respectively, are seven ages, for each of which an angel sounds a trumpet and breaks a seal as related in the final book of the Bible. Joachim affirmed that his age, the fifth, was about to conclude with the advent of the sixth angel marked by the 'sign of the living God' (*L'angelo*, 19ff).

According to Stanislao da Campagnola, the *Poverello* from Assisi received unawares 'the inheritance of the message with which the prophet from Sila had announced the advent of the friars minor and the "spirituales" of the age of the Eternal Gospel, but [threw] himself with success into the actual practice of the evangelical life.'[19] In his biography of St Francis of Assisi, Tommaso da Celano called the saint the 'Seraphim of Assisi' or the 'Seraphic Father,' terms that present *in nuce* a recognition of St Francis as the *alter Angelus* of the Apocalypse but also make the connection that becomes explicit only by the time of Giovanni da Parma (*L'angelo*, 145). For his Joachinian ideas, Giovanni da Parma was forced to renounce leadership of the Franciscan order in 1257 and was censored by his successor, St Bonaventure of Bagnoregio. St Bonaventure avoided the delicate subject of Joachim's prophecy while maintaining the identification of St Francis as the angel of the sixth seal by referring directly to the text of the Apocalypse and by citing the stigmata as proof of the sign of the living God.

However, Campanella is not as much interested in the figure of St Francis per se as much as he is in recovering the seven ages of history as set forth by Joachim of Flora.[20] In his philosophical poems, Campanella alludes to the same progression of ages, including the pouring out of the ampulla of God's wrath, the task of the fifth apocalyptic angel:

> La scuola inimicissima del vero ...
> Tornando in terra il Senno trïonfante,
> l'ampolla del quinto angelo, versante
> giusto sdegno, terribile e severo,
> di tenebre fia cinta; e l'impie labbia,
> le lingue disleal co' fieri denti
> stracceransi l'un l'altro per gran rabbia.
>
> [May the school, most inimical to the truth ...
> Upon the triumphant Intellect's, return to earth
> pouring out the ampulla of the fifth angel,
> righteous disdain, terrible and severe,
> be girded with darkness; and the impious lips,
> the disloyal tongues with their fierce teeth
> will tear one another apart in great rage.] (51.1, 6–11)

But perhaps the most pertinent example is Campanella's reference to the breaking of the seventh seal in the third poem, to which I have already alluded briefly:

> The holy Church, having the First Intellect
> as her guide, and the book that God wrote when
> He composed the world, and opening His concepts,
> unsealing now the seven seals
> will call the whole universe together
> revolving towards the living Temple (3.94–9).

The wisdom, revealed by the unsealing of the divine book, has the capacity to unite the entire creation of God to its Maker. This opened wisdom, no longer mysterious and unknowable, marks the conclusion of the fourth evangelist's long weeping:

> E finir di Giovanni il lungo pianto,
> avendo il gran Leon giudeo gli onori
> d'aprir il fatal libro, uscendo fuori
> il bianco corridor del primo canto.

> Le prime anime belle in bianche stole
> incontran lui, che, su la bianca nube,
> vien cinto da' suo' bianchi cavalieri.
> Taccia il popol moresco, che non vuole
> udir il suon delle divine tube.
> L'alba colomba scaccia i corbi neri.
>
> [And [I see] the end of John's long weeping,
> the great Leo the Jew having the honours
> of opening the fatal book, from which comes
> the white horse of the first song.
> The first beautiful souls in candid robes
> meet him, who on a white cloud
> comes girded by his white knights.
> Let the Moors be silent who refuse
> to hear the sound of the divine horns.
> The white dove scatters the black crows.] (55.5–14)[21]

Moreover, Campanella associates the sound of these divine horns with that which his own resounding name makes:

> Dal ciel la gloria del gran Dio rimbomba:
> egli è sonora tromba ...
> *Mia squilla* è ebra – per troppo desio
> di cantar vosco, o stelle, il grande Dio:
> gloria all'omnipotente Signor mio!
>
> [The glory of the great God echoes from heaven:
> it is a loud trumpet ...
> *My ringing is inebriated* – from too much desire
> to sing with you, oh stars, the great God:
> glory to my omnipotent Lord!] (85.1–2 and 87–9, emphasis mine)

However, the allusion in the pseudonym to the seventh trumpet is not without its problems. Campanella never fixes a single definition to his name. There remains always a semantic mobility, almost a magic mysteriousness in Campanella's rhetoric.[22] Words, as he says in a note on the very first sonnet, 'non arrivano a dir l'essenza delle cose' ['do not arrive at communicating the essence of things'].

Unlike the other poetic self-commentators analysed in this study,

Campanella wrote no prose proem, *argomento*, or other prefatory word in which to situate the self-exegetical perspective. This in itself is a telling indication of the function of Campanella's self-commentary. It wilfully repels the kind of prose frame that might give the impression of an intention to fix the poetry absolutely. Campanella adopts the unpredictable, non-sequential, and anti-narratorial form of the self-gloss in order to indicate not the mysterious quality of spiritual conversion, as in the case of Benivieni, but the nature of prophecy.

In theoretical terms, the spatial and identificational distancing that Campanella adopts permits a place of intersection for what Jacques Derrida would call 'le flot du langage ... le flot de la révélation' ['the flow of language ... the flow of revelation'].[23] On the one hand, the numerous reevocations of the self-referential term *Squilla* emphasize the poetic subjectivity of the compositions. On the other hand, the deliberate choice of a different pen name paradoxically distances the historic figure of Campanella. The poet is in some way emptied out of an actual identity to become the mere instrument of enunciation of the divine message. This distancing allows for that opening onto a voice from beyond, a prophetic voice.

The author's act of renaming himself goes hand-in-hand with the act of self-commentary. Because the poet in his self-gloss re-elaborates in different words the vision of his poems, the self-commentary becomes a kind of translation. Walter Benjamin's reflections in 'The Task of the Translator' can help in understanding the allusive quality of the self-commentary. Truth, the pure language that is no longer whole, Benjamin states, is like a broken vase. But it can be partially pieced together or recreated from the fragments:

> Fragments of a vessel, which are to be glued together, must match one another in the smallest details, although they need not be like one another. In the same way a translation, instead of resembling the meaning of the original, must lovingly and in detail incorporate the original's mode of signification, thus making both the original and the translation recognizable as fragments of a greater language, just as fragments are part of a vessel.[24]

The truth of pure language emerges in its inexact, though rigorous, nature. The poetic language, with its plurality of expressive possibilities, comes closer to that truth than a scientific language.

Campanella expresses himself by means of the poetic word whose inexact complexity of symbols, metaphors, allegories, and so forth, endeavours to approximate the prophetic word. His desire to render 'the chaos of all things into one,' together with his mission to fuse theology and natural science, causes Campanella to unite the poetic word (that is, the poetry) with his 'scientific' language of self-exposition. The addition of this self-translation paradoxically only highlights the ulterior fragmentation of language, the breakage of the 'pure language,' in seeking to retrieve it.

Campanella's attempt at translation, from the choice of the pseudonym to the rewording of his poetic expression in the exposition, renders his work wilfully estranged from the actual earthly time of southern Italy at the beginning of the seventeenth century. It speaks instead from a future, apocalyptic horizon. In such a way Campanella confronts the risk of ineffability in his mission to announce the perceived biblical Truth in the context of human history and language. Just as Boccaccio's self-gloss shifted his work's temporal axis by creating the sense that it was an ancient relic, Campanella's self-gloss aims to shift the work's temporal axis to an unspecified, apocalyptic future.[25] Commentary is a retrospective on the original text. It involves a turning back of one's gaze to bring into focus the writing of the past. In this sense, it is a proleptic vision. The self-commentary makes of this lyric and proleptic vision a new horizon from which to project a future-oriented perspective. The opening of the lyric by means of the self-interpretive discourse becomes the way in which these poets attempt to overcome the finitude of their individual human subjectivity.

Poet-commentators in the Italian Middle Ages and Renaissance, fearing accusations of unbridled personal and artistic pride, hastened to dispel the suspicion of authorial presumption before it could take root in the reader's mind. There are moments in the *Scelta* when Campanella too steps back and acknowledges the risks of presumption inherent in his project. A notable instance arises in poem 9, 'Contra il proprio amore scoprimento stupendo' ['Against self-love, wondrous discovery'], in which Campanella condemns a Machiavellian way of thinking of oneself as author of the universe ['autor dell'universo']. It is significant that Campanella uses the term *author*. As he states elsewhere, the world is the book in which the Eternal Intellect wrote His own concepts; men, relying on books for their learning, fall into error because these books are twice removed from the living body of wisdom that is God's creation.[26] Instead, Campanella insists that the nature of his project is to bring the *true* wisdom to others. He even presents in his proemial poem a sort of genealogy, 'Io che nacqui dal Senno e di Sofia ...' ['I who was born of Intellect and Wisdom ...']. Aside from serving to distance the poet from his actual identity, and therefore from misguided self-love and authorial self-promotion, the genealogy is also intended to suggest in the reader's mind a tenuous but evocative comparison with genealogies of biblical figures.

In this same first poem Campanella implicitly acknowledges another risk of presumption. While Lorenzo used the figure of Phaeton to signal his awareness of the risks of presumption, Campanella chooses Phaeton's half-brother Prometheus. Prometheus was the son of Clymene by the Titan Iapetos, and his name has been interpreted to mean 'the one with foreknowledge' (*pro* = before or fore, *manthano* = to know).[27] With Athena's help Prometheus lit a stalk from the wheels of Apollo's sun chariot and gave humankind the gift of fire. It was his own act of creating the world, and for his excessive presumption, Zeus had him chained and tortured. Prometheus represents the reformer of mankind, the one who brings light to the darkness. He is also, as Pietro Pomponazzi had written in his *De Fato* [On Fate], the philosopher who, while impelled to learn the mysteries of God, is gnawed by ceaseless cares and derided, persecuted, and considered foolish (even sacrilegious) by the common masses (3.7). This figure of daring originality and creativity is the prophet whose mission it was to mediate between heaven and mankind for the greater good of the latter, even at the cost of great personal sacrifice. According to Campanella, the prophet, like Prometheus, *inflames* people to virtue ['fa le genti di virtù infiammarsi'] (2n).[28]

Turning back to Campanella's choice of pseudonym, it hardly seems openly exalting. Rather, he opts for a name that parodies his diminutive surname: the pealing of a little bell.[29] Campanella may have meant to evoke by his pseudonym an edifying symbol, as the *tintinnabulum* used to invite the faithful to the Eucharistic celebration. Campanella uses the symbol visually as well, signing some of his letters with a sketch of a bell. In one example, the bell sketch appears between the words, 'The [sketch of the bell] of the glories of Your Holiness,' which are repeated with variations that echo the semantic level of the name, as for example, 'Tuorum sonitus elogiorum, Frater Thomas Campanella.'[30] Sometimes accompanying portraits of the poet consist of drawings of a bell hanging from a star. Descending from the clouds and reaching out to ring the bell is a hand, presumably God's own, and the writing: 'Propter Sion non tacebo' ['For Zion I will not be silent']. Not by chance the citation refers to the mission of the prophet as described in the context of Isaiah 62:1.

There are still other indications that the critical valorization of Campanella's self-commentary must involve an eye to some prize other than the poetic laurel. The compositions bring together the vastness of his thought – from the *Metafisica*, the 'Philosopher's Bible,' to the ideal human domain of the *City of the Sun*, and of his experience, of a destiny that he persisted in considering unique and special.[31] In the seven protrusions of his skull, Campanella believed that the seal of his predestination was evident. Seven, in fact, is a particularly significant number in his numerology, as he confirms in *Profezia di Cristo* [Prophecy of Christ]. In the number seven is hidden true wisdom: 'è nascosta la vera sapienza.'[32] Campanella sought models for his poetic inspiration in the prophets because, as I suggested earlier, he believed that the true poets, those who sing the truth, are actually prophets:

> Ut quid ergo poëtae vocantur vates, et Aratus a sancto Paulo vocatur poëta, et Epimenides, poëta Cretensis, propheta vocatur, et poësis prophetia passim dicitur a doctissimis viris, si iocus est poëtica et nugandi ars? Equidem vereor David, cum sancto Hieronymo, nuncupare poëtam et lamentationes metricas Ieremiae elegias, si poëta est qui fingit, non qui vera canit.

> [Why then are poets called prophets and poetry is sometimes called the prophecy of the wise men if it is a joke and a diversion? In truth, I would hesitate to call David a poet, as St Girolamo does, and to define as elegies the lamentations in verse by Jeremiah if a poet is one who invents, not one who sings true things.] (*Poëtica latina*, 974)[33]

Campanella's choice of pen name becomes an integral part of the underlying poetics behind the philosophical poems. If Campanella intends by *Squilla* its significance as a verb, and thinks of himself in the role of the divine messenger, he effects with his choice an especially fitting metonymic figure. From 'Campanella' to 'Squilla' one moves from the object to the sound itself, from the 'I' of the poet to the message, and from there, in some sense, towards the pure *Logos*. All of these possible significances resound in Campanella's poetic choices, in a poetic and wilfully prophetic language that remains provocative and open.

7

Invocation, Interpretation, Inspiration

> The style of Dante has a peculiar lucidity – a *poetic* as distinguished from an *intellectual* lucidity. The thought may be obscure, but the word is lucid, or rather translucent ... Undoubtedly there is an opacity, or inspissation of poetic style throughout Europe after the Renaissance.
>
> – T. S. Eliot

T. S. Eliot's comments on poetic style could not be more true where poetic self-commentary is concerned. Self-commentary does indeed persist after the Renaissance. However, there is a palpable sense that after this period it no longer dwells within the poetic sphere. In positing a point from which to observe the poetry objectively, self-interpretation is cut off from that poetic sphere. It no longer attempts to radiate a truth from within, but rather reflects upon it. Medieval and Renaissance poetic self-commentaries intuit poetry's radical status as interlocutor in a peculiar dialogue with an other voice. The kind of poetic self-commentary that the six authors of this study exemplify is possible only when there is an understanding and valorization of the not-entirely-rational quality posed by its purposefully disjunctive and dynamic inquiry. The self-interpretive works in the era and spirit of the new sciences might be said to seek an *intellectual* lucidity and not a *poetic* one.

The purpose of this study, however, is not to trace the history of philosophical, religious, and scientific bases of hermeneutic change. An especially distinguished approach to such an enormous undertaking, and one to which I am indebted in my understanding of the dissolution of a Renaissance interpretive sensibility in the early seventeenth century, is Louis Dupré's study: *Passage to Modernity: An Essay in the Hermeneutics of Nature and Culture*.[1] In particular, Dupré argues convincingly for a shift in the perception of what it means to interpret texts after the nominalists' contribution. He goes on to locate the other temporal extreme of this current of thought in the Baroque:

> Despite tensions and inconsistencies, a comprehensive spiritual vision united Baroque culture. At the centre of it stands the person, confident in the ability to give form and structure to a nascent world. But – and here lies its religious significance – the centre remains vertically linked to a transcendent source from which, via a descending scale of mediating bodies, the human creator draws his power. This dual centre – human and divine – distinguishes the Baroque world picture from the vertical one of the Middle Ages, in which reality descends from a single transcendent point, as well as from the unproblematically horizontal one of later modern culture, prefigured in some features of the Renaissance. The tension between the two centres conveys to the Baroque a complex, restless, and dynamic quality.[2]

These same tensions animate the form of early poetic self-commentary, but the imposed distance in the Cartesian scientific perspective forces a shift from the transcendent or dual centre. The characteristic hostility towards exegesis of new scientists like René Descartes or Francis Bacon betrays a decided bias in favour of reflective reasoning over reading and commenting. They condemn marginal glosses as impotent and lacking the potential to found new knowledge. Not surprisingly, poetic self-commentary also noticeably falls into disfavour.

Nevertheless, many examples of self-glossed works written after the Renaissance come to mind, including Alessandro Tassoni's *Dichiarazioni del signor Gasparo Salviani alla* Secchia rapita (Declarations by Gasparo Salviani on the *Stolen Bucket*, 1630), Benedetto Menzini's *Poetica e satire di Benedetto Menzini con annotazioni* (Poetics and Satires by Benedetto Menzini with Annotations, published posthumously in 1718), and Antonio Conti's *Prose e poesie del Signor Abate Antonio Conti* (Prose and Poetry by Antonio Conti, Abbot, 1739). On a strictly formal level, each appears to perpetuate the mixed genre of the poetic self-commentary. On closer inspection, however, these later works have less in common with the poetic self-commentary, and resemble, or strive to resemble, more closely standard commentary.

Tassoni composed and published his *Secchia rapita* at nearly the same time that Campanella's *Scelta* appeared. While Tassoni and Campanella had vastly different intellectual formations, literary objectives, and personal temperaments, they shared some common cultural and poetic interests. Both had a keen interest in astrology, and both encountered difficulties with the Inquisition. Like Campanella, Tassoni struggled to get his works past the censors. He also sparred with Church authorities when his maid and lover – mother of his illegitimate son – suffered torture at their hands, accused of letting her son play with a diabolical toy. Campanella exhorted poets to base their epic works on true deeds instead of fables, naming the exploits of Christopher Columbus as an exemplar; Tassoni attempted to fulfil Campanella's plea by beginning his poem on the discovery of America, *L'oceano*. Most importantly, however, both authors chose to write commentaries on their own verse, although those commentaries differ radically in tone and intent.

Tassoni's work really belongs to a much different literary genealogy and represents a break from the kind of self-commentary we have examined thus far. The *Secchia rapita* (sometimes translated as the *Stolen Bucket*, other times as *The Rape of the Bucket*, which emphasizes the kindred nature of this work and Alexander Pope's *The Rape of the Lock*, 1712) first appeared in 1622. Subsequent editions differed noticeably: not until 1630 did the work present itself in its definitive form, in the last edition overseen by the poet before his death in 1635.[3] In this edition appears for the first time a prose apparatus, the so-called declarations by Gaspare Salviani. While Tassoni attributes the 'dichiarazioni' to his friend, it is clear that they come from Tassoni's own pen.[4]

Tassoni defines his poem in twelve cantos in *ottava rima* as 'heroisatiricomic' ['questa sua invenzione nuova di poetare "eroisatiricomica"'] (254). By definition, mock-heroic or heroicomic poems depend for their humorous effect on the disparity between the high register of their language and form (usually epic poetry), and the low register of their subject matter. In the case of Tassoni's poem, the parody depends on the positing of an insignificant historical battle between the warring city-states of Bologna and Modena – the Petroniani and Gemignani respectively – in 1393, recounted as if it were the Trojan War or the Crusades. Moreover, instead of the fate of the Greeks or of the whole of Christendom being at stake, the heroicomic war is fought over possession of a wooden, worm-eaten bucket. Even the mythical gods of Mount Olympus take sides in the dispute, which serves as a forum for a satiric send-up of the political disputes and bickering in the literary circles of Tassoni's own time.

The declarations in Tassoni's poem underscore the distance between registers in several ways. In some instances they juxtapose history with chivalric literature, as for example: 'Questo non è capriccio del poeta, come l'hanno tenuto alcuni, ma istoria vera cavata dalle croniche del Lancillotto' ['This is not the whim of the poet, as some people have held, but a true story taken from the chronicles of Lancelot'] (*Dichiarazione* 1.12.5).[5] Other declarations invoke philosophical authority in mock defence of the poem's tone: 'Aristotile insegnò all'epico ch'egli poteva usare la varietà delle lingue; onde il poeta qui si serve della regola per introdurre il ridicolo' ['Aristotle taught that poets can use a variety of languages in the epic, so here the poet observes the rule in order to introduce the ridiculous'] (*Dichiarazione* 1.23.5).

It is probably not insignificant that Tassoni calls the prose apparatus he appends to the poem 'declarations.' He thus ironically implies a will to *clarify* passages of the poem. The careful reader, however, appreciates that Tassoni is not primarily intent on clarification, but rather uses the apparatus as another venue for comic or satirical expression. The declaration of 3.49.1, for example, is concerned less with explaining the grossly over-Petrarchanized language of the octave than with deflating the reputation of the Countess Laura Cesi with the stinging assessment of her beauty as 'sol che tramonta' ['a sun that is setting']. Despite their avowed intention, other declarations do not avert the satirical effect in the poem but rather emphasize the ridicule all the more. Particularly entertaining examples of redoubled ridicule appear in the declarations of 1.52.1 and 10.60.7.[6]

Tassoni's declarations differ from poetic self-commentaries not simply in their satiric tone, however, but also in their essential perspective from the 'self.' I have said that the declarations underscore the difference between high and low registers in the heroicomic work. They further emphasize a distance already present in the poem. That distance is the place of critical perspective. In visual perspective, for instance, the viewer must step away from an object in order to behold it and to make the perspective possible. In a similar way, Tassoni's work posits two diametrically opposed registers, the effect of which – that is, the humor or satire – results from the author's critical appreciation for that space. He looks on his object from without. In other words, Tassoni has pre-digested the non-correspondence in registers and represents it to his readers. He has separate roles as poet and perspective-giver, unlike the poetic self-commentator intent on the ever-questioning, internal exploration in poetry and prose. The differentiation of authorial roles for Tassoni seems to parallel the Cartesian split of the philosophical subject.

Outside of Italy, among the examples of self-commentative writing after the Renaissance are the searing satires of the so-called Scriblerians. The group numbered among its members Alexander Pope (1688–1744), Jonathan Swift (1667–1745), and John Arbuthnot (1667–1735). The Scriblerian Club took its name from Martinus Scriblerus, a fictitious author who embodies the overpreening intellectual rigidity and monistic materialism of early eighteenth-century academic pedantry – a primary target for the group's wittily sharp barbs. Martinus is but the most famous and well developed of a small legion of fictitious authors who mercilessly poke fun at the philosophical and political establishment.

Pope's self-glosses on his *Dunciad* offer one of the most entertaining glimpses of Martinus's handiwork. The falsely punctilious marginalia take over the pages of the 1,754-line poem in four books. While the verse sings the Dulness that conspires against the poet, the glossators focus on such petty concerns as the status of the letter E, the purported chronology of the poem, the stupidity of supposed previous commentators, and tangents of the most imaginative kind. In short, Pope effectively portrays the glossators as missing the point of the poetic word's spirit despite their purported precision, appeals to reasons, and careful documentation. Pope succeeds in taking to task his real-life ideological adversaries by taking their weapons away from them, pre-empting the petulant and fussy commentative jabs at his work by means of satirical self-commentary.

In the Scriblerian self-commentary the prose upstages the poetry. Pope's self-commentary and others like it serve as the battleground for ideological forces that spin centrifugally away from the poem, thus negating the variously unifying procedures of the earlier works examined in the present study. The medieval-Renaissance self-commentator invites the outside commentator to enter into a special spirit of poetic interpretation seeking an elusive truth, while the Scriblerian author places the outside commentator in the position of the dunce. By the time of the satiric self-commentary, the outside commentator is deliberately relegated to the outside of the text. The reflective distance necessary for outside critics to perceive the satire is precisely the characteristic that condemns them to the outside and trumps any intervention they could make. Today when self-commentary is evoked, the reader is more likely to think of the tyranny of the author's satirical distance and circumscription of the critic's role, rather than the much freer role that earlier poetic self-commentators beckon the reader to play.

Menzini's *Poetica e satire con annotazioni*, like Tassoni's *Secchia*, displays this critical, reflective distance, but in a much less entertaining way. Among the works collected in the volume are two self-annotated poems, the *Arte Poetica*, divided into five books and written in *terza rima*, and twelve *Satire*, which showcase the author's pedanticism as professor of eloquence and his rigid moralism as cleric. Most of the annotations, especially of the *Arte Poetica*, aim to distinguish between good and bad poetic precedents, to illustrate how Menzini's poetry follows the good ones, and generally to display literary erudition. Moreover, if the reader consults the 1808 Milanese edition, in which the author's annotations are accompanied by those of Francesco del Teglia and others designated as 'd'Incerto' ['of uncertain [origin]'] (11), one can see just how successfully Menzini emulates the standard commentary in his self-annotations. The unique quality of the earlier poetic self-commentary is nowhere to be found in Menzini's examples.

There is still a satirical tone in Menzini's works, but the satire itself is not necessary to achieve the critical distance, the disjunction of the poetic and hermeneutic spheres that the reader sees in the mixed genre of poetry and prose by post-Renaissance authors. Antonio Conti, in his *Prose e poesie*, presents coldly abstract and highly technical philosophical notions in verse, which seem to serve primarily as cues for the discursive prose that plods heavily through disquisitions on spiritual, philosophical, and scientific authorities from Thomas Aquinas to Nicholas Malebranche, from Aristotle to Gottfried Leibniz, and from Dionysius the Areopagite to Isaac Newton. Conti also praises the certainties that Descartes' *cogito* can help illuminate. Conti's prose does not take the fragmentary form of glosses, nor is it interspersed with the poetry like a prosimetrum. Rather, Conti's prose reads more like an independent treatise, formally separated under headings like 'Annotazioni su i Sonetti Filosofici' ['Annotations on the Philosophical Sonnets'] or 'Annotazioni su i Sonetti Teologici' ['Annotations on the Theological Sonnets'] with separate dedications and prefaces by the author.

Gregorio Piaia sees – seemingly almost triumphantly – in Conti's form of divorcing the self-commentary from its poetic text a Hegelian 'rivincita del "servo" (l'ipotesto) nei riguardi del testo-padrone' ['revenge of the "servant" (the hypotext [that is to say the commentary]) on the text-master [the poetry]'].[7] According to Piaia, 'L'intero autocommento del Conti si distingue per la ricchezza e la pregnanza delle annotazioni filosofico-teologiche, che in certi casi forniscono un sostanziale 'di più' rispetto al testo poetico' ['Conti's entire self-commentary distinguishes itself for the richness and fecundity of the philosophic-theological annotations, which in some cases provide a substantial *something more* with respect to the poetic text'].[8]

However, if we compare Conti's poetic self-commentary to that of Campanella, which of the four Renaissance texts considered here Conti's most resembles, the purposeful proximity of Campanella's self-commentary to his verse, as well as many other factors – including the undisclosed authorial intent – not shared by Conti's primarily didactic treatment, brings to Campanella's work an essence that verges on the prophetic, where as Conti seems to have endeavoured to prove beyond a reasonable doubt some 'truth' contained in his poetry. I would argue that it is instead precisely in the problematic procedure of poetic self-commentary heralded by the Renaissance poet-commentators that the potential for expressing this *something more* is glimpsed. It would be possible, of course, to cite many more examples of poets writing prose interpretations or self-glosses of their verse in the modern Italian tradition, as well as in other national literary traditions.[9] While I would not necessarily go so far as to fix here any temporally definitive, Foucault-inspired break between an 'age of commentary' and an 'age of criticism,' I do perceive a difference in the mode of poetic self-commentary of Renaissance authors and that of these later writers.

Poetic self-commentary is not alone among Renaissance literary forms to become effectively extinct. Dialogue likewise did not survive the passage to modernity, despite the fact that it has seemingly undergone a Renaissance of its own from the twentieth century.[10] Self-interpretation and theories of the self enjoy a remarkable popularity today, yet their discourses share very little in common with the kinds of poetic/self-commentative insights the writers of this study communicate. Perhaps Renaissance genres of poetic self-commentary and dialogue share a similar fate because they both engage the intersection of logic and literature.[11] Dialogue is an activity that seeks a truth in the space of the *in-between*, between two dialectical perspectives, not unlike the way that self-commentary reads between the lines of the poetic word.

In this study I have relied on the reader's willingness to think about the form of poetic self-commentary as a symbolic mode in and of itself. Indeed, one might even go so far as to call poetic self-commentary a 'symbolic form' (Cassirer). Focusing critical attention almost exclusively on what the self-commentaries say about the poetry has in the past hindered the study of these works and others like them. By raising the issue instead of how self-commentaries relate to the poetry, readers can begin to understand why the form exists – why it is not simply trying to baffle and why it is never expendable. Considering the inherent significance in these works' form also makes the authors' excuses for writing them clearer, even more shocking, especially where authors liken the form of their works to sacred texts.

I have insisted that the reader consider this form of mixed genre as a potential allegory for Gospel parables, Socratic dialogue, or eschatological prophecy, for instance. However, this procedure has actually been less abstracting than it might seem at first glance. It recuperates an originally non-differentiated role of the *mantis-prophetes*, or poet-divulger, in its emblem, Hermes' Lyre.

By Plato's time the two roles had become noticeably distinct, as is evident from this passage of the *Timaeus*:

> That divination [*mantike*] is the gift of heaven to human unwisdom we have good reason to believe, in that no man in his normal senses deals in true [*aletheia*] and inspired [*entheos*] divination, but only when the power of understanding is fettered in sleep or he is distraught by some disorder or, it may be, by divine possession [*enthousiasmos*]. It is for the man in his ordinary senses to recall and construe the utterances, in dream or in waking life, of divination or possession, and by reflection to make out in what manner and to whom all the visions of the seer betoken [*semaino*, that is to make understood by a sign, to indicate] some good or ill, past, present, or to come. When a man has fallen into frenzy and is still in that condition, it is not for him to determine the meaning of his own visions and utterances; rather the old saying is true, that only the sound in mind can attend to his own concerns and know himself. Hence it is the custom to set up spokesmen [*prophetai*] to pronounce judgment [*kritai*] on inspired divination. These are themselves given the name of diviners by some who are quite unaware that they are expositors of riddling oracle [*ainigmoi*] or vision and best deserve to be called, not diviners, but spokesmen of those who practice divination.[12]

Bruno, perhaps more obviously than any of the other poetic self-commentators, recognizes the disjunction of these roles of poet/enthusiast and commentator/declarer/critic and attempts in the *Heroic Frenzies* a reunification of them. Within his work are the poems of the *mantis*, as well as the interpretations – the speaking in-between – of the *kritai*, who also display literally the function of the expositor of *ainigmoi*, the absent emblems.

The witnessing function that Campanella claims in order to prove the truth and authority of his enunciations ('Or, c'han visto i miei sensi, / non più opinante son, ma testimonio, / né sciocche pruove ho de' secreti immensi') also echoes this Platonic context, but once again the self-commentator plays on the proximity of the two roles of *theoros* (the one who observes the vision, *thea*, and takes the message back to the *polis*) and *entheos* (the one having god within). Of course, poetic self-commentators explicitly question the Platonic notion that the *entheos* cannot also declare (or be the *prophetes*) or discern the meaning (in the role of *kritai*) of the poetic or divinely inspired message. While the works of Bruno and Campanella most literalize the drive to reappropriate a pre-Platonic understanding of the Hermetic figure, and perhaps for this very reason mark the beginning of the end of the poetic self-commentative form, all six of the medieval and Renaissance authors in this study intuit this understanding in their own ways. They also can *semaino*, plant or point out, to us as interpreters a challenging way of approaching our task.

Notes

Introduction

1 Citations of the *Vita Nuova* in the original Italian are taken from the most recent critical edition by Guglielmo Gorni (Turin: Einaudi, 1996). English translations are by Dino S. Cervigni and Edward Vasta (Notre Dame and London: University of Notre Dame Press, 1995). Gorni divides the work into only thirty-one chapters, instead of the canonical form of forty-two chapters that Michele Barbi established (Opere minori di Dante Alighieri – Edizione critica, Società Dantesca Italiana. Florence, 1907) and Cervigni and Vasta followed. For this reason, the reference numbers after the Italian and English citations rarely match.
2 This is the only footnote by Campanella on this poem. In Campanella's even more laconic moods, he simply writes, 'È chiaro' ['It is clear'] as in the self-commentary on poem 60. This and all subsequent English translations of Campanella are mine.
3 'Premessa,' in Gianfelice Peron, ed., *L'autocommento. Atti del XVIII Convegno Interuniversitario (Bressanone, 1990)* (Padua: Esedra Editrice, 1994), 1–10 at 2.
4 *Paratexts: Thresholds of Interpretation*, trans. Jane E. Lewin (Cambridge and New York: Cambridge University Press, 1997).
5 Thus on this point my view differs substantially from Anthony Grafton's: 'Nor does the historian's apparatus derive from late medieval and Renaissance authors' commentaries on their own works. The historian who builds a literary house on a foundation of documents does not address the same task as *the author of a religious, literary, or scientific work who tries to fix the text's message unequivocally for posterity*. The one explains the methods

and procedures used to produce the text, the other the methods and procedures that should be used to consume it.' *The Footnote: A Curious History* (Cambridge and London: Harvard University Press, 1997), 32–3, emphasis mine. Religious exegesis and scientific exposition may indeed try to fix the text's message unequivocally, but this cannot be the intent of the most poetic of the self-commentaries.

6 The Italian is from *Teseida delle nozze d'Emilia*, a cura di Alberto Limentani (Milan: Mondadori, 1992). English translation is by Bernadette Marie McCoy, *The Book of Theseus* (New York: Medieval Text Association, 1974), 7.30n.

7 Limentani, ed., *Teseida delle nozze d'Emilia*, 440.

8 *The Autobiography of Lorenzo de' Medici the Magnificent: A Commentary on My Sonnets*. Together with the text of *Il Commento* in the critical edition of Tiziano Zanato. Trans. James Wyatt Cook. Medieval and Renaissance Texts & Studies 129 (Binghampton, N.Y.: Center for Medieval and Early Renaissance Studies, 1995), 191n.

9 *English and Italian Literature from Dante to Shakespeare: A Study of Source, Analogue, and Divergence* (New York and London: Longman, 1995), 144 (my emphasis). See also Amilcare A. Iannucci's introduction to the volume of essays he edits on Dante: 'Baranski also broaches a subject which many of the other authors in this volume (Ascoli, Picone, and Iannucci, in particular; cf. Iannucci's "Autoesegesi dantesca") discuss, namely Dante's "autocommentary," which is designed both to guide and to cut off independent critical analysis.' *Dante: Contemporary Perspectives* (Toronto and Buffalo: University of Toronto Press, 1997), xiv.

10 Zanato, ed., *Autobiography of Lorenzo de' Medici*, 40–1.

11 This is Mario Martelli's procedure, for example, in 'Questioni di cronologia laurenziana,' *Lettere italiane* 18 (1966): 249–61 at 252. See also Zygmunt G. Baranski, 'Dante commentatore e commentato: Riflessioni sullo studio dell'*iter* ideologico di Dante,' *Letture classensi* 23 (1994): 135–58 at 146: 'Il poeta, la cui esperienza di autore è caratterizzata dal 'perpetuo sopraggiungere della riflessione tecnica accanto alla poesia' (Gianfranco Contini), resta la migliore guida e il migliore commentatore della propria opera e del proprio sviluppo intellettuale.' However, the frequency with which scholars present this sort of premise has made it almost formulaic.

12 Marianne Shapiro, 'Poetry and Politics in the *Comento* of Lorenzo de' Medici,' *Renaissance Quarterly* 26(4) (1973): 444–53 at 448. Leonid M. Batkin finds similar fault with Lorenzo's lack of historical content: 'Ma quale storico potrebbe supporre niente del genere, se disponesse soltanto di questa testimonianza falsamente confidenziale che si riduce a un catalogo retorico nel quale è riconoscibile un unico cenno concreto, quello alla

scomunica papale' (*L'idea di individualità nel Rinascimento italiano*, trans. Valentina Rossi [Bari: Laterza, 1992], 64).

13 This is the first occurance of *autocommento* that Salvatore Battaglia records in the *Grande dizionario della lingua italiana* vol. 1 (Turin: Unione Tipografico-Editrice Torinese, 1961), 854.

14 The prose of Dante's *Vita Nuova* is made up of a narrative, which recounts the story of his love for Beatrice and his early development as a poet, and the so-called divisions, those more structural descriptions of his poems' forms, that is, 'Questo sonetto à tre parti. Nella prima parte dico sì come io trovai Amore e quale mi parea; nella seconda dico quello ch'elli mi disse ...' (4.13) ['This sonnet is divided into three parts. In the first part I state how I found Love. In the second I say what He said to me ...'] (9). According to Michele Barbi, many of the pre-1600 editions of Dante's 'little book' exclude some or all of the divisions. See his critical edition of the *Vita Nuova* (1907) and his book, *Dante nel Cinquecento* (Pisa: 1890). Exclusion of the divisions profoundly distorts the reader's understanding of the *Vita Nuova*, since even the placement of the divisions influences their meaning. After the mention of Beatrice's death, for example, Dante proclaims that he will switch the order of the poems and the divisions so that the poems will appear more widowed after they are written. I will explore this issue in greater detail in chapter 1.

15 The notion that the hidden matter is valuable and what is apparent should not be prized recurs with insistent frequency in the most disparate rearticulations, from Socrates' physical appearance and the Silenus *topos*, to the secrecy of esoteric wisdom and the mystery of Christian revelation. Peter Dronke traces the 'poets as liars' view in *Fabula: Explorations into the Uses of Myth in Medieval Platonism* (Leiden and Cologne: E.J. Brill, 1974). Dante alludes to a similar self-consciousness of the poet in *Vita Nuova* 25, in which he states that a true poet is always able to reveal what is hidden in his verse. This notion rests on a classical ideal, that is, that one is present to oneself. By the time of Coluccio Salutati (1331–1406), the attitude towards the poet's self-consciousness had changed considerably. On this subject, see Arthur Field, *The Origins of the Platonic Academy in Florence* (Princeton: Princeton University Press, 1988), 250.

16 María Rosa Menocal, in *Writing in Dante's Cult of Truth: From Borges to Boccaccio* (Durham and London: Duke University Press, 1991), 30, describes Dante's *Vita Nuova* as being made up of the prose narration, the poetry, and 'a pseudoscientific and remarkably banal explication of the poem's structure and "divisions."' Benivieni biographer Caterina Re questions the self-commentator's excuse for writing his glosses, 'Ma di quanto maggior buon

senso, pover'uomo! avrebbe dato prova, rifiutandoli [i componimenti lirici di amore terreno] semplicemente come opera di cui la coscienza lo biasimava, senza assoggettare sè e il lettore alla *tortura* di quest'esegesi!' (*Girolamo Benivieni fiorentino: Cenni sulla vita e sulle opere* [Città di Castello: Casa Tipografico-Editrice S. Lapi, 1906], 188, emphasis is mine).

17 Readers of modern self-commentaries, especially those inscribed within novels, such as Laurence Sterne's *Tristram Shandy* and James Joyce's *Finnegans Wake*, take for granted one kind of manifestation of this poetic or fictive status of the self-commentative apparatus.

18 Dronke also leaves off where the present study begins, with Dante, the author whom L. Jenaro MacLennan called, not inaccurately, 'el primero que se autocomenta,' 'Autocomentario en Dante y comentarismo latino,' *Vox Romanica* 19 (1960): 82–123 at 92. However, I will qualify the cases of Boethius and Capella later in this Introduction.

19 (New York: Columbia University Press, 1958), 15–66.

20 Battista Guarini, Benedetto Varchi, and other Renaissance theorists of genre did not shy away from the idea of departing from Scholastic determinations and creating new genres when necessary in order to most approximate in some cases the capacity to interpret and to represent the whole of creation.

21 Genuine dialogue, as Hans Georg Gadamer has shown, eludes the purely subjective: 'What emerges in its truth is the *logos*, and this is neither yours nor mine, but rather exceeds the subjective opinion of the partners in the discussion to such an extent that even the leader of the discussion always remains the ignorant one.' *Truth and Method*, 2nd ed., trans. Joel Winsheimer and Donald G. Marshall (New York: Continuum, 1998), 350.

22 Another important difference between the prosimetrical self-commentary and the self-gloss forms are the break in narrative or entire lack thereof in the self-gloss type. In *Footnote*, Grafton touches on the interruption that glosses cause: 'More than one recent critic has pointed out that footnotes interrupt a narrative. References detract from the illusion of veracity and immediacy that Ranke and so many other nineteenth-century historians wished to create, since they continually interrupt the single story told by an omniscient narrator (Noel Coward made the same point more memorably when he remarked that having to read a footnote resembles having to go downstairs to answer the door while in the midst of making love)' (69–70). There is also the issue of the difference in person between the prosimetrical and self-gloss self-commentaries. The former is usually couched throughout in the first person, while the self-gloss generally uses first person in the verse and the third person in the commentary.

23 There is no lack of successful outside commentaries that read into the primary text more than what the original author necessarily intends. The *Ovide moralisé* is a striking example. Looming large, however, is the risk of these kinds of 'commentaries' either becoming primary texts themselves, mostly divorced from the works on which they are supposedly dependent, or being labelled as irresponsible scholarship. There is seemingly no room for these kinds of examples in Northrop Frye's valiant attempt to separate the ideas of commentary and primary text: 'Good commentary naturally does not read ideas into the poem; it reads and translates what is there, and the evidence that it is there is offered by the study of the structure of imagery with which it begins ... The failure to make, in practice, the most elementary of all distinctions in literature, the distinction between fiction and fact, hypothesis and assertion, imaginative and discursive writing, produces what in criticism has been called the "intentional fallacy," the notion that the poet has a primary intention of conveying meaning to a reader, and that the first duty of a critic is to recapture that intention ... But a poet's primary concern is to produce a work of art, and hence his intention can only be expressed by some kind of tautology' (*Anatomy of Criticism: Four Essays* [Princeton: Princeton University Press, 1957], 86).

24 Walter Benjamin makes this point in his justly famous essay, 'The Task of the Translator,' in *Illuminations*, ed. Hannah Arendt, trans. Harry Zohn. 1st ed. (New York: Harcourt, Brace & World, 1968).

25 Frye, *Anatomy of Criticism*, 334.

26 *Unediting the Renaissance: Shakespeare, Marlowe, Milton* (London and New York: Routledge, 1996), 3.

27 See the discussion on Gower by A.J. Minnis and A.B. Scott in *Medieval Literary Theory and Criticism c. 1100–c. 1375: The Commentary Tradition* (Oxford: Clarendon Press, 1988), 379ff.

28 Thomas H. Cain gives an overview of the ongoing debate on the identity of E.K. in his introduction to *The Yale Edition of the Shorter Poems*, ed. William A. Oram et al. (New Haven and London: Yale University Press, 1989), 6. The nature of the glosses, which 'should aim to assist the reader, but often seem to confuse, mislead, or misinform [and generally] raise unhelpful assistance to a new power' argue for renewed consideration of the glosses in the light of theories of poetic self-commentary.

29 James Simpson has examined various medieval Latin and English scientific works in prosimetrical form in *Sciences and the Self in Medieval Poetry: Alan of Lille's* Anticlaudianus *and John Gower's* Confessio amantis (Cambridge: Cambridge University Press, 1995).

30 Peter Dronke examines the *satura* in greater detail in *Verse with Prose from*

168   Notes to pages 17–28

Petronius to Dante: The Art and Scope of the Mixed Form (Cambridge and London: Harvard University Press, 1994). Dante's understanding of *comedìa* also recalls in some way Capella's view of *satura*. On this comparison, see William Franke, *Dante's Interpretive Journey* (Chicago: University of Chicago Press, 1996), 96.

31 In its most recent English translation, the work has been given the highly misleading title of *The Autobiography of Lorenzo de' Medici the Magnificent*.

32 *Footnote*, 110–11. Grafton's reference is to W. Rehm, 'Jean Pauls vergnügtes Notenleben oder Notenmacher und Notenleser,' *Späte Studien* (Bern and Munich: Francke, 1964), 7–96.

Chapter One

1 The *Vita Nuova*'s status as the first book of Italian literature is the premise for Dominico DeRobertis' *Il libro della 'Vita Nuova'* (Florence: Sansoni, 1961).

2 The chapter from Charles S. Singleton's *Essay on the "Vita Nuova"* (Baltimore: Johns Hopkins University Press, 1949), titled 'The Book of Memory' brings to the fore some of these complexities.

3 Giuseppe Mazzotta elaborates on these etymologies concerning textual interpretation in *Dante's Vision and the Circle of Knowledge* (Princeton: Princeton University Press, 1993). 'Hugh of St. Victor defines two words – commentary and gloss – which are part of Dante's hermeneutical lexicon as follows: "Commentaries (*commentaria*) are so named as from *cum mente* (with the mind) or from *comminiscor* (call to mind); for they are interpretations, as, for example, commentaries on the Law or on the Gospel. Certain persons say that the word 'comments' should be restricted to books of the pagans, while 'expositions' should be kept for the Sacred Books. The word 'gloss' is Greek, and it means tongue (*lingua*), because, in a way, it bespeaks (*loquitur*) the meaning of the word under it" (*Didascalicon*, IV, xvi)' (270).

4 See Gorni's glosses on '*Incipit Vita Nova*' in *Vita Nova* (Turin: Einaudi, 1996), 3–4.

5 The second reason Boccaccio gives, while curious in itself, cannot concern us here: 'La seconda ragione è che, secondo che io ho udito giá ragionare a persone degne di fede, avendo Dante nella sua giovanezza composto questo libello e poi essendo col tempo nella scienza e nelle operazioni cresciuto, si vergognava aver fatto questo, parendogli opera troppo puerile; e tra l'altre cose di che si dolea averlo fatto, si ramaricava d'avere inchiuse le divisioni nel testo, forse per quella medesima ragione che

muove me. Laonde io non potendolo negli altri emendare, in questo che scritto ho n'ho voluto sodisfare l'appetito de l'autore.' ['The second reason is that, according to what I have heard discussed by people worthy to be believed, Dante, having in his youth composed this little book and then with time having grown in thought and experience, was ashamed to have written this, since it seemed to him an excessively puerile work; and among the other things which it pained him to have done, he regretted having included the divisions in the text, perhaps for the same reason that moves me. Therefore, not being able to do anything about the rest, I wanted at least to satisfy the author's desire in this that I have written.'] I quote the Italian from the appendix of Domenico Guerri, *Il commento del Boccaccio a Dante: Limiti della sua autenticità e questioni critiche che n'emergono* (Bari: Laterza & Figli, 1926), 227–8; the English translation is my own. It is possible to find clues to understanding how Boccaccio viewed commentary in some of his other works on poetry. See, for example, *Genealogia deorum gentilium* 15.6: 'Habent enim civiles et canonice leges preter textus multiplices, hominum nequitia semper auctos, apparatus suos a multis hactenus doctoribus editos. Habent phylosophorum volumina diligentissime commenta composita. Habent et medicinales libri plurimorum scripta, omne dubium enodantia. Sic et sacre lictere multos habent interpretes; nec non et facultates et artes relique glosatores proprios habuere, ad quos, si oportunum sit, volens habet, ubi recurrat, et quos velit, ex multis eligat. Sola poesis, quoniam perpaucorum semper domestica fuit, nec aliquid afferre lucri avaris visa sit, non solum per secula multa neglecta atque deiecta, sed etiam variis lacerata persecutionibus a se narrata non habet!' ['The great text of both civil and canon law has grown in bulk throughout generations of human failing, by editorial apparatus from many a doctor. The books of the philosophers also carry with them their commentaries compiled with great care and zeal. The books of medicine are filled with marginal notes from countless pens that resolve every doubt, and so with sacred writings, and their numerous expositors; so also with the liberal and the technical arts – each has its own commentary, from which anyone may select on occasion according to his preference. Poetry alone is without such honour. Few – very few – are they with whom it has dwelt continuously. Money-getters have found it unprofitable. It has therefore been neglected and scorned for many centuries, nay even torn by many persecutions and stripped of the aids given to the other arts.'] Not only does Boccaccio want to remedy this state of affairs in his own poetic project, he also wishes to apply his concept of commentary to his editing of Dante's *Vita Nuova*.

6 Barbi details the permutations of the various editions in this and in his updated 1932 edition (Edizione Nazionale delle Opere di Dante. Florence: Bemporad e figlio, 1932).
7 Domenico Guerri, whose *Il commento alla 'Divina Commedia' e gli altri scritti intomo a Dante*. A cura di Domenico Guerri, Vol. 1. (Bari: Laterza, 1918), is dedicated to Benedetto Croce, states, 'Devo giustificare il corsivo delle divisioni, che certamente non fu nell'intenzione di Dante di distinguere dal resto, come provano le particolari compenetrazioni e il fatto generale che ad esse è assegnata una propria funzione costitutiva del libretto, dove, dal transito in poi, son preposte ai versi invece di seguire, affinché questi apparissero più vedovi. Mi sono permesso questo arbitrio, di cui si ha esempio già nel '300 (Boccaccio), perché in una edizione commentata, il contenuto di dette divisioni è ricompreso e ampliato nelle note, sicché il lettore di esse che non cerchi alcun moto lirico in quei tratti che, per sé, hanno natura e intendimenti didattici.' Proponents of this line of idealistic thought parallel Boccaccio's editorial procedure by making a distinction between the 'moto lirico' and the 'intendimenti didattici,' devaluing the latter as a detractor from a certain aesthetic ideal. Joseph Anthony Mazzeo has rightly identified the limitations of such a position: 'the philosophy and theology of the poem are as much poetry as anything else and serve not to simplify our moral judgments but to complicate them, by forcing us to relate the judgment of the system with the life, history, and action of the characters' (*Medieval Cultural Tradition in Dante's* Comedy [Ithaca: Cornell University Press, 1960], 5).
8 This viewpoint is expressed in different ways by many scholars writing in the 1950s and 1960s. See, for example, Luigi Pietrobono, *Saggi danteschi* (Torino: Società Editrice Internazionale, 1954): 'Alle rime della *Vita Nuova* Dante fa seguire quasi sempre codeste divisioni, che non dicono quasi nulla, è vero; ma provano che egli mirava innanzi tutto alla chiarezza' (35), and Aldo Vallone, *La prosa della 'Vita Nuova'* (Florence: Felice Le Monnier, 1963), for whom Dante's purpose in writing the divisions is to 'rendere piana la lettura' (40).
9 Scholars continue to advance Gianfranco Contini's opinion with little elaboration: 'Dante fu il primo autore italiano a fornire un commento 'storico' delle proprie rime volgari (quello letterale consistente in una 'divisione' tematica dei testi è francamente meno rilevante).' Edoardo Sanguineti's view that the *Vita Nuova* ultimately tends towards the prosaic has found rearticulation even in a study of strikingly different aim and tenor. See Deborah Parker, *Commentary and Ideology: Dante in the Renaissance* (Durham and London: Duke University Press, 1993): 'Commentary

in the *Vita Nuova* is presented within a broad framework that includes both the poems themselves and the narrative surrounding them. It is not simply an external apparatus for extracting intention; it serves as a heuristic device to clarify and enhance the poet's conception of Beatrice' (27–8).

10 *Il nome della storia: Studi e ricerche di storia e letteratura* (Naples: Liguori, 1982), 58.

11 Mark Musa, in his 'Essay on the *Vita Nuova*' in *Dante's* Vita Nuova, states: 'I wonder if [Dante] might not have had an artistic interest [as opposed to a hermeneutic one] in breaking down a poetic structure into conceptual units' (96). Robert Pogue Harrison attempts to exclude this possibility when, after quoting this passage of Musa's study in *The Body of Beatrice* (Baltimore and London: Johns Hopkins University Press, 1988), he states: 'I cannot see what artistic purpose the *divisioni* could have, but I am in accord with Musa that "there are few interpretations, allegorical or otherwise, contained in the *divisioni* of the *Vita Nuova*"' (185).

12 Peter Dronke's discussion of Alan of Lille's influence on Dante seems appropriate in this regard: 'the reader cannot rest content with the poem's "base images," but [must] rise beyond them "to the contemplation of *supercelestial* forms." A theophany, that is, can allow the perception even of forms as they exist in the divine realm.' Mere narratives 'have no hidden meanings, they are not theophanies' (*Dante and Medieval Latin Traditions* [Cambridge and New York: Cambridge University Press, 1986], 9).

13 Glauco Cambon, among others, rightfully calls attention to secular literary traditions that emphasize the need for interpreting obscure language: 'In the case of Dante, however, the existence of a circle of initiates, the "Fedeli d'Amore" ("Devotees of Love") as he calls them, having a hierarchy of their own that prevents his giving too many explanations about the poems and their inspiring object, and the attendant use of a rather exclusive style which is a kind of *trobar clus*, posits the problem of spontaneity versus convention. While Valli rejects any spontaneity or even poetry, treating as he does the whole *dolce stil nuovo* literature as religious and political communication in code with no literary aim except protective mystification, I see in the experimental use of literary convention, as expounded in Chapter XXV of the *Vita Nuova* and again in Treatise II of the *Convivio* (where allegory is discussed), Dante's need to sharpen his expressive instrument in view of the upsetting and exhilarating quality of the experience he had to clarify for himself and his connoisseur friends ... Thus I equate the polarity "convention-spontaneity" (or "coded message-love poetry," to put it in terms of the two warring schools) with the formula "experiment-experience," experiment as such leading to further, that is,

literary, experience, and experience in turn feeding on literary experiment, in an endless circle' (*Dante's Craft: Studies in Language and Style* [Minneapolis: University of Minnesota Press, 1969], 19–20).
14 Singleton, *Essay*, 55–77.
15 This is not the first occasion in which Dante finds Love's words difficult to understand. See also 1.14: 'nelle sue parole dicea molte cose, le quali io non intendea se non poche' ['He spoke of many things, of which I understood only a few'] (3.3).
16 All citations of the Bible in Latin are from the Vulgate text as they appear in Alberto Colunga and Laurentio Turrado, eds., *Biblia Sacra Vulgatae Editionis* (Madrid: Edizioni San Paolo, 1995). For the English translation I refer to Douay-Rheims *Holy Bible*, translated from the Latin Vulgate (The Old Testament first published by the English College at Douay, A.D. 1609, and the New Testament first published by the English College at Rheims, A.D. 1582) (Baltimore: John Murphy Company, 1914). Dante's focus on interpretive difficulties and on mistaken interpretations, such as the public perception of the object of Dante's love in the screen ladies, might be manifestations of the 'strategic use of misunderstandings' that is seen as a key device of Johannine rhetoric. 'The misunderstandings of characters (e.g., 2:20; 3:4) enforce a sharp distinction between insiders and outsiders, those who understand Jesus and those who do not' (Stephen D. Moore, *Literary Criticism and the Gospels: The Theoretical Challenge* [New Haven and London: Yale University Press, 1989], 49).
17 See also Matthew 25:29, Mark 4:11 and 4:24, and Luke 8:9 and 8:18.
18 Thomas C. Stillinger, *The Song of Troilus: Lyric Authority in the Medieval Book* (Philadelphia: University of Pennsylvania Press, 1992), calls to mind an important way of understanding the procedure of *divisio textus*, one of which Dante must certainly have been aware: '*divisio* is *in malo*, the condition that separates humanity from God; *in bono*, one process by which humanity reaches toward God' (78). For the insiders of Christ's disciples who understand, division is superfluous. It cannot help them to attain God. For those outside, however, division is precisely the means of approaching the essence of the word through language itself.
19 See, for instance, the entry for 'divisioni' in the *Enciclopedia dantesca*. Harrison also elaborates on the concept in *The Body of Beatrice*, 56.
20 In addition to Robert Harrison's viewpoint, *The Body of Beatrice*, 62, one could call to mind the objections voiced by María Rosa Menocal in *Writing in Dante's Cult of Truth*, to which I have already alluded: 'There are three formally distinct presentations of what might be crudely described as the

"same material": a prose narration of "what happened"; the poem(s) that formed the lyrical reaction to the event(s); and finally, and most mysteriously for almost all critics, a pseudoscientific and remarkably banal explication of the poem's structure and "divisions"' (30). Not only are the divisions accused of not denuding the poetry, but they have also been accused of 'reading into' the poetry 'something that they could not possibly mean' (Musa, 178).

21 Cf. also Matthew 18:1, Mark 9:36, Luke 9:46, 10:21, and 12:1.
22 Stillinger treats this aspect at length in *The Song of Troilus*.
23 Dante will continue to elaborate these concerns with writing as 'that which is outside' as late as the *Comedy*, as Giuseppe Mazzotta points out in 'Theology and Exile' in *Dante's Vision*: 'Dante evokes a view of writing, not as a self-enclosed and definite entity, but as an experience that exceeds the boundaries of "home." More textually, he responds by a reference to the activity of writing and glossing, as if the words he writes down transcend the perimeter of the literal and need a commentary: writing is an allegory, as it were, the sense of which will be disclosed by future glosses' (176). In other words: 'There is a sense in which all commentary is itself an act of exile. All exegesis and gloss transports the text into some measure of distance and banishment. Veiled in analysis and metamorphic exposition, the *Ur*-text is no longer immediate to its native ground. On the other hand, the commentary underwrites – a key idiom – the continued authority and survival of the primary discourse. It liberates the life of meaning from that of historical-geographical contingency. In dispersion, the text is homeland' (George Steiner, *Real Presences: Is there Anything in What We Say?* [London and Boston: Faber and Faber, 1989], 40).
24 I have relied heavily for my English renderings of the *Convivio* on the published translations by Christopher Ryan and by Richard H. Lansing. Citations in the original refer throughout to Franca Brambilla Ageno's critical edition of the *Convivio* (Società Dantesca Italiana, vol. 2 [Florence: Le Lettere, 1995]). I resist translating 'quasi comento' as 'almost a commentary' because Dante's prose does not fall short of being a real commentary. Rather, it is something different, a sense that I try to render more effectively as 'something of a commentary.'
25 The opinion of A.J. Minnis and A.B. Scott on this point has come to be widely accepted (*Medieval Literary Theory and Criticism c. 1100–c. 1375: The Commentary Tradition* [Oxford: Clarendon Press, 1988], 377).
26 Foundational studies in the consideration of Dante's *Convivio* in terms of the *accessus ad auctores* tradition are provided by Bruno Nardi, *Dal*

'Convivio' alla 'Commedia': Sei saggi danteschi (Rome: Istituto Storico Italiano per il Medio Evo, 1992) and Mazzeo, *Medieval Cultural Tradition in Dante's Comedy.*

27 Albert Russell Ascoli, in his study 'The Unfinished Author: Dante's Rhetoric of Authority in *Convivio* and *De vulgari eloquentia,*' in Rachel Jacoff, ed., *The Cambridge Companion to Dante* (Cambridge and New York: Cambridge University Press, 1993), suggests that Dante 'will act precisely as *compiler* of the wisdom of others, which he has previously distilled in a series of philosophical canzoni, and then as a humble prosaic *commentator* on his own poems (I, iii, 2) – both typical medieval roles which, as he makes explicit, invoke a metaphorical servitude toward the master-discourse of the (classical) *auctor*' (55).

28 I have cited the original from *Dialogus super auctores*, in the critical edition of the *Accessus ad auctores* by R.B.C. Huygens (Leiden: E.J. Brill, 1970), 75 (emphasis mine). The translation is by Minnis and Scott, *Medieval Literary Theory*, 43. St Bonaventure also paints a picture of the hypothetical commentator: 'Someone else writes the words of other men and also his own, but with those of other men comprising the principal part while his own are annexed merely to make clear the argument, and he is called the commentator, not the author. Someone else writes the words of other men and also of his own, but with his own forming the principal part and those of others being annexed merely by way of confirmation, and such a person should be called the author' (Minnis and Scott, *Medieval Literary Theory*, 229).

29 Critics, including Giovanni Busnelli and Giuseppe Vandelli and Maria Simonelli, agree that 'fortezza' means 'difficoltà,' and both Ryan and Lansing render the phrase 'the difficulty of my commentary.' While Dante is apparently trying to excuse the 'forte' quality of his commentary, it should not necessarily be taken as a negative characteristic of his prose, as I hope to show. I suggest instead the possible translation, 'gravity.'

30 Various scholars have explored the problem of authority in medieval texts. See, for instance, Judson Boyce Allen, *The Friar as Critic: Literary Attitudes in the Later Middle Ages* (Nashville: Vanderbilt University Press, 1971); Jacqueline T. Miller, *Poetic License: Authority and Authorship in Medieval and Renaissance Contexts* (New York: Oxford University Press, 1986); or A.J. Minnis, *Medieval Theory of Authorship* (Philadelphia: University of Pennsylvania Press, 1988).

31 Implicated in the status of author are etymological reverberations that tie the term to 'agere' ['to make,' referring to the one who creates the work], 'augere' ['to augment,' referring to the one who is both creator and authenticating witness of the act of creation], and the Greek 'autentim,' [one who

deserves faith or imitation]. Dante adds to these 'auieo' ['to link words together'], cf. *Convivio* 4.6 and Albert Russell Ascoli, 'The Vowels of Authority: Dante's *Convivio* IV.vi.3–4,' in Kevin Brownlee and Walter Stevens, eds., *Discourses of Authority in Medieval and Renaissance Literature* (Hanover: University Press of New England, 1989),' 23–46.

32 See Minnis, *Medieval Theory of Authorship*, in particular the chapter 'Academic Prologues to "Auctores."' Dante becomes one of the first 'moderns' to be considered an *auctor* worthy of commentary, as Boccaccio, for instance, makes a point of demonstrating with his *Commento alla 'Divina commedia'* and the *Vita di Dante*.

33 Minnis, *Medieval Theory of Authorship*, vii: 'Scholastic Scriptural exegesis was a central force in the re-shaping of literary values in the later Middle Ages. The central event, from my point of view, was the emergence (in Bible commentaries) of the view that the human author possessed a high status and respected didactic/stylistic strategies of his very own – in short, *auctoritas* moved from the divine realm to the human.'

34 Of course, the potential of self-commentary as a medium for revelation, the unveiling and 'reveiling' of truth in every sense of the term, is not an innovation for Dante in the convivial prose; it underwrites the message of his more 'fervid and passionate' *Vita Nuova* as well.

35 Furthermore, Dante continues: 'Lo dono veramente di questo comento è la sentenza delle canzoni alle quali fatto è, la qual massimamente intende inducere li uomini a scienza e a vertù, sì come si vedrà per lo pelago del loro trattato' ['the true gift of this commentary lies in the meaning of the canzoni for which it is made, meaning which is intended above all to lead men to knowledge and virtue, as will be seen in the full course of their treatment'] (1.9.7).

36 'E non è qui mestiere di procedere dividendo, e a littera esponendo; ché, volta [la] parola fittizia di quello ch'ella suona in quello ch'ella 'ntende, per la passata esposizione questa sentenza fia sufficientemente palese' ['And it is not necessary to continue dividing and giving a word-for-word commentary, since now that its fictitious word has been transformed from what it sounds like it is saying to what it actually means, the true meaning will be easy enough to grasp given the previous exposition'] (2.12.10). On this subject, see Salvatore Battaglia 'Dante tra *Vita nuova* e *Convivio*' in *Filologia e letteratura* 11(2) (1965): 113–28, especially 120. Also relevant in this regard is *Convivio* 2.1.10–12, which emphasizes first the need to understand the form, and then to move beyond it: 'Ancora: è impossibile, però che in ciascuna cosa, naturale ed artificiale, è impossibile procedere alla forma, sanza prima essere disposto lo subietto sopra che la forma dee stare; sì come impossibile la forma dell'oro è venire, se la materia, cioè lo

suo subietto, non è digesta e apparecchiata ... è impossibile procedere, se prima non è fatto lo fondamento, sì come nella casa e sì come nello studiare: onde, con ciò sia cosa che 'l dimostrare sia edificazione di scienza, e la litterale dimostrazione sia fondamento dell'altre, massimamente dell'allegorica, impossibile è [al]l'altre venire prima che a quella' ['Furthermore, this would be impossible because in anything whatever, natural or artificial, it is impossible to make progress without first laying the foundation, as, for instance, in the case of a house or of knowledge. Since, then, knowledge is built up by a series of demonstrations, and demonstrating the literal meaning is the foundation for doing the same with regard to the others, especially the allegorical, it is impossible to come to the other meanings without first coming to the literal one,' trans. Christopher Ryan].

37 'Veramente io sono stato legno sanza vela e sanza governo, portato a diversi porti e foci e liti dal vento secco che vapora la dolorosa povertade' ['I have indeed been a ship lacking sail and rudder, carried to various ports and river mouths and shores by the parching wind raised by painful poverty'] (1.3.5); then subsequently: 'lo tempo chiama e domanda la mia nave uscir di porto; per che, dirizzato l'artimone della ragione all'òra del mio desiderio, entro in pelago con isperanza di dolce cammino e di salutevole porto e laudabile nella fine della mia cena' ['Conditions bid and command my ship to leave port. So, having set the sail of reason to catch the breeze of my desire, I put out to sea with hopes of a pleasant journey and of a safe and honourable arrival at the conclusion of my supper'] (2.1.1).

38 To assert, as Richard Lansing does, that Dante 'relinquishes his role as a poet of love to recast himself as poet of moral rectitude, undertaking a high mission to achieve nothing less than to civilize the ruling classes of Italy' is to fall short of a full appraisal of the *Convivio*'s significance. I must disagree with his further assertion: 'In the last analysis, the *Convivio* is essentially a practical, not a theoretical work, one that conceives of philosophy as a means of fostering fellowship among the factious communes and municipalities and of instilling an underlying sense of civic responsibility and a shared body of knowledge in those who are best able to lead Italy out of her present chaos.' 'Dante's Intended Audience in the *Convivio*,' *Dante Studies* 110 (1992): 17–24 at 21 and 23 respectively.

39 See also the *Vita Nuova* 40.6–7 and 41.5 on the subject of the pilgrim outside the homeland.

40 Among those who stress the strangeness of the *Convivio* within the

Dantean corpus is Zygmunt G. Baranski 'Dante commentatore e commentato: Riflessioni sullo studio dell'*iter* ideologico di Dante,' *Letture classensi* 23 (1994): 135–58, 'Le cose cambiano radicalmente con il *Convivio*. La ragione e le sue strutture analitiche dominano ... Come ho già notato, ci troviamo di fronte a un atto di revisione, per non dire di propaganda, e, quindi, dobbiamo leggere il *Convivio* con avvertenza, come documento di un grande entusiasmo, una celebrazione, ed una ricerca appassionata nelle tradizioni poco pacifiche dell'aristotelismo ... L' 'alto sale' (*Par.* II, 13) del Paradiso separa il "sacrato poema" (*Par.* XXXIII, 62) dal "quasi comento" (*Conv.* I, iii, 2).'

41 See, for instance, Charles S. Singleton, *Essay on the 'Vita Nuova' and Journey to Beatrice* (Cambridge: Harvard University Press, 1958; Baltimore: Johns Hopkins University Press, 1977); Giuseppe Mazzotta, *Dante, Poet of the Desert: History and Allegory in the 'Divine Comedy'* (Princeton: Princeton University Press, 1993); John Freccero, *Poetics of Conversion*, ed. Rachel Jacoff (Cambridge: Harvard University Press, 1986), and Guy P. Raffa, *Divine Dialectic: Dante's Incarnational Poetry* (Toronto: Toronto University Press, 2000).

42 For an examination of this aspect, see Daniel J. Ransom, '*Panis Angelorum*: A Palinode in the *Paradiso*,' *Dante Studies* 95 (1977): 81–94. It also seems to me to suggest Martianus Capella's personification, Satura, in the first book of his *De nuptiis*, in which Satura represents, not satire, but a mixed dish of verse and prose. See Peter Dronke's discussion of Capella in *Verse with Prose from Petronius to Dante: The Art and Scope of the Mixed Form* (Cambridge and London: Harvard University Press, 1994), especially 28–9.

43 Cf. also the Old Testament reference to the banquet of Wisdom in Proverbs 9:2–6.

44 One could call to mind that, among others, Augustine associated the fish and loaves with books and commentary, the multiplication of the loaves being the exposition of the Mosaic Law in many volumes. See Frank Kermode, *The Genesis of Secrecy: On the Interpretation of Narrative* (Cambridge and London: Harvard University Press, 1979), 36–7.

45 For ease of reference, I refer in these pages to the Gospel according to John.

46 I leave aside the many metaphors of light (including those of clarification, darkness and shadow, the rising and setting sun, etc.), which could be compared against similar passages in the Bible and medieval biblical exegesis to the same ends.

47 Perhaps it is possible to see in the *Vita Nuova* an early anticipation of this divine self-testimony in the words of the God of Love (12.7).

48 Mark 4:13: 'Et ait illis: Nescitis parabolam hanc? Et quomodo omnes parabolas cognoscetis? ['And he saith to them: Are you ignorant of this parable? and how shall you know all parables?'].
49 For a more in-depth treatment of the complex issues surrounding the use of parables, see, for instance, N. Perrin, *Jesus and the Language of the Kingdom: Symbol and Metaphor in New Testament Interpretation* (Philadelphia: Fortress Press, 1976), 89–193.
50 Piero Cudini, in his introduction to the 1990 edition of the *Convivio* (Milan: Garzanti, 1990), xxvii, defines this role of receiver-dispensator in terms of Dante's philosophical program. Cambon suggests something of the kind in his discussion of Dante's view of the vernacular: 'In Catholic terms, we could say that this beloved medium is in fact, to Dante, the element of a sacrament, and even, to some extent, the divine presence inherent therein. The living language, as contrasted to the fixed dead one, is the aptest medium for a communion that is both ritual and everyday intercourse' (26). After quoting *Convivio* 1.13.11–12, he says: '[Dante] is the son of language, language being identified with his parents. Then he identifies with it to the point where he is almost a sacrificial victim, and finally becomes its priestly keeper, with fatherly connotations vis-à-vis the future communicants. From sonhood to fatherhood is a normal reversal of role in the course of a life, but it is exceptional where a whole culture is concerned. Only people like Dante become the fathers of their own language after having been its offspring' (26–7).
51 The allusion is to Romans 11:33.
52 This is another way of saying, and self-consciously so, what Kermode has suggested: outsiders read, but do not perceive; insiders read and come to an understanding, but theirs is only one of many possible modes of understanding. 'No one, however special his point of vantage, can get ... into the shrine of the single sense' (*The Genesis of Secrecy*, 123). In this way even the insiders, Kermode finds, remain outside.
53 Cf. also Proverbs 13:14, 'Lex sapientis fons vitae' ['The law of the wise is a fountain of life'].
54 In *Paradise* 26.53, Dante refers to John the Evangelist as the 'eagle of Christ' in the context of his examination of the role of love (including philosophical love, l. 25) in directing man to God: 'Non fu latente la santa intenzione/ de l'aguglia di Cristo, anzi m'accorsi/ dove volea menar mia professione' ['The holy intention of the Eagle of Christ was not hidden, indeed it was plain to me whither he would direct my profession.'] The translation is by Singleton.
55 There is some *quid* of Christ-like emulation in Dante's presentation of the

vernacular commentary (1.9.10): 'Ancora, darà lo volgare dono non dimandato, che non l'averebbe dato lo latino: però che darà se medesimo per comento, che mai non fu domandato da persona' ['Again, the vernacular will give its gift without being asked, which Latin would not have done, since it will spontaneously offer itself as a commentary, which is something never asked of it by anyone'].

56 Given that Dante does not complete the *Convivio*, we should not place any special significance on the final words of the work (*Convivio* 4.30.6): 'Oh quanto e come bello adornamento è questo che nell'ultimo di questa canzone si dà ad essa, chiamandola amica di quella la cui propria ragione è nel secretissimo della divina mente!' ['What a wonderful and beautiful adornment is given to nobility in the final words of this canzone: to be called the friend of her who in her pristine form exists in the innermost depths of the divine mind']. However, it is interesting to consider on the basis of one of the etymologies of 'comento' – 'con-mente' – that Dante's own 'quasi comento' would culminate in this 'most secret recess of the divine mind,' consonant with it and pointing to that word beyond. See Dante's long commentary on the word 'mente' of v. 1 of the second canzone: 'quella fine e preziosissima parte de l'anima che è deitade' ['(From all this it will be clear what is meant by the word mind): that subtle and most precious part of the soul which is divinity,' trans. Ryan].

Chapter Two

1 Among the Boccaccio critics who have examined this emphasis are Judson Boyce Allen, Robert Hollander, Victoria Kirkham, Alberto Limentani, A.J. Minnis, Jeffrey T. Schnapp, Janet Levarie Smarr, and Giuseppe Vandelli.
2 It is interesting to note that while allusions to Dante are frequent and central to the *Teseida*'s understanding, Boccaccio never acknowledges Dante in the glosses, as he does Virgil (6.53n) and Guido Cavalcanti and Dino del Garbo (7.50n), for instance.
3 For this reason the focus of this examination rests on the *Teseida*'s self-glosses rather than Boccaccio's prosimetrical approach to self-commentary in, for example, the *Comedia delle ninfe fiorentine* (1341–1342).
4 All references to the *Teseida* are from the 1992 Mondadori edition edited by Alberto Limentani. Except where noted, the English translation is from *The Book of Theseus*, trans. Bernadette Marie McCoy (New York: Medieval Text Association, 1974).
5 Winthrop Wetherbee, 'History and Romance in Boccaccio's *Teseida*,' *Studi sul Boccaccio* 20 (1991–2): 173–84 at 174.

6 '... quei toni e a quei modi latamente lirici ed autobiografici, a quelle prolungate note elegiache ed amorose che avevano caratterizzato fino allora il cammino dello scrittore e dovevano ancora segnare cospicuamente di sé la sua avventurosa esperienza letteraria' (524).
7 'Un autografo della *Teseida*,' *Studi di filologia italiana* 2 (1929).
8 A.J. Minnis, *Medieval Theory of Authorship* (Philadelphia: University of Pennsylvania Press, 1988), xiii. See also the contributions by Limentani and Hollander in this regard. Because the form itself and not just the content of the glosses carries significance, it is not necessary to limit discussion of Boccaccian models to whether or not he would have known Lactantius's glosses of Statius's *Thebeid*.
9 Other works by Boccaccio, most notably the *Decameron*, also begin by evoking memory.
10 *Purgatorio* 30.33 and 30.48 respectively. A detailed study remains to be written on the different understanding of the consumption of the 'flames of love' in Dante and Boccaccio. See also the *Teseida* proemial writer's remark that he prays that 'colui che me vi diede' ['he who gave you to me'] can rekindle 'in voi la *spenta fiamma*' ['in you the *extinguished flame*,' my italics].
11 Dante likewise explicitly terms his *Vita Nuova* a 'little book,' or *libello*.
12 Boccaccio writes the *Filocolo*, for instance, as a labour of love at the request of the lover's lady, Maria. Dedications to or invocations of Maria, Fiammetta, or a sort of Maria-Fiammetta who represent various levels of the narrative are also present in the *Comedia delle Ninfe Fiorentine* and the *Amorosa Visione*, as Smarr indicates in her book *Boccaccio and Fiammetta: The Narrator as Lover* (Chicago: University of Illinois Press, 1986). The historical-philological debate concerning the identification of an actual Maria or Fiammetta and her role in Boccaccio's biography, however, is only one aspect of the literary interpretation of his *figure*. What interests me here is Boccaccio's call for interpretations of the works, interpretations that must go beyond the strictly literal or historical.
13 Incidentally, this is one of the few notes that moves from the third person, 'the author says' ['[L'autore] dice ...'] to the first person 'I know that' ['so che ...']. Other glosses that insert a singular, first-person perspective include 1.6, 2.10, 3.27, 3.35, 5.31, 7.50, and 12.86.
14 This famous 'indovinello veronese' is found in Codex 89, l'*Orazionale Mozarabico*, of the Biblioteca Capitolare di Verona, which dates from the eighth or ninth century.
15 Migliorini provides a lucid overview of the phrase's origin, context, and influence in his *Storia della lingua italiana* (Florence: Sansoni, 1983 [1960]),

61–4. The metaphor is common in the Middle Ages, however, as explicated by Isidore of Seville, among others.

16 An example from the gloss that compares the pagan goddess Minerva to St John the Baptist (1.60n) contains the greatest shock value: 'Minerva tenevano gli antichi che fosse dea della sapienzia, e questa oltre a ogni altro iddio era onorato in Attene, sì come i Fiorentini più che alcuno altro santo onorato San Giovanni Batista' ['The ancients believed that Minerva was goddess of wisdom and in Athens she was honoured more than any other god, just as the Florentines honour St John the Baptist more than any other saint'].

17 (Chicago: University of Illinois Press, 1986), 81.

18 Ibid., 79.

19 Boccaccio's own gloss on the fifth canto of Dante's *Inferno* makes explicit that a Gallehault is the mediator between two lovers, a function that Boccaccio will later explicitly assign to the *Decameron*.

20 'Grazie al carattere funzionale e pragmatico, l'autocommento fornisce delucidazioni sulla natura ideologica ed artistica del testo e, pertanto, ricopre un ruolo d'inquadramento e controllo; addirittura esercita un'influenza che può coincidere con una manipolazione' (Roberta Ricci, 'Il Commento d'autore: Boccaccio, Tasso, Foscolo, Saba [PhD dissertation, Johns Hopkins University, 1999], 259). I was able to read Ricci's dissertation, written in the same year as my own, only at the stage of revising my manuscript for book publication and was struck by the fact that she came to diametrically opposing conclusions about the nature of self-commentary, which, however, she vaguely defines in much broader terms.

21 I refer to Schnapp's article 'A Commentary on Commentary,' *South Atlantic Quarterly* 91(4) (Fall 1992): 813–34 at 814: '[Self-commentary] packages, frames, and embalms the poem; it attempts to fix and stabilize it forever; to shield it against misreading, criticism, and continuation; to forestall the effects of scribal corruption, emendation, and expansion. Insistently crafting the work into a discreet and singular object, a kind of self-enacting automaton, a Book almost in the metaphysical sense, it at-tempts to shut down the relatively free play that once characterized the medieval chain of textual transmission and production. And in its place it inserts an infinitely mobile, ubiquitous author able to sign and control his creations: a poet and *vate* – as the valediction proclaims him – capable of occupying every position along the chain, capable of donning every mask, female and male, ancient and modern ... However understood, commentary always seems embedded within a web of temporal issues.'

22 *Trattatello in laude di Dante*, 521, my emphasis.

23 In fact, the *Vaticano latino* 3196 is commonly referred to as the 'codice degli abbozzi.' The bound manuscript also includes drafts of letters and poems eventually excluded from the *Canzoniere*. See Manfredi Porena's introductory remarks to the *riproduzione fototipica* of Petrarca's *Il Codice Vaticano Lat. 3196*, published by the Vatican library (1941). Marco Santagata also mentions the fact that Petrarca's notes were little more than self-reminders in his introduction to the *Canzoniere*: 'In latino scrive anche le postille private e ad uso strettamente personale apposte sui libri, persino quelle relative alle rime in volgare e ai *Trionfi*' (xli). It is interesting to note the similarity with which Petrarca treats his own poetry and the books by published *auctoritates* Horace, Virgil, and others in his personal library: he habitually writes Latin comments in the margins of these books. Sometimes, as in the case of a marginal comment in the Horace manuscript, 'quod scribemus in libello,' he speaks of his own book, precisely the *Canzoniere*. See also Giuseppe Billanovich, 'L'Orazio Morgan e gli studi del giovane Petrarca.' *Tradizione classica e letteratura umanistica. Per Alessandro Perosa*. A cura di Roberto Cardini et al. (Rome: Bulzoni, 1985), 1:121–38.

24 As Ernest Hatch Wilkins documents in *The Making of the 'Canzoniere' and Other Petrarchan Studies* (Rome: Edizioni di Storia e Letteratura, 1951), 293: 'The foregoing pages have shown that Italian lyrics by Petrarch entered into circulation, during his lifetime, in many different ways: as poems addressed to friends without specific expectation of poetic answer; as *risposte* and perhaps, in a few cases, as *proposte*; as obituary tributes; as gifts; as releases to importunate *giullari*; in personal collections formed by friends or admirers (such collections consisting either exclusively of poems by Petrarch or of miscellanies in which poems by Petrarch were included); in four forms of the *Canzoniere*; presumably in personal collections (new or expanded, exclusive or inclusive) based on forms of the *Canzoniere*; in late supplements released by Petrarch; and (in two cases) in Latin versions by Coluccio Salutati.' This list does not include Petrarca's self-glosses, or the partially autograph copy of some lyrics, *Vat. Lat.* 3195, furnished with a self-commentary. The crowded marginal notes that Petrarca pens alongside the *Africa* should be considered in much the same way, as self-reminders of the development of the laborious reworking of the unfinished epic.

25 More of the passage from his introduction to the translation *Petrarch's Lyric Poems: The Rime Sparse and Other Lyrics* (Cambridge and London: Harvard University Press, 1976), 33, is certainly relevant: 'If on the one hand Petrarch subscribes to ... the humanistic cult of literary immortality and glory, on the other hand he has an acute awareness that writing poetry

involves a kind of death. This recognition has something very modern about it; it gives a measure of the distance that separates Petrarch from Dante, who gambled recklessly on the authority his poem would have as a total integration. Petrarch is always calling attention to the psychologically relative, even suspect, origin of individual poems and thus of writing itself.'

26 As Claudio Ciociola has had occasion to observe, defining Cecco d'Ascoli's work depends largely on the texts consulted, and given the sheer quantity of early editions, manuscripts, and late Quattrocento and Cinquecento incunables, the task may not be as straightforward as it might first appear. There seems to have been a Latin source, which Ciociola argues convincingly must be the product of the same author as the Latin commentaries on the Alcabizzo and Sacrobosco's *De sphera*, that is to say, Francesco Stabili, called Cecco d'Ascoli. See 'L'autoesegesi di Cecco d'Ascoli,' in *L'Autocommento: Atti del XVII Convegno interuniversitario (Bressanone, 1990)*. Quaderni del Circolo Filologico-linguistico Padovano 17. (Padua: Esedra, 1988): 31–42. Translations into the vernacular of this Latin source, which falls short of self-commenting on the whole of the *Acerba*, are abundant, but critics have yet to put together a critical edition of the *Acerba* with the self-commentary. In fact, only the first chapter of the self-commentary is accessible to scholars in any modern publication, in the studies by Hans Pflaum, and there, however, it appears divorced of the poem on which it comments. See Pflaum, 'L'*Acerba* di Cecco d'Ascoli. Saggio d'interpretazione,' *Archivum romanicum* 23 (1939): 178–241.

27 The convicted heretic from Ascoli became famous at least in part because of his scathing remarks directed at his Florentine rival, Dante. Achille Crespi, in the introduction to his edition of *L'Acerba* (Ascoli Piceno: G. Cesare, 1927), outlines the main points of contention between the two, or rather, of the almost exclusively one-sided attacks on Dante made by Cecco d'Ascoli. There is a pointed difference in the way of viewing poetry and commentary: 'Il poema di Cecco è stato definito più volte un'enciclopedia in versi; ma non bisogna cercare la scienza nella *Divina Commedia* e l'arte nell'*Acerba*. Dante si permette di scegliere e modificare le verità della storia e della filosofia naturale per ornamento; Cecco presume che un trattato di astrologia applicata a virtù e vizi, all'anatomia, alla meteorologia divenga leggiadro con le rime' (23).

28 The recurring theme of degrees of understanding appears in, among other passages, the explication of the second canzone and sonnets 16 and 18 of part one.

29 Felice Bariola, *Cecco d'Ascoli e L'Acerba* (Florence: Tipografia della Gazzetta d'Italia, 1879): 48.

30 See, for example, Campanella's glosses on poems 37 and 59.
31 On the complex development of the various versions of the *Documenti d'amore*, see D. Goldin, 'Autotraduzione latina nei *Documenti d'amore* di Francesco da Barberino,' Atti dell'Istituto Veneto di Scienze, Lettere ed Arti. Classi di scienze morali, lettere ed arti 133 (1974–5): 371–92.
32 Of particular interest is the way in which Francesco da Barberino reverses the glossing procedure. In the *Regole d'Amore*, the poems occasionally point to the gloss. See, for example, '[le regole] son vere ognora,/ come le chiose ti diran ben quello' ['[the rules] are still true, as the glosses will surely tell you'] (2.5.17–18) and 'come diranno qui le chiose tutto' ['as the glosses here will tell all'] (9.2.14).
33 I pass over a number of other versified treatises in the vernacular with Latin self-glosses, including the *Trattato delle volgari sentenze sopra le virtù morali* (Modena: Per gli eredi Soliani, 1821) by Graziolo Bambaglioli who, like Francesco da Barberino, worked as a notary in Bologna. Not a few points of interest could be gleaned from studies of Bambaglioli's self-glosses in relation to his Latin exposition of Dante's *Inferno*. For a more detailed discussion of the Latin prosimetrical tradition, see Dronke's *Verse with Prose from Petronius to Dante: The Art and Scope of the Mixed Form* (Cambridge and London: Harvard University Press, 1994).

Chapter Three

1 Unless otherwise indicated, this and subsequent translations of the *Metamorphosis* are by Allen Mandelbaum (New York: Harcourt and Brace Co., 1993).
2 There is little reason to doubt that Lorenzo is, if not the sole editor, the guiding hand behind the anthology presented to Federigo d'Aragona probably sometime in 1476. See B.M. Scanferla, 'Per la data della Raccolta Aragonese,' *Rassegna bibliografica della letteratura italiana* 21 (1913): 244–50. Domenico De Robertis postulates two different versions of the *Raccolta*, the first composed around 1470 for Alfonso d'Aragona, containing both of the prosimetra by Dante (the *Vita Nuova* and the *Convivio*) in addition to poems by various other writers, and a second version with somewhat different contents, dedicated to Federigo d'Aragona about six years later. See 'La Raccolta aragonese primogenita,' in *Editi e rari* (Milan: Feltrinelli, 1978).
3 While some critics, such as Emilio Bigi and André Rochon, assert a brief composition time, it now seems clear, especially given Mario Martelli's convincing arguments, that Lorenzo returned to the *Comento* repeatedly in the course of his life. See Martelli's *Studi laurenziani*, Biblioteca di 'Lettere italiane' 2 (Florence, Olschki, 1965).

4 *The Dolce Stil Novo According to Lorenzo de' Medici: A Study of His Poetic Principio as an Interpretation of the Italian Literature of the Pre-Renaissance Period based on his* Commento (New Haven: Yale University Press, 1936), 89.
5 *The Autobiography of Lorenzo de' Medici The Magnificent: A Commentary on My Sonnets*. With the Italian text from the critical edition by Tiziano Zanato. Trans. James Wyatt Cook. Medieval & Renaissance Texts & Studies, vol. 129 (Binghamton, N.Y.: Center for Medieval and Early Renaissance Studies, 1995), 40–1. Unless otherwise specified, citations of the work in Italian and English are taken from this edition.
6 These issues sustain many valuable studies, including those by Martelli, Mario Fubini, Giancarlo Mazzacurati, and Zanato, for instance. Martelli, citing his friend Roberto Ridolfi, summarizes the scholarly position this way: 'Lo so. Per certi critici queste sono quisquilie: l'opera sola importa, avulsa dalla vita, dalle vicissitudini, dall'anima dello scrittore, il frutto staccato dalla sua pianta; alcuni di quei critici magari, se non fossero "laici," citerebbero il biblico *ex fructibus eorum cognoscetis eos*. Io ho sempre ritenuto, invece, che sul frutto influiscano fortemente le condizioni della pianta, la qualità del terriccio dove essa affonda le sue radici, il caldo ed il freddo, il sole e la pioggia. Per uscire di metafora, la conoscenza di tutte le circostanze nelle quali un'opera d'inchiostro è venuta a maturazione mi sembra necessaria ad intenderla; e pensi chi vuole il contrario. Io tengo per fermo, insomma, che la vita di uno scrittore sia il più valido commento all'opera sua, che un'opera possa essere intesa e valutata diversamente in un periodo piuttosto che in un altro della vita di lui' (*Studi laurenziani*, 179).
7 'More than anything else that Lorenzo wrote, *il Comento* approaches autobiography – indeed, I suggest, it *is* an autobiography, if not of the man Lorenzo was, then certainly of the man he wished others to see, and perhaps of the man he sought to become' (2–3, Cook's italics). It should be noted that given the lack of autograph evidence, the exact title of Lorenzo's work is the subject of conjecture. Zanato argues convincingly for *Comento de' miei sonetti* in 'Sul testo del *Comento* laurenziano,' *Studi di filologia italiana* 38 (1980): 71–152.
8 Much the same objection might be raised in response to those primarily concerned with unmasking the political undercurrents in the Florentine ruler's writings. William J. Kennedy's article forwards, nevertheless, a provocative hypothesis. The Petrarchan mode, Kennedy says, 'symbolically enacts a dialectic between Lorenzo's submission to the state and his domination of it. Like a Petrarchan lover Lorenzo defers to a self-proclaimed ideal that he yet tries to bend to his will ... It allows him to proclaim his personal misfortunes both as a public figure and as a private

individual. It invites the audience's sympathy with his plight, and it gives him powerful rhetorical tools to attract that sympathy. Finally it encourages a prose commentary that expands his possibilities for self-representation. The commentary permits him to fashion an *apologia pro vita sua*, an unabashed autobiographical platform upon which to shape and reshape the events of his life as he wants his Florentine audience to perceive them' ('Petrarchan Figurations of Death in Lorenzo de' Medici's Sonnets and *Comento*,' in Marcel Tetel, Ronald G. Witt, and Rona Goffen, eds., *Life and Death in Fifteenth-Century Florence* (Durham and London: Duke University Press, 1989), 47).

9 Lorenzo and his correspondents occasionally call the self-commentative prose of the *Comento* a paraphrase. See especially the 1484 letters between Lorenzo and Pico della Mirandola, some of which Eugenio Garin includes in his edited anthology, *Prosatori latini del Quattrocento* (Milan and Naples: Riccardo Ricciardi, 1952).

10 'Pensavo, oltre a questo, potere essere da qualcuno facilmente ripreso di poco iudicio, avendo consumato il tempo e nel comporre e nel comentare versi, la materia e subietto de' quali in gran parte fussi una amorosa passione' ['I thought someone could easily reprove me for poor judgment in having wasted my time composing and commenting on verses whose material and subject had for the most part been an amorous passion'] (30–1).

11 It might be possible to understand the *Comento* as a parody, along the lines that Paolo Orvieto traces in his introduction to *Tutte le opere di Lorenzo de' Medici*, I, Testi e documenti di letteratura e di lingua 14 (Rome: Salerno, 1992), xii: 'Perciò è solo ricostruendo le coordinate contenutistico-formali del genere (quindi anche i referenti culturali, perché ogni genere connota inesorabilmente una precisa atmosfera culturale) che possiamo valutare la particolare *variatio* laurenziana, spesso anche *sub specie* di contraffazione parodica: perciò caratteristiche decisamente innovative, quando non rivoluzionarie (per cui si può davvero parlare di incunaboli d'un nuovo genere), hanno opere come le *Selve* (*variatio* del genere rispetti o strambotti), il *Simposio* (versione parodica del *De amore* di Ficino), la *Nencia da Barberino* (in cui si coagula la tradizione della bucolica volgare per poi biforcarsi in filone pastorale e filone rusticale), le *Canzoni a ballo* (con ripresa e rilancio del genere a *aequivocatio* oscena) le *Canzoni carnascialesche* (che innescano il processo di trasformazione delle canzoni a ballo nei canti carnascialeschi cinquecenteschi), il *Corinto* (o [...] prototipo dell'egloga volgare), l'*Ambra* (anch'essa cultissima versione dei rispetti continuati e dei poemetti eziologici), i *Capitoli* (esaltati *revivals* degli esoterici inni alle divinità dei sommi poeti-teologi del passato: di Ermete Trismegisto, di Proclo, dei ritmi

di Boezio), ecc.' In this case, the parody would be precisely of the Dantean model of self-commentary.
12 'Parendomi, massimamente publicando questa interpetrazione, sottomettermi più tosto al giudicio degli altri, conciosiacosa che se da me medesimo avessi giudicato questi miei versi indegni d'essere letti, arei fuggito il giudicio degli altri, ma commentandogli e publicandogli fuggo, al mio parere, molto meglio la presunzione del giudicarmi da me medesimo' ['Indeed, it especially seems to me that in publishing this interpretation I submit myself rather more to the judgment of others. Because if I had myself judged these verses of mine unworthy of being read, I should have fled the judgment of others, but by commenting on them and publishing them, it seems to me, I flee far better the presumption of making my own judgment of myself'] (34–5).
13 Translated in Peter Dronke, *Fabula: Explorations into the Uses of Myth in Medieval Platonism* (Leiden and Köln: E.J. Brill, 1974), 64.
14 Ernst H. Kantorowicz explores in depth the religious, political, legal, and figurative aspects of corporate theory in his important book, *The King's Two Bodies: A Study of Mediaeval Political Theology* (Princeton: Princeton University Press, 1957).
15 Cf. *Convivio* 1.1.8–9.
16 See *Autobiography*, 38, but Lorenzo repeats the citation on page 42. The allusion is to the first poem of the *Rerum vulgarium fragmenta*. Giuseppe Mazzotta emphasizes the irony with which this sonnet is charged, within the context of Petrarca's *canzoniere*, stating that it 'comes forth as a palinode, a deliberate self-staging in which the poet, on the face of it, speaks with a voice of moral authority, the voice of a public self who finally confesses his past errors and disavows them' (*The Worlds of Petrarch* [Durham and London: Duke University Press, 1993], 58). Lorenzo's reading of Petrarca may have been influenced by the perspective Cristoforo Landino's Latin translation in his *Xandra* brings to the Petrarchan *Canzoniere*: 'Si quis at hamatis transfixus corda sagittis/ pertulerit nostri vulnera cruda dei,/ hic veniamque dabit simul et miserebitur ultro/... / Praesertim ignoscet nimium iuvenilibus annis' ['Any person who has had his heart pierced by the pointed arrows of our god of love and suffered his cruel wounds, will both grant me pardon and even pity me ... In particular he will pardon my youthful years'] (1.2.7–13). See also Martin L. McLaughlin's discussion of this issue in *Literary Imitation in the Italian Renaissance* (Oxford: Clarendon Press, 1995), 169ff.
17 Literally, 'common' ['comune'] means 'within the walls'; here the sense of being shared by the entire community is also understood.

18 For Lorenzo, Dante masterfully expresses 'molte cose teologiche e naturali' ['many theological and natural matters']; 'ha assai perfettamente absoluto quello che in diversi auttori, così greci come latini, si truova' [he 'has very perfectly performed in only one [work] that which one finds in several authors, both Greek and Roman'], and his canzoni and sonnets 'sono di tanta gravità, subtilità e ornato, che quasi non hanno comparazione' ['are of such seriousness, refinement, and adornment that they have almost no equal'] (46–9). Petrarca's style is 'grave, lepido e dolce' ['serious, sprightly, and sweet'] and treats 'cose amorose con tanta gravità e venustà ... quanta sanza dubio non si truova in Ovidio, Tibullo, Catullo, Properzio o alcuno altro latino' ['amorous matters ... with gravity and stylistic grace – more than indubitably, one finds in Ovid, Tibullus, Catullus, and Propertius or any other Latin author'] (46–9). The third crown goes to Boccaccio for his 'singulare e sola al mondo non solamente la invenzione, ma la copia et eloquenzia sua; e considerando l'opera sua del *Decamerone*, per la diversità della materia, ora grave, ora mediocre e ora bassa, e contenente tutte le perturbazioni che agli uomini possono accadere, d'amore e odio, timore e speranza, tante nuove astuzie e ingegni, e avendo a exprimere tutte le nature e passioni degli uomini che si trovano al mondo, sanza controversia giudicherà nessuna lingua meglio che la nostra essere atta a exprimere' ['unique and remarkable [invention], but also ... his fluency and eloquence ... as well. And, if one considers his work in the *Decameron*, for the diversity of the material, now profound, now ordinary, and now low, considers the way it contains all the difficulties of love and hate, fear and hope, so many new artful dodges and contrivances, and its having to express all the personalities and passions of the people that one finds in the world, without controversy one will judge no language better suited than our own for expressing them'] (48–9).

19 Pico della Mirandola was among contemporaries of Lorenzo who saw in the Magnificent's poetry the remedy for Petrarca's deficiency of content and Dante's deficiency of form. He writes in a letter dated 'Florentiae, Idibus Iuliis, 1484': 'Sunt apud vos duo praecipue celebrati poetae florentinae linguae, Franciscus Petrarcha et Dantes Aligerius, de quibus illud in universum sim praefatus, esse ex eruditis qui res in Francisco, verba in Dante desiderent. In te qui mentem habeat et aures neutrum desideraturum, in quo non sit videre an res oratione, an verba sententiis magis illustrentur ...' ['You have two celebrated poets of the Florentine vernacular: Francesco Petrarca and Dante Alighieri, concerning whom in general one should preface that among the erudite is observed a certain defect of content in Petrarch and of form in Dante. He who has mind and

ears can find nothing to be desired in you, in whose verse it is difficult to say if the style of speech or the meaning of the words shines forth more brilliantly ...'] (*Prosatori latini del Quattrocento*, a cura di Eugenio Garin. La Letteratura Italiana: Storia e testi 13. (Milan and Naples: Riccardo Ricciardi, 1952), 797).

20 Cited from the *Prosatori latini del Quattrocento*, 802.

21 It is also interesting to keep in mind that while Lorenzo must have had a copy of the *Vita Nuova* containing both the poetry and the prose, the work was not always copied or published in its entirety. In numerous early editions part or all of Dante's prose is missing. In fact, the lyrics of the 'libello' were first printed in 1527, after Lorenzo's death, in *Sonetti e canzoni di diuersi antichi autori toscani* ['Sonnets and Canzoni by Various Ancient Tuscan Authors'], but an integral edition containing the prose as well did not appear until 1576. See Michele Barbi's critical edition of the *Vita Nuova* (Florence: 1907).

22 See, for example, Orvieto's introduction to the *Comento* in *Tutte le opere di Lorenzo de' Medici*, 1: 334–5, where he links Simonetta-Giovanna to the Lucifer star that comes first in order to announce the 'luce vera' ['true light']. Lorenzo's first lady might even be seen as a conflation of the *Vita Nuova*'s Giovanna and the friend of Beatrice whose death inspires 'Piangete, amanti, poi che piange Amore' ['Weep, lovers, since love weeps']. If Lorenzo did have some such ciphered understanding of the first lady, it is primarily a literary allusion. Despite his soulful ascension by means of a death and resurrection, Lorenzo's account is largely bereft of the more Christological references which infused Dante's (and subsequently, Benivieni's) journey of the mind to God.

23 I cite the original passage from *De hominis dignitate, Heptaplus, De ente et uno, e scritti vari*, ed. Eugenio Garin (Florence: Vallecchi, 1942), 174.

24 Lorenzo will return again to the issue of the relationship between truth, appearance, rhetoric, and presumption: 'Perché nel precedente sonetto abbiamo fatto qualche menzione de' miracoli d'Amore, vorrei avere tale facultà che gli potessi fare credibili apresso di qualunque, come sono certi apresso alli gentilissimi ingegni delli inamorati. E veramente, come si può imputare a gran difetto il credere leggermente quelle cose che *prima facie* paiono impossibile, così non mi pare da aprovare la oppinione di quelli che non prestono fede ad alcuna cosa, quando exceda in qualche parte o l'uso comune o l'ordine naturale, perché spesso si è veduto nascere grandissimi inconvenienti presupponendo una cosa falsa, per parere quasi impossibile, e nondimeno pure essere vera. E, oltra questo, come el credere presto pare officio di uomo leggiere, così absolutamente el non credere

dimostra grande presunzione; perché, chi dice: "Questa cosa non può essere," presumme di sapere tutte le cose che possono essere e quanto sia la potenzia della natura' ['Because in the preceding sonnet we have made some mention of the miracles of Love, I should like to have some capacity for being able to make them as credible to someone else as they are certain to the most noble understandings of the enamoured. And truly, just as one can find a great fault in lightly believing those things that seem *prima facie* impossible, so the opinion of those who will not believe in any thing that in some measure exceeds either the common usage or the order of nature does not, therefore, to me seem warranted. For often we have seen a thing occur that has most wrongly been supposed false because it seemed almost impossible, and nevertheless has been true. And, beyond this, just as quick credulity seems the office of frivolous men, so does absolute unbelief reveal great presumption. For whoever says, "This thing cannot be," presumes to know all things that can be and how great the power of nature is'] (180–1). This position leads Lorenzo to argue for faith àmong his readers, who may esteem him as not very truthful, on the same basis that they hold belief in miracles and the witness of others' experience: 'Questo miracolo e molti altri abbiamo veduti d'Amore, e crediamo appresso e gentili cuori sarà assai credibile, el testimonio de' quali ancora appresso degli altri dovrebbe avere fede' ['These miracles of love and many others we have seen, and we believe that they will be very credible among noble hearts, whose testimony must yet make the others have faith'] (184).

25 Lorenzo is best able to illustrate this progression by means of paradox, as Orvieto notes: 'Linee tuttavia forse non omogenee [nella poesia di Lorenzo], ma certo ben profilate che contrappongono la *nóesis* intuitiva e mistica al *lógos* discorsivo e, prima ancora, una teologia negativa o apofatica ad una positiva (quella di origine aritotelica) o catafatica. Il nuovo Dio che sostanzia di sé tutte le rime di Lorenzo negli anni 1477–83, è l'Innominabile, l'Abisso. Con parallela regressione della poesia di Lorenzo da una fase catafatica (la fase filosofica) ad una fase apofatica: allora al sonetto-sillogismo si sostituirà il sonetto-inno, semplice e puro canto d'amore e di ringraziamento; allora il paradosso cercherà di esprimere l'ineffabile' (*Tutte le opera*, xxi). Any study of Renaissance literary paradoxes should not ignore the considerable contribution of Rosalie L. Colie, *Paradoxia Epidemica: The Renaissance Tradition of Paradox* (Princeton: Princeton University Press, 1966).

26 This is Horace Gregory's efficacious translation.

27 *Metamorphosis* (New York: Mentor, 1960 [Viking Press, 1958]). Curiously enough, Lorenzo's 'Argumento' will end with his exposition of the etymol-

ogy of 'cura': '"cura" non vuole dire altro se non quella cosa che arde e consuma il cuore' ['"care" means nothing except "that thing that burns and consumes the heart"'] (72).

28 This argument also has a familiar ring to it, when we remember the attention Lorenzo devoted to discussions of the variety of human occupations.

29 'E però, guardando tra fiore e fiore, vidi tra gli altri quello piccolo fiore che vulgarmente chiamiamo "tornalsole" e da' Latini detto *clytia*; nel quale fiore, secondo Ovidio ...' ['And therefore, looking from flower to flower, I saw among the others that little flower that in the vernacular we call "sunflower" and by the Latins called "*clitia*." Into that flower, according to Ovid ...'] (62–3).

30 Lorenzo's eclogues would also no doubt be of interest in this regard. I am thinking of the 'Apollo e Pan' one in particular.

31 Marsilio Ficino insists on this play on Lorenzo's name in the proem of his *De triplici vita*, going so far as to draw a link between his dedicatee and the mythic god Apollo: 'His vero tu medicinae libris ignosce, precor, indulgentissime Laurenti, si dum medicus esse volo, nescio quomodo etiam nolens sum, et si non bonus saepe poeta. Nam et Phoebus idem est medicinae repertor poesisque magister, vitamque ille suam nobis non tam per herbas quam per citharam cantumque largitur. Ipsa quinetiam Venus apud astrologs musicum aeque parit et medicum' ['But I beg you, good-natured Lorenzo, to pardon these books of medicine, if while trying to be a doctor, I am, somehow or other, willy-nilly a poet, and often not a good one. For one and the same Phoebus is the discoverer of medicine and the master of poesy, and he gives us of his life not only by herbs but gives birth equally to the musician and the doctor'] *Three Books on Life*. Critical Edition and Trans. Carol V. Kaske and John R. Clark. Medieval & Renaissance Texts & Studies vol. 57. (Binghamton: Renaissance Society of America, 1989), 104–5.

32 The translation is by Mark Musa, *Dante's* Vita Nuova (Bloomington and London: Indiana University Press, 1973).

33 Lorenzo, in speaking to his friend about the nature of the departed lady, confirms this association: 'l'anima di quella gentilissima o è transformata in questa nuova stella o si è coniunta con essa; e, se questo è, non pare mirabile questo splendore' ['the soul of that most noble lady either has been transformed into this new star or has been joined with it. And, if this is the case, this splendour does not seem marvelous'] (60–1).

34 Orvieto, *Tutte le opere di Lorenzo de' Medici*, 1:353: *Silv*. I, Proem. 1–2, 'Diu multumque dubitavi an hos libellos ... congregatos ipse dimitterem.'

35 In point of fact, doubt is a primary motivation for any commentary: glosses of poems can serve to clarify meanings perceived as open to conflicting interpretations. It is also possible to see in Lorenzo's words of doubt an oblique reference to Dante's discussion of the 'doubtful words' in the *Vita Nuova* (7.14), as discussed in the chapter on Dante.

36 Lorenzo's assertion refers back to Dante's discussions of language, particularly in the *De vulgari eloquentia* and the *Convivio*. For treatment of the language question, especially as it relates to issues of politics and power, see Marianne Shapiro, 'Poetry and Politics in the *Comento* of Lorenzo de' Medici,' *Renaissance Quarterly* 26(4) (1973): 444–53.

37 *Inf.* 17.100–14: 'Come la navicella esce di loco / in dietro in dietro, sì quindi si tolse; / e poi ch'al tutto si sentì a gioco, là 'v' era 'l petto, la coda rivolse, / e quella tesa, come anguilla, mosse, / e con le branche l'aere a sé raccolse. / Maggior paura non credo che fosse / quando Fetonte abbandonò li freni, / per che 'l ciel, come pare ancor, si cosse; / né quando Icaro misero le reni / sentì spennar per la scaldata cera, / gridando il padre a lui "Mala via tieni!" / che fu la mia, quando vidi ch' i' era / ne l'aere d'ogne parte, e vidi spenta / ogne veduta fuor che de la fera' ['As the bark backs out little by little from its place, so Geryon withdrew thence; and when he felt himself quite free, he turned his tail to where his breast had been, and, stretching it out, moved it like an eel, and with his paws gathered the air to himself. I do not think that there was greater fear when Phaeton let loose the reins, whereby the sky, as yet appears, was scorched, nor when the wretched Icarus felt his loins unfeathering by the melting wax, and his father cried to him, "You go an ill way!" than was mine when I saw that I was in the air on every side, and saw extinguished every sight, save of the beast']. English translation, here and subsequently, by Charles S. Singleton. The character of Virgil will remind Dante the protagonist of this flight in *Purgatorio* 27.22–4: 'Ricorditi, ricorditi! E se io / sovresso Gerion ti guidai salvo, / che farò ora presso piú a Dio?' ['Remember, remember ... and if on Geryon I guided you safely, what shall I do now nearer to God?'].

38 *Inf.* 26.118–26: '"Considerate la vostra semenza: / fatti non foste a viver come bruti, / ma per seguir virtute e canoscenza." / Li miei compagni fec' io sì aguti, / con questa orazion picciola, al cammino, / che a pena poscia li avrei ritenuti; / e volta nostra poppa nel mattino, / de' remi facemmo ali al folle volo, / sempre acquistando dal lato mancino' ['"Consider your origin: you were not made to live as brutes, but to pursue virtue and knowledge." With this little speech I made my companions so keen for the voyage that then I could hardly have held them back. And turning our stern to the morning, we made of our oars wings for the mad flight, always gaining on the left'].

Chapter Four

1 For biographical data I am indebted to Caterina Re's book, *Girolamo Benivieni fiorentino: Cenni sulla vita e sulle opere* (Città di Castello: Casa Tipografico-Editrice S. Lapi, 1906) and Cesare Vasoli's updated information in his entry for the *Dizionario biografico degli italiani*, from which I have condensed the following account.

2 If Benivieni was known as the *other* Orpheus, the illusion is not necessarily to the ancient figure of Orpheus. Marsilio Ficino also played an orphic role in the Medici circle. See Cosimo de' Medici's letter to Ficino, perhaps drafted by Ficino himself, in Ficino's *Opera omnia* 2 vols. (Turin: Bottega d'Erasmo, 1962–): 608: 'Vale, et veni non absque Orphica lyra.'

3 Citations of Benivieni's self-commented *canzoniere* are to the unedited incunabulum published in Florence by Antonio Tubini, Lorenzo (de Alopo) Veneziano and Andrea Ghirlandi on 7 September 1500. I am thankful to the Beinecke Rare Books and Manuscripts Library at Yale University for its generous support in the form of a 1997 summer research grant, which allowed me to transcribe the volume in its entirety. I have selectively modernized spelling (using v's where appropriate, instead of u's, as in 'vive' for 'uiue,' and inserting accent marks, but leaving unchanged Benivieni's inconsistent gender-number agreement between articles, nouns, adjectives, and participles and his spelling of recognizable words, such as 'belleza') and punctuation. The English translations of Benivieni's text are my own. In addition to the proem, the *Commento* consists of three parts. In the first part there are twenty-two sonnets and three canzoni; in the second part, twenty-three sonnets and two canzoni; and in the third part, forty-five sonnets and five canzoni. Altogether these total a hundred compositions, ten of which are canzoni. In my references to the *Commento* I use Benivieni's numbering, giving first the identification of the form of poetry (sonnet or canzone, given that they are mixed together randomly, and each form proceeds from number one, i.e. 'Canzona 2' comes after 'Sonetto 5' in the first part), followed by the book (i.e., in which of the three parts of the *Commento* the poem appears), then the poem's number, and finally, in the case of the *canzoni*, the stanza, where appropriate. This should make reference to the work considerably easier than the use of folio numbers, should the *Commento* be republished in a modern edition. For considerations of the pastoral self-commentary see Francesca Battera, 'Per l'esegesi della III egloga di Gerolamo Benivinti [sic],' *Studi e problemi di critica testuale* 38 (Aprile 1989): 45–69. On Benivieni's commentary on the penitential psalms, see Olga Zorzi Pugliese, 'Il *Commento* di Girolamo Benivieni ai *Salmi Penitenziali*,' *Vivens Homo* 5(2) (1994): 475–94.

4 Here I am speaking of degrees of emphasis, of course, not of absolute mutual exclusion of the characteristics of the two periods.

5 Benivieni states that he writes his self-commentaries because he is unable to recall and burn the earlier versions of works he deems manifestations of the immoral errors of his youth. He reforms his works by rewriting them. Benivieni's prefatory letter to Luca della Robbia in the 1519 edition of his *Opere* is not an atypical example of his explanation for the procedure: 'L'alma al suo primo ben converte e tira, senza che hora così dalle amorevoli tue persuasioni invitato e dalli errori della mia adolescentia admunito io havessi dinuovo affaticare la mente di chi legge con la explanatione delle ineptie di quella, cioè d'epsa mia adolescentia. Delle quali ineptie, ineptie veramente puerile perché poi che a Dio piacque di illustrare in qualche modo con lume della sua gratia le tenebre della mia cecità, io ho sempre reputato e reputo non piccola parte la sequente Buccolica, dovevo e non immeritamente fare quando lecito stato mi fussi, così di questa, come io già feci di quelle, cioè d'epse mie ineptie puerile, uno sacrificio a Vulcano. Ma perchè questo per l'essere stata già più volte impressa e in molte copie e varij luoghi disseminata, era et è impossibile con tanta più mia satisfactione, cedo hora a epse tue amorevoli persuasioni quanto essendomi tolta la facultà di poterla supprimere a ognihora, più mi stimola la memoria di alcuni suoi concepti.' *Opere*, f. 69r. ['My soul converts and strives towards its first Good, and if I hadn't been invited now by your loving persuasions and admonished for my youthful errors, I would not have to weary the mind of the reader with an explanation of the trifles of it, that is of my youth. Since God was pleased to illustrate in some way the shadows of my blindness with the light of His grace, I have always believed and believe that I should have made a sacrifice to Vulcan when I could have of not a small part of the following *Buccolica*, as I did already of those truly puerile trifles. But because it was already printed various times and disseminated in many copies and places, its burning was and is impossible for me to carry out to my satisfaction. So I yield now to your persuasions, and because the capacity to suppress it was denied me at every pass, the memory of some of its concepts urges me on all the more.']

6 Benivieni names some of these women in the poems' 'argumenti,' including Simonetta (identified as Giuliano de' Medici's love), 'una gentil fanciulla el cui vero nome è Stella' ['a noble maiden whose true name is Stella'] (53), 'una gentile fanciulla alhora habitante sotto l'Alpe di Mugello, el cui nome era Fiametta' ['a noble maiden now living beneath the Alpe di Mugello, whose name was Fiametta'] (56), and another referred to as Coreta in the section that follows the 'Amor fuggitivo.' It is worth noting

that along with the majority of the early lyrics of the Sessoriano text appear in the same hand some brief introductory remarks that contextualize the poems and resemble in some ways Benivieni's 'argumenti' of the *Egloghe*, hence my use of the term.

7 Precisely how Benivieni's text changes from the Sessoriano version to that of the *Commento* will form the subject of a future study. A brief glance at the 'argumenti' and their respective commentaries in the *Commento* attests to the complex nature of the transition. In some cases, Benivieni retains the original sense of the early 'argumento.' For example, sonnet 9 ('Così volge Fortuna, o cure Humane') of the Sessoriano is introduced with the statement, 'Descriptione de la medesima cosa [la conditione della humana miseria da la velocità del tempo]' ['Description of the same thing [the condition of human misery from the velocity of time]']. The sonnet of the same title appears in the *Commento* as 2.16, accompanied by the statement, 'Descrive la anima per le presente Sonetto la humana miseria dalla velocità del tempo e dalle sue qualità' ['The soul describes in the present sonnet human misery from the velocity of time and from its qualities']. In other cases, such as that of 'Venuto è el tempo hormai, hor el momento' (sonnet 12 in the Sessoriano, 2.11 in the *Commento*), Benivieni changes completely the meaning of the 'argumento.' From 'contrarij effecti di longa e vana speranza' ['the contrary effects of long and vain hope'], Benivieni's revised commentary becomes a lesson on being careful about placing one's hopes on temerarious or evil objectives. In still other cases, Benivieni combines both of these procedures, as in 'Lasso hor non veggio più in qual parte io vada' ['Alas I now do not see anymore in which way I go'] (Sessoriano canzone 2, *Commento* canzone 2.1). Here Benivieni opens his subsequent commentary by stating, 'Due sono e fini e gli obiecti della presente Canzona' ['Two are the ends and the objectives of the present canzone']. The first end proceeds from the earlier 'argumento,' the second adds a new moralizing significance. Moreover, the 'argumenti' of this edition of Benivieni's youthful love lyrics resembles the 'argumenti' of his *Egloghe* in the author's association of the works' form with their expression of the significance of love and its earthly association.

8 Like the expositor of the *Ovide moralisé*, Benivieni doubles back on the poetry, emphasizing divine love rather than explicating its original meaning tied to earthly love. For a more detailed discussion of the *moralisé* procedure, see Rita Copeland, *Rhetoric, Hermeneutics, and Translation in the Middle Ages: Academic Traditions and Vernacular Texts* (Cambridge and New York: Cambridge University Press, 1991), especially 110ff.

9 See Eugenio Garin, 'Marsilio Ficino, Girolamo Benivieni e Giovanni Pico,'

Giornale critico della filosofia italiana 23 (1–2) (1942): 93–9. However, I agree with Pugliese that it is important not to exaggerate Benivieni's supposed 'dull plagiarism' and 'lack of originality.'

10 In the original, Benivieni typically capitalizes the first two or three letters of the repeated phrase from the poem in order to signal the citation.

11 Benivieni signals the end of such digressions with a variation on the statement, 'Hammi trasportato alquanto oltre a el termino del mio primo consiglio la dolceza del ragionare di quello primo, vero e incommutabile bene, senza la gratia del quale ogni nostro pensiero e ogni nostra operatione sarebbe vana, inutile e inefficace. Tornando adunque con lo aiuto necessario di quello al proposito nostro' ['The sweetness of reasoning about the first, true, and unchangeable Good, without whose grace all our thoughts and all our actions would be in vain, useless, and without effect, has taken me quite far beyond the boundary of my first intent. So returning with His necessary aid to our subject'].

12 Published in the same volume following the *Commento* are two short works, a *Deploratoria del prefato Hieronymo Benivieni allo Illustre Principe Iohanni Pico Mirandulano*, consisting of eight chapters in terza rima, and the *Amore di Hieronymo Benivieni Fiorentino allo Illustre Signore Conte Messer Niccolò Vicecomite da Coreggio*, which Benivieni prefaces with a dedicatory letter and 'argumento.' The *Amore* itself consists of 119 octaves.

13 Although my own emphasis is on Benivieni's poetic precedents, I do not deny strong religious influences on his work, especially from St Bonaventure. In this regard, see Olga Zorzi Pugliese, 'Benivieni's *Commento* and Bonaventure's *Itinerarium*: Autobiography and Ideology,' *Rivista di storia e letteratura religiosa* 30 (2) (1994): 347–62.

14 See the proem: 'Havendo io già per lungo spatio decorsa la mia gioventù sotto lo imperio di quello amore, per la cui calamitosa victoria suole el senso della ragione triumphare, cominciai meco medesimo a considerare la miseria dello stato mio. Imperochè raguardando io alla dignità della humana natura, e alli inifniti beneficii a quella da Dio conceduti. Et da altra parte repentendo meco medesimo dove e con quale servitù, come e con quanti miei damni e ingratitudine io havessi in prima con la deformatione di quella offesa la bontà di Dio, pensai meco medesimo di porre fine in quanto a me fussi possibile a e miei ciechi e male ordinati desiderii' ['Having for a long time passed my youth in decline under the aegis of that [earthly] love, for whose calamitous victory sense usually triumphs over reason, I began to consider the misery of my state. Considering the dignity of human nature and the infinite graces conceded to it by God, I regretted where and with what servitude, how and to what extent of ruin

and ingratitude I had offended the goodness of God by my deformation of that dignity of human nature. So I thought to myself to put an end to my blind and badly ordered desires as much as it is possible for me'].

15 The *Dialogo di Antonio Manetti, cittadino fiorentino, circa al sito, forma et misure dello* Inferno *di Dante Alighieri, poeta excellentissimo* by Hieronymo Benivieni. A republication of the work appears with an introduction by Nicola Zingarelli in the 'Collezione di Opuscoli Danteschi inediti o rari' (Città di Castello: S. Lapi, 1897).

16 Dante's version reads: 'Allor fu la paura un poco queta,/ che nel lago del cor m'era durata/ la notte ch'i' passai con tanta pieta./ E come quei che con lena affannata,/ uscito fuor del pelago a la riva,/ si volge a l'acqua perigliosa e guata,/ così l'animo mio, ch'ancor fuggiva,/ si volse a retro a rimirar lo passo/ che non lasciò già mai persona viva' ['Then the fear was somewhat quieted that had continued in the lake of my heart through the night I had passed so pieously. And as he who with labouring breath has escaped from the deep to the shore turns to look back on the dangerous waters, so my mind which was still fleeing turned back to gaze upon the pass that never left anyone alive']. All translations of *The Divine Comedy* are by Charles S. Singleton, 6 vols. Bollinger Series 80. (Princeton: Princeton University Press, 1991 [1970]).

17 The number retains special significance for Benivieni: 'Con ciò sia che havendo per insino da principio promesso di introducere qualche volta realmente e fuori di ogni ombra la anima perigrina in ella sua patria Hierusalem superna, et essendo già epse nostre Canzone e Sonetti saliti, come si vede, per tre gradi, cioè per virtù della sanctissima Trinità alla perfectione di quello numero, per el quale etiam in elle sacre lettere mysticamente si significa epsa nostra patria Hierusalem celeste, cioè ad epso numero centenario, meritamente hora fermeremo el piè della amorosa nostra intentione e discorso sopra questo ultimo grado, cioè in epsa subiecta Canzona, come in quella per la quale apertamente si insinui, secondo che poco innanzi diciavamo, e si demonstri lo ascenso reale della anima a el suo sposo, che è el primo e solo vero e essentiale suo fine e obiecto' ['Having promised from the beginning to introduce sometimes truly and without any shadow the pilgrim soul to its country celestial Jerusalem, and given that our canzoni and sonnets have risen, as can be seen, these three steps, that is by virtue of the most holy Trinity to the perfection of that number, in which in sacred letters mystically signifies our country of the celestial Jerusalem, that is the number 100, worthily we will now stop the foot of our amorous intention and discourse on this last step, that is in this canzone, as in that for which openly is insinuated,

according to what we just now were saying, and is shown the real ascension of the soul to its Bridegroom, who is its first and only true and essential end and objective'] (canzone 3.5.1).

18 The phrase 'come altrui piacque' returns, of course, in *Purgatorio* 1 in the mouth of Cato, a pagan who is saved, thus making a scathing intrapoetic commentary on Ulysses' cause for damnation.

19 The metaphor of ship navigation is one that Benivieni adopts frequently. See also: 'Con ciò sia adunque che la piccola mia navicella dopo uno lungo e laborioso discorso sia ultimamente a el desiderato porto per divina gratia arrivata' ['Thus my little boat, after a long and laborious discourse, is finally at its desired port having arrived by divine grace'] (proem) and 'non con poco timore ardisco di mettere hora la mia troppo per sè fragile barchetta in tanto pelago, quanto è questo dello amore divino, in el quale solo quelli possono senza alcuna offensione navighare' ['not with a little fear I dare to put now my boat, which is too frail in itself, in such a whirlpool, which of divine love this [whirlpool] is, in which only those can navigate who are without offence'] (canzone 1.1), etc. In each instance, Benivieni is careful to counter Ulysses' impiety with such references as that to the working of God's grace and his own fear of God. On the 'bark of genius' *topos*, see Ernst Robert Curtius's appendix in *European Literature in the Latin Middle Ages*, trans. Willard R. Trask (Princeton: Princeton University Press, 1990); and John Freccero's *The Poetics of Conversion*, ed. Rachel Jacoff (Cambridge: Harvard University Press, 1986), especially 146, where Freccero makes explicit the association between the *ingegno* and the itineraries of the mind and the journey of the poem itself. Freccero continues: 'The distance that separates Ulysses' point of shipwreck from the pilgrim's survival (the *Convivio* from the *Purgatory*) is measured by the descent into Hell. The descent into the self, *intra nos*, is the prerequisite for the kind of transcendent knowledge that all men desire.' Benivieni's journey likewise descends into the self and its sinful nature before the soul can pursue its union with God in the third part of the *Commento*.

20 Cf. the *Convivio* on working for the good of others and Lorenzo on working for the good of *oneself* and of others.

21 Beyond the mere mention of the *Convivio* (*Commento*, canzone 1.1.1), the banquet metaphor also recurs at various points throughout Benivieni's commentary, as for example in the prose of canzone 1.1.1, when he mentions the 'mensa' ['table'] at which the 'vivande ... da Dio preparate' ['foods ... prepared by God'] are served.

22 As I have noted, Lorenzo de' Medici continued to work on his *Comento* until close to his death in 1492, eight years before Benivieni's *Commento*

was published. Benivieni makes a more explicit reference to Lorenzo's *Comento* in his preface to the *Bucoliche*. There he also does not hesitate to read Lorenzo's self-commentary in the same morally allegorizing light as his own, by insisting that Lorenzo's lady is Poetry personified: *'ò nella descriptione della sua donna, cioè epsa Poesia, ò nella transformazione di quella'* ['either in the description of his lady, that is Poetry, or in its transformation'], *Opere* 73r.

23 I do not entertain the possibility that Benivieni's early poetry was coded to praise a homosexual love for Pico. Among others, Re refutes readings that contend there are suggestions in the *Bucolica* of 'una relazione meno che onesta fra i due' (*Girolamo Benivieni*, 77–8).

24 The sonnet in question is number five in the manuscript of the Codice Sessoriano 413. Benivieni dedicates it to Giuliano de' Medici as a gesture of consolation for Simonetta's death. It begins, 'Se morta, vive ancora colei che in vita.' In reference to a sonnet on the death of Benivieni's brother Domenico, Re states: 'in origine fu scritto per altra persona, per una donna, e amata da un altro, cui il poeta, giovane ancora, voleva gradire. La donna era la bella Simonetta, ritratta dal Botticelli col pennello, dal Poliziano nel verso armonioso, la bella Simonetta, donde mosse, o si finse mossa, la poesia del Magnifico' (55).

25 This passage is from Benivieni's letter to Niccolò Vicecomite da Coreggio, which serves as the preface to the *Amore*, published along with the *Commento* and *Deploratorio*. In this passage, 'effrenata' recalls again the 'senza freno' of the Ulysses canto. However, it is also a term heavily invested with Platonic resonances. I am thinking in particular about the notion of the two horses of human reason, which Michael J.B. Allen studies in great detail in *Marsilio Ficino and the Phaedran Charioteer* (Berkeley and Los Angeles: University of California Press, 1981).

26 Gerhart B. Ladner, *The Idea of Reform: Its Impact on Christian Thought and Action in the Age of the Fathers* (Cambridge: Harvard University Press, 1959), 197ff.

27 Like the best of Benivieni's metaphors, the veil is not strictly an abstract notion. The poet never loses sight of the literal level. In fact, he states that one of the most important reforms Savonarola instituted is in the Florentine citizens' customs and *modesty in dress* (canzone 3.4.1), which included headcoverings for ladies.

28 In this sense Benivieni may be said to have learned the lessons of the most prominent Florentine commentators, including Cristoforo Landino, especially well. Poetic philosophers, such as Dante and Virgil, Landino taught, secretly probe and adapt themselves to the individual reader's intellect,

and by delighting the mind with poetry, they lead each soul by means of philosophy to the good life. The poet allures 'the soul with but another form of what it had hitherto enjoyed: thus the soul, deceived by mixed poetic styles, is carried along, until suddenly that which it thought it was enjoying is found to be something else entirely, something higher and better, and the soul discovers that the previous "life" it was enjoying is inadequate. "Whatever men have done and whatever they have known," Landino explained before his lectures on Dante and Virgil, "the poetic discipline adorns with wonderful figments and carries over into another species." The poets "mix together the greatest seriousness with the greatest delight, and leave the hearers in a stupor." This is eloquence, to be sure, but an eloquence especially suited to the nature of the soul: this poetic, allegorical eloquence thus [did not serve philosophy] by taking obscure philosophical tenets and making them clear.' Arthur Field on Cristoforo Landino in *The Origins of the Platonic Academy of Florence* (Princeton: Princeton University Press, 1988), 264. The veil, then, because it partially obscures, prompts the beholder's desire to examine what lies beneath it.

29 Cristoforo Landino, among others, expounds this notion in his first lecture on Dante in 1456. Field discusses the lecture at greater length in *The Origins of the Platonic Academy of Florence*, 240ff.

30 Benivieni alludes to Dante's portrayal of Francesca da Rimini, as well as to the great deliverance in *Purgatorio* 2.46ff in his citation of Psalm 113 ('In exitu Israel de Aegypto'). In addition, Benivieni's very next words are 'Ma perché nè io sono Iosue, nè epsa anima Israel' ['But since I am neither Joshua, nor this soul Israel'], which pull together again an Exodus allusion (3:11) of Moses ('Who am I that I should go to Pharaoh and lead the Israelites out of Egypt?') as well as a Dantean one ('Io non Enea, io non Paulo sono,' *Inferno* 2.32).

31 Ladner, *Idea of Reform*, 40ff.

32 It is interesting to note the emphasis on order and precept of civil rule, which reflects Benivieni's reduction of poetry in the *Commento* to a prescribed series of spiritual steps: 'Havendo già come per lo argumento della precedente Canzona vedemmo, epso servo di Dio e vero Propheta Frate Hieronymo Savonarola in gran parte reformata la nostra città, e non solo quanto al ben vivere et alle cose dello spirito, ma anchora quanto per queste era necessario al publico e civile governo di quella' ['This servant of God and true prophet, Girolamo Savonarola, had reformed a good part of our city, as we saw in the commentary on the previous canzone, and the reform did not concern only good living and the things of the spirit, but

also concerned the things pertinent to the city's public and civil governance'] (canzona 3.4.1).

33 On the link between the Medusa and the *rime petrose*, see John Freccero, *The Poetics of Conversion*. Incidentally, Dante also insists on a deeper meaning hidden beneath the veils of his verse in the context of this passage: 'O voi ch'avete li 'ntelletti sani,/ mirate la dottrina che s'asconde/ sotto 'l velame de li versi strani' (vv. 61–3) ['O you who have sound understanding, mark the doctrine that is hidden under the veil of the strange verses!'].

34 This same concern for protecting the text from certain readers while communicating his message to others appears, for instance, in Marsilio Ficino's *Commentary on Plato's Symposium on Love*, trans. Sears Jayne (Dallas: Spring Publications, Inc., 1985): 'Therefore stay away from these heavenly feasts, stay away, I say, you profane people, who are covered with earthly filth, who are completely enslaved to Bacchus and Priapus, and who trample the heavenly gift of love in the dirt and mud, like swine. But you virtuous guests, and all others dedicated to Diana and Pallas, who rejoice in the freedom of a guiltless soul, and in the endless pleasures of the intellect, you are welcome to come and listen carefully to the divine mysteries revealed to Socrates by Diotima' (107–8).

35 According to Sears Jayne, in his concise and highly accessible introduction to the English translation of the text.

36 'Havendo io ... alcuni versi raccolti e in uno quasi corpo di amore celeste e divino reformati, et dubitando che se così nudi, cioè senza alcuna altra expositione in publico si monstrassino che e' loro quantunque per sè puri e inviolabili concepti non fussero da alcuni huomini animali etiam in contrarii sensi distorti ...' ['Having gathered together some poems and reformed them in almost a body of celestial and divine love, and doubting that they should show themselves in public naked, that is without an exposition, since their concepts, though in themselves are pure and inviolable, could be distorted into contrary senses by some bestial men ...'].

37 Francesco Bausi, in his introduction to Poliziano's *Stanze*, proposes in passing another reading: 'Negli stessi anni, Lorenzo de' Medici apriva il suo *Comento de' sonetti* proprio con questo evento, con la morte di Simonetta (cui dedicava i primi quattro sonetti dell'opera, con le relative prose esplicative), avvertendo che un tale inconsueto esordio possedeva una profonda motivazione filosofica, connessa con la riconosciuta necessità di morire alle cose imperfette onde potersi innalzare a quelle più perfette; ossia, ancora una volta, onde passare dalla vita attiva a quella

contemplative, dall'impegno nella *civitas hominis* alla beatitudine della *civitas Dei*' (xiv). In any case, it is important not to expect from the self-commentary, or even from certain commentaries, like Pico's on Benivieni's canzone on love, a clarification of philosophical minutiae. For a contrasting view on the subject, see John Charles Nelson, 'The Commentary of Giovanni Pico della Mirandola on Benvieni's *Canzone d'Amore*,' in *Renaissance Theory of Love: The Context of Giordano Bruni's* Eroici furori (New York: Columbia University Press, 1958). 'The utility – indeed, the necessity – of such a commentary is occasioned by the poem's obscurity, an inevitable result of the ambitious attempt to concentrate into 154 verses a large body of Neoplatonic doctrine' (56).

Chapter Five

1 Among Bruno's other works of mixed form one could mention the *Spaccio de la bestia trionfante* (Expulsion of the Triumphant Beast), the *Cena de le cenere* (The Ash Wednesday Supper), *De la causa, principio e uno* (On the Cause, Principle and One), and *De l'infinito universo e mondi* (On the Infinite Universe and Worlds), which are works in dialogue form, and in which Bruno also liberally intersperses poems by other authors, including Ariosto, Tasso, Tansillo, Lucretius, and Ovid. Illustrations sometimes accompany the dialogues, and epistolary proems frequently precede the works.
2 In references to this work I adopt both the fundamental critical edition in two volumes by Giovanni Gentile: *Dialoghi italiani*, 2nd ed. (Firenze: Sansoni, 1985) and the edition by Simonetta Bassi, with introduction by Michele Ciliberto (Roma-Bari: Laterza, 1995). English translations of the work sometimes have the title *Heroic Enthusiasts*, other times the *Heroic Frenzies*. Unless otherwise specified, English translations of the work in the present study are by Paul Eugene Memmo, Jr, *The Heroic Frenzies*, Studies in the Romance Languages and Literatures, vol. 50 (Chapel Hill: University of North Carolina Press, 1964).
3 Pasquale Sabbatino rightly emphasizes Bruno's deliberate refusal to contextualize his dialogues: 'La dimensione spaziale, elemento fondamentale nel dialogo diegetico del primo Cinquecento, viene del tutto annullata negli *Eroici furori*. I personaggi, esistenti solo in quanto voce dialogante, non hanno una scena, privata o pubblica. Affiorano dalla memoria personale del Bruno – ad eccezione del Tansillo che appartiene anche alla memoria pubblica – e vengono situati in uno spazio di cui non si danno le coordinate e non si mettono a fuoco dettagli. Siamo di fronte a spazi

mentali più che reali' (*Giordano Bruno e la 'Mutazione' del Rinascimento*. Biblioteca dell"Archivum Romanicum' 254. Serie I – Storia-Letteratura-Paleografia (Florence: Leo S. Olschki, 1993), 88).

4 For a detailed discussion of the process of the *Eroici furori*'s publication, see Giovanni Aquilecchia's philological discussion of Bruno's works in *Oeuvres complètes* (Paris: Les Belles Lettres, 1999), xlvii–l.

5 *An Apologie for Poetrie*, ed. Evelyn S. Shuckburgh (Cambridge: Cambridge University Press, 1928), 8: 'the Morrall Philosopher standeth upon the naturall vertues, vices, and passions of man ... The Lawyer sayth what men have determined. The Historian what men have done. The Grammarian speaketh onely of the rules of speech ... Onely the Poet, disdayning to be tied to any such subiection, lifted up with the vigor of his owne invention, dooth growe in effect into another nature, in making things either better than Nature bringeth forth, or, quite anewe, formes such as never were in Nature ... so as hee goeth hand in hand with Nature, not inclosed within the narrow warrant of her gifts, but freely ranging onely within the Zodiack of his owne wit.' On heroic poetry, see 32–3ff.

6 John Charles Nelson addresses this and other literary influences on Bruno's *Heroic Frenzies* in *Renaissance Theory of Love: The Context of Giordano Bruno's Eroici furori* (New York: Columbia University Press, 1958), especially 164ff.

7 Incidentally, a poet who does follow through with his determination to call his collection of poems a *Cantica* is Tommaso Campanella. His *Scelta* of philosophical poems is derived from his much larger *Cantica*, which unfortunately, does not seem to have survived. See the discussion of Tommaso Campanella's poetic self-commentary in chapter 6.

8 'L'una [ragione] per il timor ch'ho conceputo dal rigoroso supercilio de certi farisei, che cossì mi stimarebono profano per usurpar in mio natural e fisico discorso titoli sacri e sopranaturali' (Argomento) ['One [reason was] for the fear which I conceived of the austere frown of certain pharisees, who would judge me profane for usurping sacred and supernatural titles in my natural and physical discourse']. Bruno's fear of censure is modelled on Dante's in the *Convivio* and Lorenzo's in his *Comento* and does not necessarily have to be explained in terms of actual 'Farisei,' that is, the Puritans, according to Yates, 'The Religious Policy.'

9 In a similar way, Bruno evokes the concepts of the emblems without ever actually representing them visually.

10 The ironic tone in this passage can be better understood if one remembers the other instances in Bruno's works in which he stresses his capacity to understand other authors better than they do themselves. Among these are

Ramón Lull's art of memory and Copernicus's discovery. Bruno claims in *The Ash Wednesday Supper* that as a mathematician, Copernicus did not understand the full meaning of his discovery as Bruno himself has.
11 Bruno was greatly influenced by St Thomas Aquinas. At an early age Bruno entered the Dominican convent in Naples where the saint is buried, and he came to revere him as a great magus. See Frances A. Yates, *Giordano Bruno and the Hermetic Tradition* (Chicago: University of Chicago Press, 1964), 251.
12 Giovanni Gentile noted that Bruno might be trying to distinguish the form of his own sonnets from those of others by inserting a seven-syllable line, usually as the penultimate line. See Gentile's edition of Bruno's dialogues (955). Ferruolo also examines metrical variations of sonnets in 'Sir Philip Sidney e Giordano Bruno' (697ff).
13 The other interlocutors are: Cicada in the first five dialogues; Cesarino and Maricondo in Part two, dialogues one and two; Liberio and Laodonio (2.3), Severino and Minutolo (2.4); and Laodomia and Giulia (2.5). For more detailed information concerning their historical identities see V. Spampanato, *Vita di Giordano Bruno* (Messina: Principato, 1921). The unusual structure Bruno establishes between the unified first five dialogues and the crowd of contextless interlocutors of the second five dialogues probably reflects his wider philosophical interests of the one and the many, for instance. Sabbatino states: 'La linea della inamovibilità degli interlocutori nella prima parte cede il passo alla linea della *variatio* nella seconda parte. La stabilità degli interlocutori dà ai primi cinque dialoghi continuità narrativa e alla prima parte unitarietà, mentre la variazione degli interlocutori divide e isola i secondi cinque dialoghi – sulla base dei personaggi sono raggruppabili solo i primi due e i successivi vantano priena autonomia – e rende la seconda parte un aggregato di più poli' (*Giordano Bruno*, 85).
14 Socrates' insistence on knowing thyself is also a crucial motif throughout the *Heroic Frenzies*, since the search for wisdom in the visible forms must always lead to a deeper search within the self: '*Cesarino*: Come intendi che la mente aspira alto? verbi grazia, con guardar sempre alle stelle? al cielo empireo? sopra il cristallino? *Maricondo*: Non certo, ma procedendo al profondo della mente, per cui non fia mistiero massime aprir gli occhi al cielo, alzar alto le mani, menar i passi al tempio, intonar l'orecchie de simulacri, onde più si vegna exaudito; ma venir al più intimo di sé, considerando che Dio è vicino, con sé e dentro di sé più ch'egli medesimo esser non si possa' (2.1) ['*Cesarino*: How do you understand that the mind aspires to raise itself? For example, would it be by turning towards the stars, or the empyrean, or the crystalline heaven? *Maricondo*: Certainly not,

but by proceeding to the depths of the mind; and in order to accomplish this, it is not at all necessary to gaze wide-eyed toward the sky, to raise one's hands, to direct one's steps toward the temple, wearying the ears of statues with the sounds we make; but it is necessary to descend more intimately within the self and to consider that God is near, that each one has Him with him and within himself more than he himself can be within himself'].

15 It is true, as Sabbatino says, that 'l'insistenza sul motivo del dialogare stando fermi non è certo un dato innocuo nelle mani del Bruno. Per un antiartistotelico dichiarato il dialogare stando seduti diviene un *topos* antiperipatetico' (*Giordano Bruno*, 91). However, this implicit criticism is aimed at only a certain type of Aristotelianism, a pedantic one. The invitation to discuss while walking at the end of many of the dialogues aims to call attention to the contrast between Bruno's form of inquiry and that of the pedants. In another context, Yates speaks of the distinction Bruno makes between Aristotle and his followers: 'Aristotle himself, unlike the stupid Aristotelians his followers, was one who did see deep truths but veiled them in obscure language. In a moment of divination, Aristotle half guessed that the earth moves when he used in the *Meteorologica* the words "propter solem et circulationem." Here Aristotle was not speaking as a philosopher, but "as a diviner, or as one who understood but did not dare to say what he understood, or as one who saw but did not believe what he saw" (*Cena*, V)' (*Giordano Bruno and the Hermetic Tradition*, 251).

16 Michele Ciliberto rightly summarizes, 'Non è lineare – o scontato – il cammino che dalla filosofia porta alla poesia; né può essere spiegato e compreso alla luce di spiegazioni puramente filosofiche, dell'intelletto; o di motivazioni di carattere esteriori, qualunque ne sia la natura: è questo che Bruno intende comunicare a chi lo legge, arrestandosi, consapevole, su un limite strutturale che egli vuole in questa maniera ribadire. Quello delle Muse è una "grazia," un "dono" destinato a un "eletto" che sta come "sospeso" proprio perché è cosciente di quello che gli accade, del suo significato, della responsabilità che gli è toccata. Egli sa, dopo un lungo cammino, che nella sua vita "è avvenuto" qualcosa che potrà portarlo oltre se stesso.' From his introduction to Simonetta Bassi's edition of the *Eroici furori* (Rome and Bari: Laterza, 1995), ixl–xl.

17 See Sidney, *An Apologie for Poetrie*, 19–20: 'For conclusion, I say the Philosopher teacheth, but he teacheth obscurely, so as the learned onely can understande him; that is to say, he teacheth them that are already taught: but the Poet is the foode for the tenderest stomacks, the Poet is indeed the right Popular Philosopher.'

18 In fact, from the 'lowest ebb of the sciences ... have bred the scum of

opinions, themselves the causes of the vilest habits and works' ['ora che siamo stati nella feccia delle scienze, che hanno parturita la feccia delle opinioni, le quali son causa della feccia de gli costumi ed opre, possiamo certo aspettare de ritornare a meglior stati'] (2.1). It would seem that Bruno sees the only possibility of harmony and truth in the frenzy of a search within the same spirit, accessible through poetry. The same distrust of science is betrayed in other remarks, such as: 'Più possono far gli maghi per mezzo della fede, che gli medici per via de la verità' (1.5) ['Magicians can do more by means of faith than doctors by means of the truth.']

19 See David Quint, *Origin and Originality in Renaissance Literature* (New Haven: Yale University Press, 1983), 146–7: 'While the [proposing of] silence as a preferable mystical mode seems to eliminate poetry altogether, Bruno does not criticize an allegorical language of praise as such, but rather praise that stops short of its infinite divine object by presenting itself as a finished act ("compita e perfetta azione"). The poem can never become equal to the God it tries to celebrate, and once the poem suggests that it has somehow completed its allegorical function – that is has made a definitive and finite statement about divinity – it merely obscures human understanding, casting smoke instead of light. True understanding of the divine derives from the allegorical act itself, the poem that points beyond its own letter in an act of signification which can never be completed. This refusal to stop the allegorical process authorizes Bruno's literary enterprise, for it defines knowledge of God in terms of the process by which the mind recognizes and refuses its limitations. If words and mental images cast darkness upon the understanding which searches beyond them toward the divine, allegory becomes analogous to the experience of the nine men who are blinded by matter while on their spiritual quest. In both cases the never-ending mystical process itself is substituted for a final revelation. The zeal to keep the process going, what Bruno in his elevation of the will over the intellect calls "studio ed ardire," is the vital allegorical as well as contemplative principle.'

20 Like Lorenzo de' Medici, Bruno places a higher premium on courageously attempting a daunting task and failing, rather than not taking the chance and foregoing such a task in the first place.

Chapter Six

1 I refer to the critical edition by Lina Bolzoni for all citations from Campanella's *Scelta*: *Opere letterarie di Tommaso Campanella* (Turin: UTET, 1977).

The English translations of Campanella are my own. Unfortunately, an English readership of Campanella's poetry must otherwise still depend on the Victorian translation by John Addington Symonds, *The Sonnets of Michael Angelo Buonarroti and Tommaso Campanella* (London: Smith, Elder & Co., 1878). This rendition, while very lyrical, is antiquated and incomplete, and misleads the reader by attributing the self-commentary to the work's first editor, Tobia Adami. Given the widespread popularity of Symonds's study, it may be surprising to an English readership that Campanella's *Scelta* is included in a study of *self*-commentaries. The mere fact that the current study places Campanella's *Scelta* within a tradition of poetic self-commentaries represents a new way of considering this text.

2 Campanella may also be suggesting that these seemingly easy passages may not be so simple after all.

3 On the Hermetic tradition, see for example, D.P. Walker's *Spiritual and Demonic Magic from Ficino to Campanella* (London: Warburg Institute, University of London, 1958).

4 Dante alludes to the same biblical passage in his *Convivio*, as I have shown.

5 One could compare this use of 'stuol' ['crowd'] to that in poem 75.8:7–8: 'Dunque, mente / tanto *stuol* di profeti che tu mandi?' ['Then that crowd of prophets that You send lies?']. Campanella uses the term *stuol di profeti* here with evident sarcasm. He shows elsewhere as well that wise men know more than they manifest openly and that the use of parables can help the poet to say various things at once: 'Parabola mirabile per intendere come il mondo diventò pazzo per lo peccato, e che gli savi, pensando sanarlo, furon forzati a dire e fare e vivere come gli pazzi, se ben nel lor segreto hanno altro avviso' (13n). ['[It's a] wondrous parable to understand how the world became crazed because of sin, and that wisemen, believing to heal it, were forced to say and do and live like madmen, though they secretly have other beliefs].

6 Campanella must certainly be aware that he cannot simply declare himself a prophet: he must be considered one by others. However, he does not adopt the more typical stance, such as that represented by Jonah, who repeatedly resists the call to prophesy. On Dante's similarly ambiguous oscillation between the two voices of poetry and prophecy, see Giuseppe Mazzotta's *Dante, Poet of the Desert: History and Allegory in the* Divine Comedy (Princeton: Princeton University Press, 1979).

7 Boccaccio, in his proem discourse to Fiammetta, presents a contrasting vision of the witness, one who is unreliable. In making his case for the truth of poetry, Boccaccio contrasts it with the words of his lady. The truth

may not be present in Fiammetta's testimony based on experience, since she can lie ('se non mentiste'). See the discussion on Boccaccio's self-commentary in chapter 2.

8 For a detailed study of Campanella's trials, tortures, and years in prison, see Luigi Amabile's two studies, *Fra Tommaso Campanella, la sua congiura, i suoi processi e la sua pazzia*, 3 vols. (Napoli, 1882) and *Fra Tommaso Campanella ne' Castelli di Napoli, in Roma ed in Parigi*, 2 vols. (Naples, 1887). On the subject of dissimulation, Thomas Cerbu, in 'Dissimulation on Display': The Feint of Power in Campanella's *Scelta*,' in Ronald Bogue and Mihai I. Spariosu, eds., *The Play of the Self* (Albany: State University of New York Press, 1994), 203–19, argues that Campanella writes the self-commentary in order to establish 'an equivalence between a reformed Campanella of 1613 and the reader, as against the author of the poems. The commentary literally dis/played for himself as much as for the reader what lay behind the poems by giving a content to what had been allegedly dissimulated. As proof of his good faith, the commentary logically extended the resolve already present in certain poems to expose his and the revolt's failure as self-deception' (205). Like Joseph Scalzo's reading ('Campanella, Foucault, and Madness in Late-Sixteenth Century Italy,' *Sixteenth-Century Journal* 21 (1990): 359–71), and unlike my own, Cerbu's political reading of the *Scelta*'s self-commentary makes of Campanella a shrewd gamesman and opportune liar, from whom one can learn to transform 'dissimulation from a principle of human action into one of metaphysical order' (216).

9 As an aside, I mention that a worthy subject for another study would be to examine the parallels between Campanella's self-commentary and the variations between his Italian and Latin versions of *Città del sole*. Campanella subsequently recontextualizes these in his larger philosophical project, the *Philosophia realis*. Such a study might better illuminate the nature of Campanella's conversion.

10 Moreover, this sonnet makes reference to poem 46.1–4, Campanella's personal version of the 'Pater noster,' which emphasizes the fundamental theme of the earth's transformation into the heavenly realm: 'Padre, che stai nel Ciel, santificato / perché sia il nome tuo, venga oramai / il regno tuo; che in terra sia osservato / il tuo voler, sì come in Ciel fatto hai' ['Father, who are in heaven, hallowed may your name be, your kingdom come now, may your will be obeyed on earth, as you have made it in heaven'].

11 Prophecy is in *Etymologies* 7.8.1: '[prophetae] quos gentilitas vates appellant, hos nostri prophetas vocant, quasi praefatores, quia porro fantur et de

futuris vera praedicunt.' It properly derives from 'speaking in the place of' God.

12 Campanella understands the seven protrusions as a mark from God, as I have discussed previously. Incidentally, Campanella writes some of his other works under pen names as well. He signs, for example, his *A Venezia* (which Gaspare Scioppio will later title the *Antiveneti*), in which Campanella speaks for the Church's mission against Venice's political designs, as Temisquilla Settimontano. This pseudonym contains within it a sort of ciphered warning: 'temi,' in Temi-squilla suggests the imperative form of the verb 'temere' (to fear). On the *Antiveneti*, see Luigi Firpo, ed., *Tutte le opere di Tommaso Campanella* (Verona: Mondadori, 1954), lxxix.

13 Some critics, such as Rodolfo de Mattei, even suggest that the pseudonym is a matter of personal taste: 'Non può sorprenderci che si riscontri in qualche [manoscritto] del Campanella un pseudonimo. A parte i pericoli, l'uso dei pseudonimi non dovette esser lontano dal gusto del Campanella: si pensi al nome "Settimontano Squilla," sceltosi dal frate nei *Canti*, e anche attribuitogli nelle corrispondenze degli amici.' *Studi campanelliani* (Florence: Sansoni, 1933), 94.

14 Campanella's pen name is easily identifiable with him from his exegetical observations: 'Perché l'autore scrisse ch'ogni cosa sente più o meno, quanto basta alla sua conservatione, come appare da' libri *De sensu rerum*. E perché nella sua *Metafisica* ...' ['Thus the author wrote that every thing feels more or less, as much as is necessary for its survival, as it appears in the books *De sensu rerum*. And thus in his *Metafisica* ...'](23.1n), or 'secondo che l'autore scrive nella *Città del Sole*' (25.5n), ['According to what the author writes in the *Città del Sole*'] etc.

15 See also the self-commentary on Poem 2, 'A' poeti,' ['To the Poets'] in which Campanella rails against those poets who falsify history in the name of poetic inventiveness: 'E grida lor contro, che tornino al prisco poetare. E perché pensano che le favole sono degne di cantarsi per l'ammirazione, dice che più mirabili sono l'opere di Natura. E qui condanna Aristotele, che fece la favola essenziale al poeta: poiché questa si deve fingere solo dove si teme dir il vero per conto de' tiranni, come Natan parlò in favola a David; o a chi non vuol sapere il vero, si propone con gusto di favole burlesche o mirabili; o a chi non può capirlo, si parla con parabole grosse, come Esopo e Socrate usâro, e più il santo Vangelo. Talché l'autore lauda quella favola solo che non falsifica l'istoria' ['So he exhorts them to return to ancient poetry. Also, because they think that fables deserve to be sung in admiration, he says that the works of nature are more admirable. Here he

condemns Aristotle, who made the fable essential to the poet, since the fable should be made up only when there is a fear of speaking the truth against tyrants, as Nathan spoke in fables to David; or, for those who do not want to know the truth, burlesque or marvelous fables within the bounds of good taste are proposed; or for those who cannot understand the truth, one should speak in thick parables, like those used by Aesop and Socrates, and also the holy Gospels. Thus the author praises only the fable that does not falsify history'].

16 In this regard, see also the poem excluded from the *Scelta* (108.15–29): 'A poco a poco rende / sua vita il mondo al primo Creatore; / viene il giorno fatale al malfattore; / ritorna il Redentore / a riveder il conto del suo gregge. / Par mal annunzio a chi lo guida e regge / con durissima legge; / e perché taccia il vero in carcer tetro / io sto; ma, con san Paolo e con san Pietro, / canto un occulto metro, / che nel secreto orecchio alle persone / la CAMPANELLA mia fa che risone: / ch'or l'Eterna Ragione / pria tutti i regni uman compogna in uno, / che renda il caos tutte cose all'uno' ['Little by little the world surrenders / its life to the first Creator; / the fatal day comes to the malefactor; / the Redeemer returns / to recount his flock. / It does not seem to bode well to those who lead and rule / with harshest law; / and so that the truth is silenced, in gloomy prison / I stay; but with saints Paul and Peter, / I sing a hidden meter, that in the secret ears of the people / my CAMPANELLA [LITTLE BELL] makes resound: / that now may Eternal Reason / before all the human kingdoms compose in one, / that chaos surrender all things to the one']. Campanella uses the capital letters in the original.

17 For a more ample treatment of this theme and its association with St Francis of Assisi, see Stanislao da Campagnola, *L'angelo del sesto sigillo e l'Alter Christus: Genesi e sviluppo di due temi francescani nei secoli xiii–xiv* (Rome, 1971).

18 Dante describes Joachim of Flora in this way in *Paradise* 12.140–1. The frequency with which Campanella cites the prophetic writings of Joachim in his poems and other works reinforces the notion of his importance for the poet. See also Firpo's note to poem 124. Other prophetic writers dear to Campanella include St Bridgett and the Sibyls.

19 *L'angelo*, 118–19: 'l'eredità del messaggio con cui il profeta della Sila aveva annunciato l'avvento dei 'minores' e degli 'spirituales' dell'età dell''Evangelium aeternum,' ma gettandosi con realismo esecutivo nella pratica della vita evangelica.' It is important to underline that the relationship between Joachim's message and St Francis's activity is not direct, but part of a latent suggestion for interpretation: 'La "novitas franciscana"

non ha perciò né intenti né atteggiamenti che denuncino un mondo in rovina e prossimo alla catastrofe, né toni profetici che siano di preludio e di inizio ad una palingenesi apocalittica, nella quale il carisma di una intellezione profonda, spirituale che, superando la comprensione gerarchico-sacramentale dell'età vigente del Nuovo Testamento, aprisse la via all'epoca di un Vangelo diverso, per la lettera e per lo spirito, da quello di Cristo, dominio di un "Ordo novus" di contemplativi, di poveri e di solitari, di fanciulli e di semplici.'

20 Campanella actually mentions St Francis in poem 10. It is true that the saint's relationship with nature and his active work within it must have struck a chord with Campanella (see Bolzoni's note in this regard in her critical edition of the work, 116).

21 The 'bianco corridor' is the *equus albus* of *Apocalypse* 6:2, 'nel quale Campanella credeva fosse prefigurato l'ordine domenicano dal bianco saio e, in particolar modo, la propria azione riformatrice,' notes Firpo, *Tutte le opere*, 1330.

22 'Rhetoricam quodammodo magiae portiunculam esse diximus: mentis enim scientiis utitur ad praxim, ordinando applicandoque activa passivis ad immutandos animos affectusque humanos, mirabiliter sane' ['Rhetoric is in some way a small part of magic: in fact, it uses the sciences of the mind for its practice, marvelously preparing and applying the active to the passive to change human souls and emotions.'] (from the *Rhetorica* 3, *Tutte le opere*, 742). Marziano Guglielminetti studies this theme, central also to the author's poetics, in 'Magia e tecnica nella poetica di Tommaso Campanella.'

23 *Psyché: Interventions de l'autre* (Paris: Galilée, 1988), 235.

24 *Illuminations*, ed. Hannah Arendt, trans. Harry John (New York: Harcourt, Brace & World, 1968), 78. The German original appears in *Gesammelte Schriften*, 4.1 (Suhrkamp Verlag, 1972).

25 This temporal displacement is aided by the fact that Campanella's poems are created still-born, as he indicates in poem 79.8: 'Nel prender commiato dice che queste rime sono fatte in una fossa, e però *sepolte avanti che nate*; ed esorta le genti a mutar vita e sospetto, perché non si è mosso a parlar così, se non per esperienza, e per Nume divino che l'ha insegnato, e per ragion naturale filosofica; e assicura tutti del vero' ['In taking leave he says that these poems were written in a pit, and were thus *buried before they were born*; and he exhorts the people to change their life and suspicion, because he wasn't moved to speak like this, except by experience and from what the divine deity had taught him through natural philosophic reason. And he assures everyone of the truth'] (my emphasis).

26 Romano Amerio, in his explication of poem 5, 'Anima immortale,' rightly states that 'Campanella insegna nella *Metafisica* che nel fondo dell'autocoscienza è il conoscimento di Dio e nel fondo dell'autovolizione, onde ciascuna creatura si radica nel proprio essere, è l'amore di Dio, principio di tutti gli esseri.' *Opere di Giordano Bruno e di Tommaso Campanella.* A cura di Augusto Guzzo e Romano Amerio (Milan: Riccardo Ricciardi, 1956). One should not stop here, however, but rather ask if the form of the *Scelta* also conforms to this model; that is: at the basis of the *autocommento* might there be the only partially effable message of God? Campanella's insistence on learning from the book of God's creation is the primary distinction he makes between his philosophy and one such as that of Pico della Mirandola, and is relevant in this regard. See the letter dated '[Napoli,] dal profondo Caucaso, agli 8 di luglio 1607. "Una che la ringrazia e supplica" Monsignor Antonio Querengo': 'Ecco dunque il diverso filosofar mio da quel di Pico; ed io imparo più dall'anatomia d'una formica o d'una erba ... che non da tutti li libri che sono scritti dal principio di secoli sin a mò, dopo ch'imparai a filosofare e legger il libro di Dio: al cui esemplare correggo i libri umani malamente copiati a capriccio, e non secondo sta nell'universo, libro originale ... Veramente Pico fu ingegno nobile e dotto; ma filosofo più sopra le parole altrui che nella natura, donde quasi niente apprese ... Pico ancora nelle cose morali e politiche fu scarsissimo, e tutto si diede alla nomanzia dello ebraismo ed a voltar libri; ma se non morìa così presto, diventava grande eroe della vera sapienza' ['This is thus the difference between my philosophising and that of Pico. I learn more from the anatomy of an ant or a [blade of] grass ... than from all the books that have ever been written from the beginning of time until now, after I learned to philosophise and read the book of God. Following that exemplar, I correct the human books that have been copied from it by whim, not according to what is in the universe, the original book ... Truly Pico was a noble and wise genius; but he was a philosopher of others' words and not of nature, whence he learned hardly anything ... Pico also came up very short in moral and political matters, giving himself up entirely to Jewish necromancy and rifling books. But if he had not died so young, he would have become a great hero of true wisdom'] (cited from Amerio's edition of Campanella's works, *Opere di Giordano Buono e di Tommaso Campanella*, 972).

27 For a consideration of the significance and appropriation of the Prometheus figure by other authors, see Timothy Richard Wutrich, *Prometheus and Faust: The Promethean Revolt in Drama from Classical Antiquity to Goethe* (Westport, Conn.: Greenwood Press, 1995), 7.

28 The prophet inflames people as opposed to the ignorant ones who only

claim to be wise and whose 'sventurato fuoco smorza in tutto' (poem 12.14) and whose 'ardori' are 'infami' (2.6). Campanella alludes frequently to the myth of Prometheus or to his prison, as the 'Caucaso' where Prometheus was tortured, in his other poems (including poem 80) and in many of his letters.

29 Even though *squilla* appears in the aulic works of the Italian poetic tradition, Campanella does not seem to invest the name with any particular, high literary allusion. Among the occurances of *squilla* are in Dante *Purgatorio* 8.1–6, 'Era già l'ora che volge il disio / ai navicanti e 'ntenerisce il core / lo dì c'han detto ai dolci amici addio; / e che lo novo peregrin d'amore / punge, se ode *squilla* di lontano / che paia il giorno pianger che si more.' ('Squilli,' in the masculine form, appears in *Paradiso* 20.18: 'Poscia che i cari e lucidi lapilli / ond'io vidi ingemmato il sesto lume / puoser silenzio a li angelici *squilli*,' and is glossed by Lana, l'Ottimo, Benvenuto, Buti, and others as a 'suono acuto e vibrante proprio di uno strumento musicale come la tromba'); or in works of a much different tone, such as Petrarca's *Canzoniere*, 'Spirto gentil che quelle membra reggi,' vv. 55–6: 'né senza *squille* s'incomincia assalto / che per Dio ringraziar fur poste in alto'; or Ariosto's *Orlando furioso*, 46.2: 'Sento venir per allegrezza un tuono / che fremer l'aria e rimbombar fa l'onde: / odo di *squille*, odo di trombe un suono' (my emphasis).

30 Tommaso Campanella, *Lettere*, Vincenzo Spampanato, ed. (Bari: Laterza, 1927), 298 and 343.

31 Verzera, *Profilo*: 'chi aveva scritto *Degli heroici furori* non poteva indietreggiare davanti alla luce di un rogo. Campanella è diverso ... perché convinto di dover assolvere una missione insostituibile, perché preso dal giuoco di una sorta di finzione scenica che lo vuole attore e protagonista sino al limite estremo di quella giornata terrena che il Creatore gli ha elargito, che gli uomini non possono abbreviare o troncare, perché egli sa che il suo destino lo chiama a lottare e a combattere contro la perfidia dei nuovi farisei, che vogliono aver ragione di lui, e non riusciranno a piegarlo' (19).

32 Tommaso Campanella, *La profezia di Cristo*, ed. Romano Amerio, (Rome: Centro Internazionale di Studi Umanistici, 1973), 35. In the number of tortures he underwent in prison Campanella saw the same significant number, *Scelta* 75.6:–8 'le membra sette volte tormentate' ['my limbs tortured seven times']

33 Campanella compares himself on occasion to the prophets. See, for example, the passage from the *Lettere*, 22: 'Son accusato per ribello ed eretico, per lo che otto anni cominciano che sto sepolto "*donec veniret verbum eius*":

e le dico che la ribellion mia è come quella d'Amos profeta nel settimo dove scrive l'empio sacerdote Amasia: *"rebellat contra te Amos, o rex Ieroboam."'* ['I am accused of being a rebel and heretic for which I have been buried now starting my eighth year *"donec veniret verbum eius"*: and I tell you that my rebellion is like that of Amos the prophet in the seventh [chapter] where the impious priest Amasia writes: "rebellat contra te Amos, o rex Ieroboam"'].

Chapter Seven

1 (New Haven and London: Yale University Press, 1993.)
2 Ibid., 237.
3 According to Giorgio Rossi in *La secchia rapita, L'oceano e le rime*, Alessandro Tassoni (Bari: Laterza, 1930): 'È noto che su un esemplare di questa edizione il Tassoni aggiunse le note che uscirono poi col nome di Gaspare Salviani; e che questa copia accomodata secondo le intenzioni ultime dell'autore è quella che servì di originale all'edizione veneta del 1630, ultima fatta lui vivo. È appunto questa edizione stampata a Venezia nel 1630 da Giacomo Scaglia, e soltanto questa, che si deve considerare definitva e deve essere riprodotta da chiunque si accinga a dare una nuova edizione della *Secchia*' (353).
4 Rossi's 1904 study, *Studi e ricerche tassoniane* (Bologna: Nicola Zanichelli, 1904), summarizes the philological debate, showing convincingly that the declarations could not in fact belong to Salviani or anyone other than Tassoni.
5 All translations of Tassoni are mine. For a complete English translation of the *Secchia rapita*, one must resort to the translation by James Atkinson published in 1825, *La Secchia rapita: or The Rape of the Bucket: An Heroicomical Poem in Twelve Cantos* 2 vols. (London: J.M. Richardson, 1825). Unfortunately for my purposes, however, Atkinson does not recognize the annotations by Gaspare Salviani as self-commentary, but treats them as standard commentary: 'The *Secchia rapita*, according to Gaspare Salviani, was written by Alessandro Tassoni in 1611' (v). He does not translate or reproduce the self-commentary in his edition.
6 It would seem that not everyone is privy to Tassoni's joke. I mention in passing the case of Pellegrino Rossi's *Annotazioni alla* Secchia rapita in sequito delle già fatte da Gaspare Salviani [Annotations of the *Stolen Bucket*] (Piacenza: Giacopazzi Stampator, 1738). The work, which consists solely of Rossi's 'annotazioncelle,' shows moments in which Rossi may be stifling a smile or offering an instance of dry wit. For example, the note on

2.66 reads: 'se poi [Sardegna] sia altrettanto ricca d'uomini bugiardi, come dice il Tassoni, mi rimetto alla grave di lui autorità' ['if Sardinia is just as rich in lying men, as Tassoni says, I submit to his grave authority.'] On the whole, however, the annotations are oddly straightforward, according to the purpose Rossi asserts in his prefatory remarks to his 'amico lettore' ['friendly reader']: 'non essendo bastanti per renderlo chiaro, e in molte parti intelligibile quelle pochissime note, che v'intrecciò Gaspare Salviani, ne viene altresì ... dono' ['those very few notes that Gaspare Salviani provided, not being sufficient to render the text clear, and in many parts intelligible, I make a gift of others.']

7 'L'autocommento nei sonetti filosofici di Antonio Conti,' in Gianfelice Peron, ed., L'autocommento. Atti del XVIII Convegno Interuniversitario (Bressanone, 1990) (Padua: Esedra Editrice, 1994), 91.

8 Ibid., 83–4.

9 Two of the most intriguing are Ugo Foscolo's experiment with commentary and self-commentary in *Vestigi della storia del sonetto italiano* and Umberto Saba's *Storia e cronistoria del 'Canzoniere.'* This inquiry also does not take into account the many literary or satirical glosses on prose texts, like those rendered famous by James Joyce or Laurence Sterne. See, for example, Anthony Grafton's *The Footnote: A Curious History* (Cambridge and London: Harvard University Press, 1997) and Shari Benstock, 'At the Margin of Discourse: Footnotes in the Fictional Text,' *PMLA* 98(1) (1983): 204–25.

10 According to Jon R. Snyder: 'Like many other kinds of literature popular in the Renaissance, however, dialogue did not survive the advent of modernity. The Earl of Shaftesbury, in his "Advice to an Author" (1710), already felt very sure of himself in bluntly remarking that "dialogue is at an end"; and, notwithstanding some notable exceptions (such as Paul Valéry), the status of dialogue as a part of the literary system did not further improve with the passage of time. Yet in the twentieth century the term "dialogue" has become a catchword across a broad spectrum of disciplines, from anthropology to hermeneutics to literary theory to psychoanalysis, that together constitute the Western human sciences' (*Writing the Scene of Speaking: Theories of Dialogue in the Late Italian Renaissance* [Stanford: Stanford University Press, 1989], viii).

11 Snyder, *Writing the Scene of Speaking*, 14: 'A heightened critical awareness after 1550 in Italy of the intricacy and ubiquity of fiction – presaging the appearance of Baroque literary culture – helps to make an encounter with the problem of dialogue, as the intersection of logic and literature, a potentially explosive one.' This same problematic has been examined from

many different perspectives, including most notably from that of the changes in the understanding of the symbolic mode. See Angus Fletcher, *Allegory: The Theory of a Symbolic Mode* (Ithaca: Cornell University Press, 1964).

12 *Timaeus* 71e–72b, trans. Francis M. Cornford (New York: Macmillan, 1985). For the etymologies of the Platonic terms in relation to their use in critical discourse, see George A. Kennedy, ed., *The Cambridge History of Literary Criticism*, vol. 1. (Cambridge and New York: Cambridge University Press, 1989), 24–9.

Bibliography

Defining Poetic Self-Commentary vis-à-vis Other Metapoetic Categories

Allen, Judson Boyce. 'Commentary and Criticism: Formal Cause, Discursive Form, and the Late Medieval Accessus.' *Acta conventus neo-latini lovaniensis.* Munich: Leuven University Press, 1973. 29–48.
- *The Ethical Poetic of the Later Middle Ages: A Decorum of Convenient Distinction.* Toronto: University of Toronto Press, 1982.
- *The Friar as Critic: Literary Attitudes in the Later Middle Ages.* Nashville: Vanderbilt University Press, 1971.

Bagni, Paolo. '*Res ficta non facta*: Il campo concettuale del commento.' *Studi di estetica* 1 (1973): 113–63.

Bakhtin, Mikhail M. *The Dialogic Imagination: Four Essays.* Ed. Michael Holquist. Trans. Caryl Emerson and Michael Holquist. Austin: University of Texas Press, 1981.

Battistini, Andrea. *Lo specchio di Dedalo: Autobiografia e biografia.* Bologna: Il Mulino, 1990.

Beaujour, Michel. 'Speculum, Method, and Self-Portrayal: Some Epistemological Problems.' In John D. Lyons and Stephen G. Nichols, eds., *Mimesis: From Mirror to Method, Augustine to Descartes.* Hanover and London: University Press of New England, 1982: 188–96.
- *Poetics of the Literary Self-Portrait. Studies in French Culture and Civilization.* Trans. Yara Milos. New York: New York University Press, 1991.

Benjamin, Walter. "The Task of the Translator." *Illuminations.* Ed. Hannah Arendt. Trans. Harry Zohn. 1st ed. New York: Harcourt, Brace & World, 1968: 69–82.

Benstock, Shari. 'At the Margin of Discourse: Footnotes in the Fictional Text.' *PMLA* 98(1) (1983): 204–25.

Bentivoglio, Bruno, e Guglielmo Gorni, eds. *Il commento al testo lirico (Pavia, 25–26 ottobre 1990). Schifanoia: Notizie dell'Istituto di Studi Rinascimentali di Ferrara* 15–16 (1995). Modena: Franco Cosimo Panini Editore, 1995.

Bettarini, Rosanna. 'Postille e varianti nella canzone delle visioni.' *Studi Petrarcheschi* 2 (1985): 159–84.

Biblia Sacra Vulgatae Editionis. Ed. Alberto Colunga and Laurentio Turrado. Madrid: Edizioni San Paolo, 1995.

Boethius. *The Consolation of Philosophy*. Trans. Richard Green. New York: Macmillan, 1962.

– *De Consolatione Philosophiae, Opuscula Teologica*. Bibliotheca Teubneriana. Ed. Claudio Moreschini. Munich and Leipzig: K.G. Saur Verlag, 2000.

Brand, Charles P. 'Poet, Poem, and Public in the Italian Renaissance.' In Ronald G. Popperwell, ed., *Expression, Communication, and Experience in Literature and Language*. Leeds: W.S. Maney & Son, 1973: 57–71.

Brush, Craig. *From the Perspective of the Self: Montaigne's Self-Portrait*. New York: Fordham University Press, 1994.

Bruss, Elizabeth W. *Autobiographical Acts: The Changing Situation of a Literary Genre*. Baltimore: Johns Hopkins University Press, 1976.

Capella, Martianus. *Martianus Capella: Martiani Minnei Felicis Capellae De Nuptiis Philologiae et Mercurii*. Ed. James Willis. Leipzig: BSB B.G. Teubner Verlagsgesellschaft, 1983.

– *Martianus Capella and the Seven Liberal Arts: The Marriage of Philology and Mercury*. Vol. 2. Trans. William Harris Stahl and Richard Johnson, with E.L. Burge. New York: Columbia University Press, 1977.

Censori, B., and E. Vittori. 'Il commento all'*Acerba* in un codice casanatense del secolo XV.' In B. Censori, ed., *Atti del I Convegno di studi su Cecco d'Ascoli*. Florence: Giunti-Barbèra, 1976: 231–6.

Colie, Rosalie L. *Paradoxia Epidemica: The Renaissance Tradition of Paradox*. Princeton: Princeton University Press, 1966.

– *The Resources of Kind: Genre Theory in the Renaissance*. Berkeley and Los Angeles: University of California Press, 1973.

Copeland, Rita. 'Literary Theory in the Later Middle Ages.' *Romance Philology* 41 (1987): 58–71.

– *Rhetoric, Hermeneutics, and Translation in the Middle Ages: Academic Traditions and Vernacular Texts*. Cambridge and New York: Cambridge University Press, 1991.

Crane, Ronald S., ed. *Critics and Criticism: Ancient and Modern*. Chicago: University of Chicago Press, 1952.

Croce, Benedetto. *Poesia e non poesia. Scritti di storia letteraria e politica 18.* Bari: Laterza, 1935.
Curtius, Ernst Robert. *European Literature and the Latin Middle Ages.* Trans. Willard R. Trask. Princeton: Princeton University Press, 1990 [1953, 1983].
De Robertis, Domenico. 'Commentare la poesia, commentare la prosa.' *Il commento ai testi: Atti del Seminario di Ascona, 2–9 ottobre 1989.* A cura di Ottavio Besomi e Carlo Caruso. Basel-Boston-Berlin: Birkhäuser Verlag, 1992: 169–213.
Dronke, Peter. *Verse with Prose from Petronius to Dante: The Art and Scope of the Mixed Form.* Cambridge and London: Harvard University Press, 1994.
Dunn, Kevin. *Pretexts of Authority: The Rhetoric of Authorship in the Renaissance Preface.* Stanford: Stanford University Press, 1994.
Fedi, Roberto. *La memoria della poesia: canzonieri, lirici e libri di rime nel Rinascimento.* Rome: Salerno, 1990.
Ferguson, Margaret W. *Trials of Desire: Renaissance Defenses of Poetry.* New Haven: Yale University Press, 1983.
Fish, Stanley. *Self-Consuming Artifacts: The Experience of Seventeenth-Century Literature.* Berkeley and Los Angeles: University of California Press, 1972.
Fletcher, Angus. *Allegory: The Theory of a Symbolic Mode.* Ithaca: Cornell University Press, 1964.
Folena, Gianfranco. 'Premessa.' In Gianfelice Peron. ed., *L'autocommento. Atti del XVIII Convegno Interuniversitario (Bressanone, 1990).* Padua: Esedra Editrice, 1994: 1–10.
Folkenflik, Robert, ed. *The Culture of Autobiography: Constructions of Self-Representation.* Stanford: Stanford University Press, 1993.
Frye, Northrop. *Anatomy of Criticism: Four Essays.* Princeton: Princeton University Press, 1957.
Gadamer, Hans Georg. *Truth and Method.* 2nd ed. Trans. Joel Winsheimer and Donald G. Marshall. New York: Continuum, 1998.
Genette, Gérard. *Paratexts: Thresholds of Interpretation.* Trans. Jane E. Lewin. Cambridge and New York: Cambridge University Press, 1997.
Grafton, Anthony. *Defenders of the Text: The Tradition of Scholarship in an Age of Science, 1450–1800.* Cambridge and London: Harvard University Press, 1991.
– *The Footnote: A Curious History.* Cambridge and London: Harvard University Press, 1997.
Greenblatt, Stephen Jay. *Renaissance Self-Fashioning: More to Shakespeare.* Chicago: University of Chicago Press, 1980.
Greene, Thomas. 'The Flexibility of the Self in Renaissance Literature.' *The Disciplines of Criticism.* Ed. Peter Demetz, Thomas Greene, and Lowry Nelson, Jr. New Haven: Yale University Press, 1968: 241–64.

- *The Light in Troy: Imitation and Discovery in Renaissance Poetry.* New Haven: Yale University Press, 1983.
- *The Vulnerable Text: Essays on Renaissance Literature.* New York: Columbia University Press, 1986.

Greenfield, Concetta C. *Humanist and Scholastic Poetics, 1250–1500.* Lewisburg: Bucknell University Press, 1981.

Guglielminetti, Marziano. *Memoria e scrittura. L'autobiografia da Dante a Cellini.* Turin: Einaudi, 1977.

Gusdorf, Georges. 'De l'autobiographie initiatique à l'autobiographie littéraire.' *Revue d'histoire littéraire de la France* 75(6) (1975): 957–94.

Häring, Nikolaus M. 'Commentary and Hermeneutics.' In Robert L. Benson and Giles Constable, with Carol D. Lanham, eds., *Renaissance and Renewal in the Twelfth Century.* Cambridge: Harvard University Press, 1982. 173–200.

Hartman, Geoffrey H. 'Literary Commentary as Literature.' *Criticism in the Wilderness.* New Haven: Yale University Press, 1980.

Hathaway, B. *The Age of Criticism: The Late Renaissance in Italy.* Ithaca: Cornell University Press, 1962.

Helgerson, Richard. *Self-Crowned Laureates: Spenser, Jonson, Milton, and the Literary System.* Berkeley and Los Angeles: University of California Press, 1983.

Hilbert, Betsy. 'Elegy for Excursus: The Descent of the Footnote.' *College English* 51 (1989): 400–4.

The Holy Bible. Douay-Rheims edition. Baltimore: John Murphy Company, 1914.

Jackson, H.J. *Marginalia: Readers Writing in Books.* New Haven and London: Yale University Press, 2001.

Jeanneret, Michel. 'Commentary on Fiction, Fiction as Commentary.' *South Atlantic Quarterly* 91(4) (1992): 909–28.

Kahn, Victoria. 'Humanism and the Resistance to Theory.' In Patricia Parker and David Quint, eds., *Literary Theory/Renaissance Texts.* Baltimore: Johns Hopkins University Press, 1986: 373–96.

Kamuf, Peggy. *Signature Pieces: On the Institution of Authorship.* Ithaca: Cornell University Press, 1988.

Kermode, Frank. *The Genesis of Secrecy: On the Interpretation of Narrative.* Cambridge and London: Harvard University Press, 1979.

Kirkpatrick, Robin. *English and Italian Literature from Dante to Shakespeare: A Study of Source, Analogue, and Divergence.* Longman Medieval and Renaissance Library. London and New York: Longman, 1995.

Marcus, Leah S. *Unediting the Renaissance: Shakespeare, Marlowe, Milton.* London and New York: Routledge, 1996.

Mathieu-Castellani, Gisèle. 'Le commentaire de la poésie (1550–1630): L'écriture du genre.' In Gisèle Mathieu-Castellani and Michel Plaisance, eds., *Les commentaires et la naissance de la critique littéraire*. Paris: Aux Amateurs de Livres, 1990.

Mazzeo, Joseph Anthony. *Renaissance and Seventeenth-Century Studies*. New York: Columbia University Press, 1964.

Miller, Jacqueline T. *Poetic License: Authority and Authorship in Medieval and Renaissance Contexts*. New York: Oxford University Press, 1986.

Minnis, A.J., and A.B. Scott, eds., with the assistance of David Wallace. *Medieval Literary Theory and Criticism c. 1100–c. 1375: The Commentary Tradition*. Oxford: Clarendon Press, 1988.

Minnis, A.J. *Medieval Theory of Authorship*. Philadelphia: University of Pennsylvania Press, 1988.

Morson, Gary Saul. *The Boundaries of Genre*. Austin: University of Texas Press, 1981.

Nelson, John Charles. 'Prose Commentaries on Verses.' *Renaissance Theory of Love: The Context of Giordano Bruno's* Eroici furori. New York: Columbia University Press, 1958: 15–66.

Noakes, Susan. *Timely Reading: Between Exegesis and Interpretation*. Ithaca: Cornell University Press, 1988.

Olney, James. *Metaphors of Self: The Meaning of Autobiography*. Princeton: Princeton University Press, 1972.

Oppenheimer, Paul. *The Birth of the Modern Mind: Self, Consciousness, and the Invention of the Sonnet*. New York: Oxford University Press, 1989.

Patterson, Lee. 'On the Margin: Postmodernism, Ironic History, and Medieval Studies.' *Speculum* 65 (1990): 87–108.

Poe, Elizabeth W. *Compilatio: Lyric Texts and Prose Commentaries in Troubadour Manuscript H (Vat. Lat. 3207)*. The Edward C. Armstrong Monographs on Medieval Literature, vol. 2. Lexington: French Forum Publishers, 2000.

Psaki, Francies Regina. 'The Medieval Lyric-Narrative Hybrid: Formal Play and Narratorial Subjectivity.' PhD dissertation. Cornell, 1989.

Quint, David. *Origin and Originality in Renaissance Literature*. New Haven: Yale University Press, 1983.

– 'Introduction.' In Patricia Parker and David Quint, eds., *Literary Theory/Renaissance Texts*. Baltimore: Johns Hopkins University Press, 1986: 1–19.

Sasso, Luigi. 'Il nome dell'autore.' *Il nome nella letteratura: L'interpretazione dei nomi negli scrittori italiani del medioevo*. Genoa: Marietti, 1990.

Segre, Cesare. 'Definizione del commento.' In Ottavio Besomi and Carlo Caruso, eds., *Il commento ai testi. Atti del Seminario di Ascona, 2–9 ottobre 1989*. Basel: Birkhäuser Verlag, 1992: 1–17.

Simpson, James. *Sciences and the Self in Medieval Poetry: Alan of Lille's* Anticlaudianus *and John Gower's* Confessio amantis. Cambridge Studies in Medieval Literature 25. Cambridge: Cambridge University Press, 1995.

Smalley, Beryl. *The Study of the Bible in the Middle Ages*. Oxford: Clarendon Press, 1941.

Spenser, Edmund. *The Yale Edition of the Shorter Poems*. Ed. William A. Oram et al. New Haven and London: Yale University Press, 1989.

Spitzer, Leo. 'Note on the Poetic and Empirical "I" in Medieval Authors.' *Romanische Literatur-Studien 1936–1956*. Tübingen: Max Niemeyer Verlag, 1959: 100–12.

Steiner, George. *Real Presences: Is there anything in what we say?* London and Boston: Faber and Faber, 1989.

Stillinger, Thomas C. *The Song of Troilus: Lyric Authority in the Medieval Book*. Philadelphia: University of Pennsylvania Press, 1992.

Weintraub, Karl J. 'Autobiography and Historical Consciousness.' *Critical Inquiry* 1 (1975): 821–48.

– *The Value of the Individual: Self and Circumstance in Autobiography*. Chicago: University of Chicago Press, 1978.

Wimsatt, Jr, William K. and Monroe Beardsley. 'The Intentional Fallacy.' *Sewanee Review* 54 (1946). Repr. in Wimsatt's *The Verbal Icon: Studies in the Meaning of Poetry*. Lexington, 1954.

Zimmerman, T.C. Price. 'Confession and Autobiography in the Early Renaissance.' In A. Molho and J.A. Tedeschi, eds., *Renaissance Studies in Honor of Hans Baron*. Florence: Sansoni, 1971: 121–40.

Dante Alighieri and Giovanni Boccaccio

Anderson, David. 'Boccaccio's Glosses on Statius.' *Studi sul Boccaccio* 22 (1994): 3–134.

Ascoli, Albert Russell. 'Neminem ante nos': Historicity and Authority in the *De vulgari eloquentia*.' *Annali d'Italianistica* 8 (1990): 186–231.

– 'Palinode and History in the Oeuvre of Dante.' In Theodore J. Cachey, Jr., ed., *Dante Now: Current Trends in Dante Studies*. Notre Dame and London: University of Notre Dame, 1995. 155–87.

– 'The Unfinished Author: Dante's Rhetoric of Authority in *Convivio* and *De vulgari eloquentia*.' In Rachel Jacoff, ed., *The Cambridge Companion to Dante*. Cambridge and New York: Cambridge University Press, 1993. 45–66.

– 'The Vowels of Authority (Dante's *Convivio* IV.vi.3–4).' In Kevin Brownlee and Walter Stevens, eds., *Discourses of Authority in Medieval and Renaissance Literature*. Hanover: University Press of New England, 1989. 23–46.

Bacci, Orazio. *Il Boccaccio lettore di Dante*. Florence: Sansoni, 1913.
Baranski, Zygmunt G. 'Dante and Medieval Poetics.' In Amilcare Iannucci, ed., *Dante: Contemporary Perspectives*. Toronto and Buffalo: University of Toronto Press, 1997. 3–22.
– 'Dante commentatore e commentato: Riflessioni sullo studio dell'*iter* ideologico di Dante.' *Letture classensi* 23 (1994): 135–58.
Barbi, Michele. *Dante nel Cinquecento*. Pisa: Bocca, 1890.
Bambaglioli, Graziolo. *Trattato delle volgari sentenze sopra le virtù morali*. Modena: Per gli eredi Soliani, 1821.
Bariola, Felice. *Cecco d'Ascoli e L'Acerba*. Florence: Tipografia della Gazzetta d'Italia, 1879.
Barolini, Teodolinda. *Dante's Poets: Textuality and Truth in the* Comedy. Princeton: Princeton University Press, 1984.
Battaglia, Salvatore. 'Dante tra *Vita nuova* e *Convivio*.' *Filologia e letteratura* 11(2) (1965): 113–28.
Bérard, Claude Cazalé. 'Boccaccio e la poetica: Mercurio, Orfeo e Giasone, tre chiavi dell'avventura ermeneutica.' *Studi sul Boccaccio* 22 (1994): 277–306.
– 'Dante e Boccaccio: Due strategie del narrare d'amore.' *Rassegna Europea di Letteratura Italiana* 4 (1994): 11–34.
Billanovich, Giuseppe. 'L'Orazio Morgan e gli studi del giovane Petrarca.' *Tradizione classica e letteratura umanistica. Per Alessandro Perosa*. A cura di Roberto Cardini et al. Rome: Bulzoni, 1985.
Boccaccio, Giovanni. *Boccaccio on Poetry. Being the Preface and the Fourteenth and Fifteenth Books of Boccaccio's* Genealogia Deorum Gentilium. Trans. and ed. Charles G. Osgood. Indianapolis and New York: Bobbs-Merrill Co, Inc., 1956.
– *The Book of Theseus*. Trans. Bernadette Marie McCoy. New York: Medieval Text Association, 1974.
– *Il comento alla 'Divina Commedia' e gli altri scritti intorno a Dante*. A cura di Domenico Guerri. Vol. 1. Bari: Laterza, 1918.
– *Teseida delle nozze d'Emilia*. A cura di Alberto Limentani. Milan: Mondadori, 1992.
Botterill, Steven. 'Dante and the Authority of Poetic Language.' In Amilcare Iannucci, ed., *Dante: Contemporary Perspectives*. Toronto and Buffalo: University of Toronto Press, 1997. 167–80.
– '"Però che la divisione non si fa se non per aprire la sentenzia de la cosa divisa" (*VN* XIV, 13): The *Vita Nuova* as Commentary.' In Vincent Moleta, ed., *La Gloriosa donna de la mente: A Commentary on the* Vita Nuova. Italian Medieval and Renaissance Studies, University of Western Australia, vol. 5. Florence: Olschki and Perth: Department of Italian, University of Western Australia, 1994: 61–76.

Cambon, Glauco. *Dante's Craft: Studies in Language and Style*. Minneapolis: University of Minnesota Press, 1969.
Charity, A.C. *Events and Their Afterlife: The Dialectics of Christian Typology in the Bible and Dante*. Cambridge: Cambridge University Press, 1966.
Ciociola, Claudio. 'L'autoesegesi di Cecco d'Ascoli.' In Gianfelice Peron, ed., *L'Autocommento. Atti del XVIII Convegno Interuniversitario (Bressanone, 1990)*. Quaderni del Circolo Filologico-Linguistico Padovano 17. Padua: Esedra, 1988. 31–42.
Croce, Benedetto. *La poesia di Dante*. Bari: Laterza, 1921.
D'Andrea, Antonio. *Il nome della storia: Studi e ricerche di storia e letteratura*. Naples: Liguori, 1982.
– *Strutture inquiete: Premesse teoriche e verifiche storico-letterarie*. Florence: Olschki, 1993.
Dante Alighieri. *Convivio*. Vol. 4 of *Opere di Dante*. Ed. Giovanni Busnelli and Giuseppe Vandelli. Florence: Felice Le Monnier, 1964.
– *Convivio*. Ed. Maria Simonelli. Bologna: Casa Editrice Prof. Riccardo Pàtron, 1966.
– *Convivio. The Banquet*. Trans. Christopher Ryan. Stanford French and Italian Studies 61. Saratoga, Cal.: ANMA Libri & Co., 1989.
– *Convivio*. Ed. Piero Cudini. Milan: Garzanti, 1990.
– *Convivio. The Banquet*. Trans. Richard H. Lansing. Garland Library of Medieval Literature. Vol. 65, ser. B. New York and London: Garland Publishing, Inc., 1990.
– *Convivio*. Ed. Franca Brambilla Ageno. Società Dantesca Italiana. Vol. 2. Florence: Le Lettere, 1995.
– *Dante's Vita Nuova*. Trans. and essay by Mark Musa. Bloomington and London: Indiana University Press, 1973.
– *The Divine Comedy*. Trans. with a commentary by Charles S. Singleton. 6 vols. Bollingen Series 80. Princeton: Princeton University Press, 1991 [1970].
– *Opere minori*. Ed. Domenico DeRobertis and Gianfranco Contini. Vol. 1:1. Milan and Naples: Riccardo Ricciardi, 1979.
– *Vita Nuova*. Ed. Michele Barbi. Opere minori di Dante Alighieri – Edizione critica, Società Dantesca Italiana. Florence: 1907 [Edizione Nazionale delle Opere di Dante. Florence: Bemporad e figlio, 1932].
– *Vita Nuova*. A cura di Edoardo Sanguineti. Milan: Garzanti, 1977.
– *Vita Nuova*. Trans. Dino S. Cervigni and Edward Vasta. Notre Dame and London: University of Notre Dame Press, 1995.
– *Vita Nova*. Ed. Guglielmo Gorni. Turin: Einaudi, 1996.
D'Ascoli, Cecco. *L'Acerba*. A cura di Achille Crespi. Ascoli Piceno: G. Cesari, 1927.

De Robertis, Domenico. 'Petrarca interprete di Dante (Ossia leggere Dante con Petrarca.)' *Studi danteschi* 61 (1989): 307–28.

Dronke, Peter. *Dante and Medieval Latin Traditions*. Cambridge and New York: Cambridge University Press, 1986.

Durling, Robert M., and Ronald L. Martinez. *Time and the Crystal: Studies in Dante's Rime Petrose*. Berkeley and Los Angeles: University of California Press, 1990.

Franke, William. *Dante's Interpretive Journey*. Chicago: University of Chicago Press, 1996.

Freccero, John. *Poetics of Conversion*. Ed. with intro. by Rachel Jacoff. Cambridge: Harvard University Press, 1986.

Gilson, Étienne. *Dante and Philosophy*. Trans. David Moore. New York: Harper Torchbooks, 1963.

Goldin, D. 'Autotraduzione latina nei *Documenti d'Amore* di Francesco da Barberino.' *Atti dell'Istituto Veneto di Scienze, Lettere ed Arti*. Classe di scienze morali, lettere ed arti 133 (1974–5): 371–92.

Guerri, Domenico. *Il commento del Boccaccio a Dante: Limiti della sua autenticità e questioni critiche che n'emergono*. Bari: Laterza & Figli, 1926.

Harrison, Robert Pogue. *The Body of Beatrice*. Baltimore and London: Johns Hopkins University Press, 1988.

Hollander, Robert. 'Dante *Theologus-Poeta*.' *Dante Studies* 94 (1976): 91–136.

– 'Imitative Distance: Boccaccio and Dante.' In John D. Lyons and Stephen G. Nichols, eds., *Mimesis: From Mirror to Method, Augustine to Descartes*. Hanover and London: University Press of New England, 1982. 83–99.

– 'The Validity of Boccaccio's Self-Exegesis.' *Medievalia et Humanitas* 8.ns (1977): 163–83.

Huygens, R.B.C. *Accessus ad auctores : Bernard d'Utrecht and Conrad d'Hirsau*. Leiden: E.J. Brill, 1970.

Iannucci, Amilcare A. 'Autoesegesi dantesca. La tecnica dell'episodio parallelo nella *Commedia*.' *Lettere italiane* 33 (1981): 305–28.

– ed. *Dante: Contemporary Perspectives*. Toronto and Buffalo: University of Toronto Press, 1997.

Kirkham, Victoria. '"Chiuso parlare" in Boccaccio's *Teseida*.' In Aldo S. Bernardo and Anthony L. Pellegrini, eds., *Dante, Petrarch, Boccaccio: Studies in the Italian Trecento In Honor of Charles S. Singleton*. Binghamton, N.Y.: Medieval and Renaissance Texts and Studies, 1983. 305–51.

Kleinhenz, Christopher. 'Dante and the Art of Citation.' In Theodore J. Cachey, Jr., ed., *Dante Now: Current Trends in Dante Studies*. Notre Dame and London: University of Notre Dame, 1995. 43–61.

Lansing, Richard H. 'Dante's Intended Audience in the *Convivio.*' *Dante Studies* 110 (1992): 17–4.

Limentani, Alberto. 'Tendenze della prosa del Boccaccio ai margini del *Teseida.*' *Giornale storico della letteratura italiana* 135 (1958): 524–51.

MacLennan, L. Jenaro. 'Autocomentario en Dante y comentarismo latino.' *Vox Romanica* 19 (1960): 82–123.

Martinez, Ronald L. 'Before the *Teseida*: Statius and Dante in Boccaccio's Epic.' *Studi sul Boccaccio* 20 (1991–2): 205–19.

Mazzeo, Joseph A. *Medieval Cultural Tradition in Dante's* Comedy. Ithaca: Cornell University Press, 1960.

Mazzotta, Giuseppe. *Dante, Poet of the Desert: History and Allegory in the* Divine Comedy. Princeton: Princeton University Press, 1979.

– *Dante's Vision and the Circle of Knowledge*. Princeton: Princeton University Press, 1993.

– 'Teologia ed esegesi biblica.' In Giovanni Barblan, ed., *Dante e la Bibbia*. Atti del Convegno Internazionale promosso da *Biblia*, Firenze, 26–8 settembre, 1986. Florence: Olschki, 1988. 95–112.

McGregor, James H. 'Boccaccio's Glosses to *Teseida* and his Knowledge of Lactantius' Commentary on Statius' *Thebaid.*' *Studi sul Boccaccio* 14 (1983–4): 302–9.

Menocal, María Rosa. *Writing in Dante's Cult of Truth: From Borges to Boccaccio*. Durham and London: Duke University Press, 1991.

Migliorini, Bruno. *Storia della lingua italiana*. Florence: Sansoni, 1983 [1960].

Milanese, Angela. 'Affinità e contraddizioni tra rubriche e novelle del *Decameron.*' *Studi sul Boccaccio* 23 (1995): 89–111.

Moore, Edward. *Studies in Dante*, 1st ser. New York: Greenwood Press, 1968 (1896).

Moore, Stephen D. *Literary Criticism and the Gospels: The Theoretical Challenge*. New Haven and London: Yale University Press, 1989.

Nardi, Bruno. *Dal 'Convivio' alla 'Commedia': Sei saggi danteschi*. Rome: Istituto Storico Italiano per il Medio Evo, 1992.

– 'La vivanda e il pane del *Convivio.*' *L'Alighieri* 6(2) (1965): 54–7.

Nolan, Edward Peter. 'Self as Other: Medieval Commentary and the Domain of the Letter.' *Now Through a Glass Darkly: Specular Images of Being and Knowing from Virgil to Chaucer*. Ann Arbor: University of Michigan Press, 1990. 83–114.

Parker, Deborah. *Commentary and Ideology: Dante in the Renaissance*. Durham and London: Duke University Press, 1993.

Perrin, Norman. *Jesus and the Language of the Kingdom: Symbol and Metaphor in New Testament Interpretation*. Philadelphia: Fortress Press, 1976.

Perrus, Claudette. 'Dante critique de Dante.' In Gisèle Mathieu-Castellani and Michel Plaisance, eds., *Les commentaires et la naissance de la critique littéraire*. Paris: Aux Amateurs de Livres, 1988. 83–9.

Pertile, Lino. 'A Desire of Paradise and a Paradise of Desire: Dante and Mysticism.' In Amilcare A. Iannucci, ed., *Dante: Contemporary Perspectives*. Toronto and Buffalo: University of Toronto Press, 1997. 148–66.

Peterman, Larry. 'Reading the *Convivio*.' *Dante Studies* 103 (1985): 125–38.

Petrarca, Francesco. *Il Codice Vaticano Lat. 3196*. Intro. Mandredi Porena. Codices e vaticanis selecti 26. Biblioteca Apostolica Vaticana, 1941.

– *Opere italiane. Il Canzoniere*. Vol. 1. A cura di Marco Santagata. Milan: Mondadori, 1996.

– *Petrarch's Lyric Poems: The Rime Sparse and Other Lyrics*. Trans. Robert M. Durling. Cambridge and London: Harvard University Press, 1976.

Pflaum, Hans. 'L'*Acerba* di Cecco d'Ascoli. Saggio d'interpretazione.' *Archivum romanicum* 23 (1939): 178–241.

Picone, Michelangelo. 'Strutture poetiche e strutture prosastiche nella *Vita Nuova*.' *Modern Language Notes* 92 (1977): 117–29.

– 'La *Vita Nuova* fra autobiografia e tipologia.' *Dante e le forme dell'allegoresi*. Ed. Michelangelo Picone. Ravenna: Longo Editore, 1987. 59–69.

Pietrobono, Luigi. *Saggi danteschi*. Turin: Società Editrice Internazionale, 1954.

Raffa, Guy. *Divine Dialectic: Dante's Incarnational Poetry*. Toronto: University of Toronto Press, 2000.

Ransom, Daniel J. '*Panis Angelorum*: A Palinode in the *Paradiso*.' *Dante Studies* 95 (1977): 81–94.

Rajna, Pio. 'Per le "divisioni" della *Vita Nuova*.' *Strenna dantesca* 1 (1902): 111–14.

Ricci, Roberta. 'Il Commento d'autore: Boccaccio, Tasso, Foscolo, Saba.' PhD dissertation, Johns Hopkins University, 1999.

Rivers, Elias L. 'Dante at Dividing Sonnets.' *Symposium* 2 (1957): 290–5.

Russo, Vittorio. 'Voi che "ntendendo" e "Amor che ne la mente": La diffrazione dei significati secondo l'auto-commento del *Convivio*.' In Gianfelice Peron, ed., *L'autocommento. Atti del XVIII Convegno Interuniversitario (Bressanone, 1990)*. Quaderni del Circolo Filologico-Linguistico Padovano 17. Padua: Esedra, 1988. 11–19.

Sarolli, Gian Roberto. *Prolegomena alla 'Divina commedia.'* Florence: Leo S. Olschki, 1971.

Schnapp, Jeffrey T. 'A Commentary on Commentary' in *South Atlantic Quarterly* 91(4) (Fall 1992): 813–34.

– 'Un commento all'autocommento nel *Teseida*.' *Studi sul Boccaccio* 20 (1991–2): 185–203.

Shapiro, Marianne. 'On the Role of Rhetoric in the *Convivio.*' *Romance Philology* 40(1) (1986): 38–64.
Singleton, Charles S. *Essay on the 'Vita Nuova.'* Baltimore: Johns Hopkins University Press, 1949.
– *Journey to Beatrice*. Dante Studies II. Cambridge: Harvard University Press, 1958; Baltimore: Johns Hopkins University Press, 1977.
– '*Vita Nuova XII*: Love's Obscure Words.' *Romanic Review* 36(2) (April 1945): 89–102.
Smarr, Janet Levarie. 'Before Fiammetta: *Teseida.*' *Boccaccio and Fiammetta: The Narrator as Lover*. Chicago: University of Illinois Press, 1986: 61–82.
Steiner, George. *Real Presences: Is there anything in what we say?* London and Boston: Faber and Faber, 1989.
Tateo, Francesco. *Questioni di poetica dantesca*. Bari: Adriatica Editrice, 1972.
Took, J.F. *Dante, Lyric Poet and Philosopher: An Introduction to the Minor Works*. Oxford: Clarendon Press, 1990.
Trovato, Mario. 'Il primo trattato del *Convivio.*' *Misure critiche* 6 (1976): 5–14.
Vallone, Aldo. 'Boccaccio lettore di Dante.' *Giovanni Boccaccio editore e interprete di Dante*. A cura della Società Dantesca Italiana. Atti del convegno su 'Giovanni Boccaccio editore e interprete di Dante' (Firenze-Certaldo, 19–20 aprile 1975). Florence: Leo S. Olschki, 1979. 91–117.
– *La prosa del 'Convivio.'* Florence: Felice Le Monnier, 1967.
– *La prosa della 'Vita Nuova.'* Florence: Felice Le Monnier, 1963.
Vandelli, Giuseppe. 'Un autografo della *Teseida.*' *Studi di filologia italiana* 2 (1929).
Vickers, Nancy J. 'Widowed Words: Dante, Petrarch, and the Metaphors of Mourning.' In Kevin Brownlee and Walter Stephens, eds., *Discourses of Authority in Medieval and Renaissance Literature*. Hanover and London: University Press of New England, 1989.
Wailes, Stephen L. *Medieval Allegories of Jesus' Parables*. Berkeley and Los Angeles: University of California Press, 1987.
Warkentin, Germaine. 'The Form of Dante's "Libello" and its Challenge to Petrarch.' *Quaderni d'Italianistica* 2 (1981): 160–70.
Wetherbee, Winthrop. 'History and Romance in Boccaccio's *Teseida.*' *Studi sul Boccaccio* 20 (1991–2): 173–84.
Wilkins, Ernest Hatch. *The Making of the 'Canzoniere' and Other Petrarchan Studies*. Rome: Edizioni di Storia e Letteratura, 1951.
Zambon, Francesco. 'Allegoria e linguaggio dell'ineffabilità nell'autoesegesi dantesca dell'"Epistola a Cangrande."' In Gianfelice Peron, ed., *L'autocommento. Atti del XVIII Convegno Interuniversitario (Bressanone, 1990)*. Quaderni del Circolo Filologico-Linguistico Padovano, 17. Padua: Esedra, 1988. 21–30.

Lorenzo de' Medici and Girolamo Benivieni

Allen, Michael J.B. *Marsilio Ficino and the Phaedran Charioteer.* Publications of the Center for Medieval and Renaissance Studies, UCLA 14. Berkeley and Los Angeles: University of California Press, 1981.
- *The Platonism of Marsilio Ficino: A Study of His* Phaedrus *Commentary, Its Sources and Genesis.* Center for Medieval and Renaissance Studies, UCLA, vol. 21. Berkeley and Los Angeles: University of California Press, 1984.
- 'The Second Ficino-Pico Controversy: Parmenidean Poetry, Eristic, and the One.' *Plato's Third Eye: Studies in Marsilio Ficino's Metaphysics and Its Sources.* Collected Studies Series. Brookfield, VT: Variorum Ashgate Publishers Company, 1995.

Batkin, Leonid M. *L'idea di individualità nel Rinascimento italiano.* Trans. Valentina Rossi. Bari: Laterza, 1992.

Battera, Francesca. 'Le egloghe di Girolamo Benivieni.' *Interpres* 10 (1990): 133–223.
- 'Per l'esegesi della III egloga di Gerolamo Beniventi.' [sic] *Studi e problemi di critica testuale* 38 (April 1989): 45–69.

Benivieni, Girolamo. *Canzone et sonetti di Girolamo Benivieni fiorentino. Come, dove, quando, e di cui prima se innamora, et quale fructo ne seguitasse.* Codice Sessoriano 413 (cart. misc. 495. XV). Biblioteca Nazionale Centrale Vittorio Emanuele, Rome.
- *Commento di Hieronymo Benivieni sopra a più sue canzone et sonetti dello Amore et della belleza divina.* Florence: Antonio Tubini, Lorenzo (de Alopo) Veneziano e Andrea Ghirlandi, 1500 [This work is also occasionally referred to as *Canzoni et sonetti con commento.*].
- *Dialogo di Antonio Manetti, cittadino fiorentino, circa al sito, forma et misure dello Inferno di Dante Alighieri, poeta excellentissimo.* Intro. Nicola Zingarelli. 'Collezione di Opuscoli Danteschi inediti o rari.' Città di Castello: S. Lapi, 1897.
- *Opere.* Florence: Per li heredi di Philippo di Giunta, 1519.

Bigi, Emilio. 'Lorenzo lirico.' *Dal Petrarca al Leopardi.* Milan: Ricciardi, 1954: 23–45.

Brownlee, Kevin. 'Phaeton's Fall and Dante's Ascent.' *Dante Studies* 102 (1984): 135–44.

Dempsey, Charles. *The Portrayal of Love: Botticelli's Primavera and Humanist Culture at the Time of Lorenzo the Magnificent.* Princeton: Princeton University Press, 1992.

De Robertis, Domenico. *Editi e rari.* Milan: Feltrinelli, 1978.

Dronke, Peter. *Fabula: Explorations into the Uses of Myth in Medieval Platonism.* Mittellateinische Studien und Texte 9. Leiden and Cologne: E.J. Brill, 1974.

Ficino, Marsilio. *Commentary on Plato's Symposium on Love.* Trans. Sears Jayne. Dallas: Spring Publications, Inc., 1985.
- *El libro dell'amore.* A cura di Sandra Niccoli. Istituto Nazionale di Studi sul Rinascimento 16. Florence: Olschki, 1987.
- *Opera Omnia.* Con una lettera introduttiva di Paul Oskar Kristeller e una premessa di Mario Sancipriano. 2 vols. Turin: Bottega d'Erasmo, 1962– .
- *Sopra lo amore, ovvero Convito di Platone.* A cura di Giuseppe Rensi. Cultura dell'anima. Lanciano: R. Carabba, 1914.
- *Three Books on Life.* Critical edition and trans. Carol V. Kaske and John R. Clark. Medieval & Renaissance Texts & Studies vol. 57. Binghamton: Renaissance Society of America, 1989.

Field, Arthur. *The Origins of the Platonic Academy of Florence.* Princeton: Princeton University Press, 1988.

Fubini, Mario. 'Nota sulla prosa di Lorenzo il Magnifico.' *Studi sulla letteratura del Rinascimento.* Florence: Sansoni, 1948. 126–37.

Garin, Eugenio. 'Marsilio Ficino, Girolamo Benivieni e Giovanni Pico.' *Giornale critico della filosofia italiana* 23. 1–2 (1942): 93–9.
- a cura di. *Prosatori latini del Quattrocento.* La Letteratura Italiana: Storia e testi 13. Milan and Naples: Riccardo Ricciardi, 1952.

Giraud, Yves F.-A. *La fable de Daphné: Essai sur un type de métamorphose végétale dans la littérature et dans les arts jusqu'a la fin du XVII siècle.* Geneva: Librairie Droz, 1968.

Greco, Aulo. 'Dante nella poesia di Lorenzo de' Medici.' *Dante nel pensiero e nella esegesi dei secoli XIV e XV.* Atti del III Congresso Nazionale di Studi Danteschi (Melfi, 27 Sept.–2 Oct. 1970). Florence: Olschki, 1975. 117–26.

Hyatte, Reginald. 'A Poetics of Ficino's "Socratic Love": Medieval Discursive Models of *Amor* in Marsilio Ficino's and Lorenzo de' Medici's Amatory Epistles.' *Fifteenth-Century Studies* 20 (1993): 99–117.

Hyde, Thomas. *The Poetic Theology of Love: Cupid in Renaissance Literature.* Newark: University of Delaware Press, 1986.

Jayne, Sears. 'Benivieni's Christian Canzone.' *Rinascimento: Rivista dell'Istituto Nazionale di Studi sul Rinascimento* 24 (1984): 153–80.

Kantorowicz, Ernst H. *The King's Two Bodies: A Study of Mediaeval Political Theology.* Princeton: Princeton University Press, 1957.

Kennedy, William J. 'Petrarchan Figurations of Death in Lorenzo de' Medici's Sonnets and *Comento*.' In Marcel Tetel, Ronald G. Witt, and Rona Goffen, eds., *Life and Death in Fifteenth-Century Florence.* Durham and London: Duke University Press, 1989: 46–67.

Ladner, Gerhart B. *The Idea of Reform: Its Impact on Christian Thought and Action in the Age of the Fathers.* Cambridge: Harvard University Press, 1959.

Lipari, Angelo. *The Dolce Stil Novo According to Lorenzo de' Medici: A Study of His Poetic Principio as an Interpretation of the Italian Literature of the Pre-Renaissance Period based on his* Comento. Yale Romanic Studies 12. New Haven: Yale University Press, 1936.

Lo Monaco, Francesco. 'Alcune osservazioni sul commento umanistico ai classici nel secondo Quattrocento.' In Ottavio Besomi and Carlo Caruso, eds., *Il commento ai testi. Atti del Seminario di Ascona, 2–9 ottobre 1989.* Basel: Birkhäuser Verlag, 1992: 103–54.

Lorenzo de' Medici. *The Autobiography of Lorenzo de' Medici the Magnificent: A Commentary on My Sonnets.* Together with the text of *Il Comento* in the critical edition of Tiziano Zanato. Trans. James Wyatt Cook. Medieval & Renaissance Texts & Studies 129. Binghamton, N.Y.: Center for Medieval and Early Renaissance Studies, 1995.

– *Tutte le opere.* vol. 1. A cura di Paolo Orvieto. Testi e documenti di letteratura e di lingua 14. Rome: Salerno, 1992.

– *Canzoniere di Lorenzo de' Medici.* A cura di Paolo Orvieto. Milan: Mondadori, 1984.

Marsh, David. 'Ovid in Tuscany: Myth and Unity in Lorenzo's *Ambra*.' *Stanford Italian Review* 11 (1992): 75–90.

Martelli, Mario. 'L'autografo laurenziano del "Comento dei Sonetti."' *La Bibliofilia* 68 (1966): 233–71.

– 'Questioni di cronologia laurenziana.' *Lettere italiane* 18 (1966): 249–61.

– *Studi laurenziani.* Biblioteca di 'Lettere italiane' 2. Florence: Olschki, 1965.

Mazzacurati, Giancarlo. 'Storia e funzione della poesia lirica nel *Comento* di Lorenzo de' Medici.' *Modern Language Notes* 104(1) (1989): 48–67.

Mazzotta, Giuseppe. *The Worlds of Petrarch.* Durham and London: Duke University Press, 1993.

McLaughlin, Martin L. *Literary Imitation in the Italian Renaissance.* Oxford: Clarendon Press, 1995.

Nelson, John Charles. 'The Commentary of Giovanni Pico della Mirandola on Benivieni's *Canzone d'amore*.' *Renaissance Theory of Love: The Context of Giordano Bruno's* Eroici furori. New York: Columbia University Press, 1958. 54–63.

Orvieto, Paolo. 'Boccaccio mediatore di generi o dell'allegoria d'amore.' *Interpres* 2 (1979): 7–104.

Ovid. *The Metamorphoses of Ovid.* Trans. Allen Mandelbaum. New York: Harcourt Brace and Co., 1993.

– *Metamorphosis.* Trans. Horace Gregory. New York: Mentor, 1960 [Viking Press, 1958].

Pellizzari, Achille. 'Un'asceta del Rinascimento: La vita e le opere di Girolamo

Benivieni.' *Dal Duecento all'Ottocento: Ricerche e studi letterari*. Naples: Società Editrice F. Perrella, 1914. 257–363.
Pico della Mirandola, Giovanni. *Commentary on a Canzone of Benivieni*. Trans. Sears Jayne. American University Studies, ser. 2, vol. 19. New York: Peter Lang, 1984.
– *De hominis dignitate, Heptaplus, De ente et uno, e scritti vari*, a cura di Eugenio Garin. Edizione Nazionale dei classici del pensiero italiano 1. Florence: Vallecchi, 1942.
– *A Platonick Discourse upon Love*. Ed. Edmund G. Gardner. Boston: Merrymount Press, 1914.
Poliziano, Angelo. *Poesie volgari*. 2 vols. Ed. Francesco Bausi. Rome: Vecchiarelli, 1997.
Pugliese, Olga Zorzi. 'Benivieni's *Commento* and Bonaventure's *Itinerarium*: Autobiography and Ideology.' *Rivista di storia e letteratura religiosa* 30(2) (1994): 347–62.
– 'Il *Chronicon* di Angelo Clareno nel Rinascimento: Volgarizzamento postillato da Girolamo Benivieni.' *Archivum Franciscanum Historicum* 73(4) (1980): 514–26.
– 'Il *Commento* di Girolamo Benivieni ai Salmi Penitenziali.' *Vivens Homo* 5(2) (1994): 475–94.
– 'Girolamo Benivieni: umanista riformatore (dalla corrispondenza inedita).' *Bibliofilia* 72(3) (1970): 253–88.
– 'Variations on Ficino's *De Amore*: The Hymns to Love by Benivieni and Castiglione.' In Konrad Eisenbichler and Olga Zorzi Pugliese, eds., *Ficino and Renaissance Neoplatonism*. University of Toronto Italian Studies. Ottawa: Dovehouse, 1986. 1:113–22.
Quercioli, R. 'Spiritualità nel *Comento* di Lorenzo de' Medici.' *Città di vita* 2 (1947): 558–64.
Re, Caterina. *Girolamo Benivieni fiorentino: Cenni sulla vita e sulle opere*. Città di Castello: S. Lapi, 1906.
Rice, Eugene F. *The Renaissance Idea of Wisdom*. Cambridge: Harvard University Press, 1958.
Ridolfi, Roberto. 'Girolamo Benivieni e una sconosciuta revisione del suo *Canzoniere*.' *La bibliofilia* 56 (1964): 213–34.
Rochon, André. *La Jeunesse de Laurent de Medicis (1449–1478)*. Paris: Les Belles Lettres, 1963.
Scanferla, B.M. 'Per la data della *Raccolta Aragonese*.' *Rassegna bibliografica della letteratura italiana* 21 (1913): 244–50
Seznec, Jean. *The Survival of the Pagan Gods: The Mythological Tradition and Its*

Place in Renaissance Humanism and Art. Trans. Barbara F. Sessions. Bollingen Series 38. New York: Pantheon, 1953.
Shapiro, Marianne. 'Petrarch, Lorenzo il Magnifico and the Latin Elegiac Poets.' *Romance Notes* 15(1) (1973): 172–5.
– 'Poetry and Politics in the *Comento* of Lorenzo de' Medici.' *Renaissance Quarterly* 26(4) (1973): 444–53.
Sturm, Sara. *Lorenzo de' Medici*. New York: Twayne, 1974.
Tateo, Francesco. *'Retorica' e 'Poetica' fra medioevo e rinascimento*. Bari: Adriatica, 1960.
Tenenti, Alberto. *Il senso della morte e l'amore della vita nel Rinascimento*. Turin: Einaudi, 1957.
Vasoli, Cesare. 'Note su alcuni 'Proemi' e dediche di Marsilio Ficino.' *Strategie del testo: Preliminari Partizioni Pause. Atti del XVI e del XVII Convegno Interuniversitario (Bressanone, 1988 e 1989)*. A cura di Gianfelice Peron. Quaderni del Circolo Filologico-Linguistico Padovano, 16. Padua: Esedra, 1995: 133–50.
Zanato, Tiziano. *Saggio sul 'Comento' di Lorenzo de' Medici*. Biblioteca dell''Archivum Romanicum,' ser. 1, vol. 153. Florence: Olschki, 1979.
– 'Sul testo del *Comento* laurenziano.' *Studi di filologia italiana* 38 (1980): 71–152.

Giordano Bruno and Tommaso Campanella

Acquilecchia, Giovanni. *Giordano Bruno*. Rome: Istituto della enciclopedia italiana, 1971.
Amabile, Luigi. *Fra Tommaso Campanella, la sua congiura, i suoi processi e la sua pazzia*. 3 vols. Naples, 1882.
– *Fra Tommaso Campanella ne' castelli di Napoli, in Roma ed in Parigi*. 2 vols. Naples, 1887.
Amerio, Romano. 'Forme e significato del principio di autocoscienza in S. Agostino e in T. Campanella.' *Rivista di filosofia neoscolastica* 23 (1931): 75–114.
– 'Il problema esegetico fondamentale del pensiero campanelliano.' *Rivista di filosofia neoscolastica* 31 (1939): 368–87.
– 'Autobiografia medica di Fra Tommaso Campanella.' *Campanella e Vico*. Aavv. Archivio di Filosofia organo dell'Istituto di Studi Filosofici, Padua: CEDAM, 1969.
Badaloni, Nicola. 'Campanella poeta.' *Ultimi studi campanelliani*. Ed. Vincenzo Paladino. Messina: EDAS, 1978: 59–70.

Bàrberi Squarotti, Giorgio. 'Per una descrizione e interpretazione della poetica di Giordano Bruno.' *Studi secenteschi* 1 (1960): 39–56.

Bolzoni, Lina. 'La restaurazione della poesia nel proemio dei 'Commentaria' campanelliani.' *Annali della Scuola Normale Superiore di Pisa: Classe di Lettere e Filosofia* 1 ns (1971): 307–44.

– 'I 'Commentaria' di Campanella ai 'Poëmata' di Urbano VIII: Un uso infedele del commento umanistico.' *Rinascimento: Rivista dell'Istituto Nazionale di Studi sul Rinascimento* 28 (1988): 113–32.

Bruno, Giordano. *Dialoghi italiani*. 2 vols. Nuovamente ristampati con note da Giovanni Gentile. Terza edizione a cura di Giovanni Aquilecchia. Florence: Sansoni, 1985 (2a ristampa).

– *Eroici furori*. Intro. Michele Ciliberto. Ed. Simonetta Bassi. Rome and Bari: Laterza, 1995.

– *The Heroic Frenzies*. Trans. Paul Eugene Memmo, Jr. Studies in the Romance Languages and Literatures, vol. 50. Chapel Hill: University of North Carolina Press, 1964.

– *Oeuvres complètes*. Ed. Giovanni Aquilecchia et al. Vol. 7. Trans. Paul-Henri Michel. Paris: Les Belles Lettres, 1999.

– *Opere di Giordano Bruno e di Tommaso Campanella*. A cura di Augusto Guzzo e Romano Amerio. Milan: Riccardo Ricciardi, 1956.

– *Opere latine*. Ed. Francisco Fiorentino, Vittorio Imbriani, C.M. Tallarigo, Felice Tocco, e Girolamo Vitelli. 3 vols. Stuttgart-Bad Cannstatt: Friedrich Fromman Verlag Gunther Holzboog, 1962 [Naples and Florence: 1879–1891].

Campagnola, Stanislao da. *L'angelo del sesto sigillo e l'Alter Christus: Genesi e sviluppo di due temi francescani nei secoli XIII-XIV*. Rome, 1971.

Campanella, Tommaso. *De libris propriis et recta ratione studendi syntagma. Opuscoli Filosofici. Testi e documenti inediti o rari pubblicati da Giovanni Gentile*. Vol. 2. Ed. Vincenzo Spampanato. Milan: Bestetti e Tumminelli, 1927.

– *Opere di Giordano Bruno e di Tommaso Campanella*. A cura di Augusto Guzzo e Romano Amerio. Milan: Riccardo Ricciardi, 1956.

– *Opere letterarie di Tommaso Campanella*. Ed. Lina Bolzoni. Turin: UTET, 1977.

– *Tutte le opere di Tommaso Campanella*. Ed. Luigi Firpo. Verona: Mondadori, 1954.

Cerbu, Thomas. 'Dissimulation on Display: The Feint of Power in Campanella's *Scelta*.' In Ronald Bogue and Mihai I. Spariosu, eds., *The Play of the Self*. Albany: State University of New York Press, 1994. 203–19.

Ciliberto, Michele. *Giordano Bruno*. Rome and Bari: Laterza, 1992.

Corsano, Antonio. *Il pensiero di Giordano Bruno nel suo svolgimento storico*. Florence: Sansoni, 1940.

Cro, Stelio. 'Tommaso Campanella and the Poetry of the Baroque.' *Romance Notes* 22(1) (1981): 88–93.

D'Elia, Francesco. 'La "terza età" gioachimita e la "Città del sole" di Tommaso Campanella.' In Antonio Crocco, ed., *L'età dello spirito e la fine dei tempi in Gioacchino da Fiore e nel gioachimismo medievale*. San Giovanni in Fiore: Centro Internazionale di Studi Gioachimiti, 1986.

De Carolis Pilotti, Laura. *Tommaso Campanella poeta*. Florence: Sansoni, 1942.

De Mattei, Rodolfo. *Studi campanelliani*. Florence: Sansoni, 1933.

Derrida, Jacques. *Psyché: Interventions de l'autre*. Paris: Galilée 1988.

Di Napoli, Giovanni. 'Il messaggio di Tommaso Campanella.' *Archivio storico per la Calabria e la Lucania* 36 (1968): 7–31.

Ellero, Maria Pia. 'Appunti sull'"Esposizione" alla "Scelta d'alcune poesie filosofiche" di Tommaso Campanella.' In Gianfelice Peron, ed., *L'autocommento. Atti del XVIII Convegno Interuniversitario (Bressanone, 1990)*. Padua: Esedra Editrice, 1994: 69–80.

Farley-Hills, David. 'The "Argomento" of Bruno's *De gli eroici furori* and Sidney's *Astrophil and Stella*.' *Modern Language Review* 87(1) (1992): 1–17.

Feldhay, Rivka, and Adi Ophir. 'Heresy and Hierarchy: The Authorization of Giordano Bruno.' *Stanford Humanities Review* 1(1) (1989): 118–38.

Ferruolo, A. 'Sir Philip Sidney e Giordano Bruno.' *Convivium* 5 nuova serie (1948).

Gentile, Giovanni. *Giordano Bruno e il pensiero del Rinascimento*. Bari: Laterza, 1925.

Getto, Giovanni. 'La poesia di Tommaso Campanella.' *Lettere italiane* 35(2) (1983): 157–66.

Grillo, Francesco. *Campanella e Dante*. Cosenza: Pellegrini, 1977.

Guglielminetti, Marziano. 'Magia e tecnica nella poetica di Tommaso Campanella.' *Rivista di estetica* 9 (1964): 361–400.

Headley, John M. 'Tommaso Campanella and the End of the Renaissance.' *Journal of Medieval and Renaissance Studies* 20(2) (1990): 157–74.

Isoldi, A.M. Jacobelli. *Tommaso Campanella. La crisi della coscienza di sè*. Milan: Fratelli Bocca Editori, 1953.

Kristeller, Paul Oskar. 'Between the Italian Renaissance and the French Enlightenment: G. Naudé as an Editor.' *Renaissance Quarterly* 32(1) (1979): 41–72.

Niccoli, Ottavia. *Profeti e popolo nell'Italia del Rinascimento*. Bari: Laterza, 1987.

Ong, W.J. 'From Allegory to the Diagram in the Renaissance.' *Journal of Aesthetics and Art Criticism* 17 (1959): 423–40.

Pastore, Annibale. 'Autocoscienza e intuizione lirica in T. Campanella.' *Sophia* 15 (1947): 50–9.

Pugliese, Olga Zorzi. 'Apocalyptic and Dantesque Elements in a Franciscan Prophecy of the Renaissance.' *PMR: Annual Publication of the Patristic, Mediaeval and Renaissance Conference*, 10 (1985). Villanova: Augustinian Historical Institute & Villanova University, 1986: 127–35.

Ruschioni, Ada. *Tommaso Campanella filosofo-poeta*. Brunello: Edizioni Otto/Novecento, 1980.
Sabbatino, Pasquale. *Giordano Bruno e la 'Mutazione' del Rinascimento*. Biblioteca dell''Archivum Romanicum' 254. Serie I-Storia-Letteratura-Paleografia. Florence: Leo S. Olschki, 1993.
Scalzo, Joseph. 'Campanella, Foucault, and Madness in Late-Sixteenth Century Italy.' *Sixteenth-Century Journal* 21 (1990): 359–71.
Sidney, Sir Philip. *An Apologie for Poetrie*. Ed. Evelyn S. Shuckburgh. Cambridge: Cambridge University Press, 1928.
Snyder, Jon R. *Writing the Scene of Speaking: Theories of Dialogue in the Late Italian Renaissance*. Stanford: Stanford University Press, 1989.
Spampanato, V. *Vita di Giordano Bruno*. Messina: Principato, 1921.
Symonds, John Addington, trans. *The Sonnets of Michael Angelo Buonarroti and Tommaso Campanella*. London: Smith, Elder & Co., 1878.
Tragella, Giovan Battista. 'T. Campanella e l'idea missionaria.' *Il pensiero missionario* 13 (1941): 302–13.
Tuscano, Pasquale. *Poetica e poesia di Tommaso Campanella*. Milan: Edizioni I.P.L., 1969.
– 'L'esperienza del carcere e le lodi delle creature al Creatore nella poesia del Campanella.' *Archivio storico per la Calabria e la Lucania* 36 (1968): 33–69.
Verzera, Antonino. *La poesia di Tommaso Campanella*. Naples: Federico e Ardia, 1968.
Walker, D.P. *Spiritual and Demonic Magic from Ficino to Campanella*. London: Warburg Institute, University of London, 1958.
Wutrich, Richard. *Prometheus and Faust: The Promethean Revolt in Drama from Classical Antiquity to Goethe*. Westport, Conn.: Greenwood Press, 1995.
Yates, Frances. *The Art of Memory*. Chicago: Chicago University Press, 1966.
– 'The Emblematic Conceit in Giordano Bruno's *De gli eroici furori* and in the Elizabethan Sonnet Sequences.' *Journal of the Warburg and Courtauld Institutes* 6 (1943): 101–21.
– *Giordano Bruno and the Hermetic Tradition*. Chicago: University of Chicago Press, 1964.
– 'The Religious Policy of Giordano Bruno.' *Journal of the Warburg and Courtauld Institutes* 3(3–4): 181–207.

Poetic Self-Commentary after the Renaissance

Ariani, Marco. *Drammaturgia e mitopoiesi. Antonio Conti scrittore*. Rome: Bulzoni, 1977.
Badaloni, Nicola. *Antonio Conti. Un abate libero pensatore fra Newton e Voltaire*. Milan: Feltrinelli, 1968.

Basile, Bruno. 'Autoesegesi e memoria poetica: Sette esposizioni del Tasso alle proprie *Rime.*' *Lingua e Stile* 7 (1972): 25–46.
Berry, Reginald. 'Absurder Projects: Scriblerus, Chaucer, and the Discommodities of Marriage.' *English Studies in Canada* 7(2) (Summer 1981): 141–55.
Besomi, Ottavio. 'L'autocommento nella "Secchia rapita."' In Gianfelice Peron, ed., *L'autocommento. Atti del XVIII Convegno Interuniversitario (Bressanone, 1990).* Padua: Esedra Editrice, 1994. 53–68.
Cappello, Giovanni. 'Le reazioni alla critica e l'autocommento (due esempi pirandelliani).' *Strumenti critici* 16(1) (1992): 103–28.
Cassirer, Ernst. *The Philosophy of Symbolic Forms.* Trans. Ralph Manheim. New Haven and London: Yale University Press, 1953.
Conti, Antonio. *Prose e poesie del Signor Abate Antonio Conti.* 2 vols. Venice: Giambattista Pasquali, 1756 [1739].
Dupré, Louis. *Passage to Modernity: An Essay in the Hermeneutics of Nature and Culture.* New Haven and London: Yale University Press, 1993.
Erickson, Robert A. 'Situations of Identity in the *Memoirs of Martinus Scriblerus.*' *Modern Language Quarterly* 26 (1965): 388–400.
Foucault, Michel. *Les mots et les choses.* Paris: Gallimard, 1966.
Gronda, Giovanna. 'Tradizione e innovazione: le versioni poetiche di Antonio Conti.' *Giornale storico della letteratura italiana* 147 (1970): 292–353.
Hammond, Brean S. 'Scriblerian Self-Fashioning.' *Yearbook of English Studies* 18 (1988): 108–24.
Kennedy, George A., ed., *The Cambridge History of Literary Criticism.* vol. 1. Cambridge and New York: Cambridge University Press, 1989.
Kenner, Hugh. *Flaubert, Joyce, and Beckett: The Stoic Comedians.* London: W.H. Allen, 1964.
Lund, Roger D. 'Martinus Scriblerus and the Search for the Soul.' *Papers on Language and Literature: A Journal for Scholars and Critics of Language and Literature* 25(2) (Spring 1989): 135–50.
– '*Res et Verba:* Scriblerian Satire and the Fate of Language.' *Bucknell Review* 27(2) (1983): 63–80.
Mancini, Albert N. 'Alessandro Tassoni: Between the Renaissance and the Baroque.' *Italian Quarterly* 54 (1970): 113–20.
Menzini, Benedetto. *Poetica e satire di Benedetto Menzini con annotazioni.* Milan: Società Tipografica de' Classici Italiani, 1808.
Nabokov, Vladimir. *Pale Fire.* New York: Random House, 1989 [1962].
Nicoletti, Giuseppe. 'Introduzione all'autobiografia italiana del Settecento.' *La memoria illuminata.* Florence: Vallecchi, 1989: 52–8.
Perkins, Jean A. *The Concept of Self in the French Enlightenment.* Geneva: Librairie Droz, 1964.

Piaia, Gregorio. 'L'autocommento nei sonetti filosofici di Antonio Conti.' In Gianfelice Peron, ed., *L'autocommento. Atti del XVIII Convegno Interuniversitario (Bressanone, 1990)*. Padua: Esedra Editrice, 1994. 81–92.

Rossi, Giorgio. *Saggio di una bibliografia ragionata delle opere di Alessandro Tassoni*. Bologna: Nicola Zanichelli, 1908.

– *Studi e ricerche tassoniane*. Bologna: Nicola Zanichelli, 1904.

Rossi, Pellegrino. *Annotazioni alla* Secchia rapita *in seguito delle già fatte da Gaspare Salviani*. Piacenza: Giacopazzi Stampator, 1738.

Scarpati, Claudio. *Il vero e il falso dei poeti: Tasso, Tesauro, Pallavicino, Muratori*. Milan: Vita e pensiero, 1990.

Tassoni, Alessandro. *La secchia rapita, L'oceano e le Rime*. A cura di Giorgio Rossi. Scrittori d'Italia 135. Bari: Laterza, 1930.

– *La secchia rapita: or The rape of the bucket: an heroicomical poem in twelve cantos*. Trans. with notes by James Atkinson. 2 vols. London: J.M. Richardson, 1825.

– *Opere*. A cura di Luigi Fassò. Milan and Rome: Rizzoli, 1942.

Unali, Lina. *Descrizione di sé. Studio sulla scrittura autobiografica del Settecento*. Rome: Lucarini, 1979.

Webber, Joan. *The Eloquent 'I': Style and Self in Seventeenth-Century Prose*. Madison: University of Wisconsin Press, 1968.

Index

accessus ad auctores, 40–1, 49, 54, 174n. 28
Adami, Tobia, 15, 207n. 1
Aeneas, 93, 200n. 30
Aesop, 209–10n. 15
Aforismi politici (*Political Aphorisms*, by Tommaso Campanella), 144
Africa (by Francesco Petrarca), 182n. 24
Ageno, Franca Brambilla, 173n. 24
Alan of Lille, 16, 68, 167n. 29, 171n. 12
Alexander VI, Pope, 97
Allen, Judson Boyce, 174n. 30, 179n. 1
Allen, Michael J.B., 199n. 25
alter Angelus, 146
Amabile, Luigi, 208n. 8
Amerio, Romano, 212n. 26, 213n. 32
Amorosa Visione, 180n. 12
Antiveneti (*A Venezia*, by Tommaso Campanella), 209n. 12
Apollo, 19, 79–80, 82–6, 88–90, 94–5, 131, 151, 191n. 31
Aquilecchia, Giovanni, 203n. 4
Aquinas, St Thomas (and his *Espositio in Psalmos*), 123–4, 158, 204n. 11
Arbuthnot, John, 157
'architectonic' poets, 144
Arendt, Hannah, 167n. 24, 211n. 24
Ariosto, Ludovico, 202n. 1, 213n. 29
Aristotle, 47, 50, 78–9, 129, 135, 138, 144, 156, 158, 205n. 15, 209–10n. 15
Ascoli, Albert R., 164n. 9, 174n. 27, 175n. 31
Atkinson, James, 214n. 5
Aurora, 84, 86

Bacon, Francis, 154
Baio, Antonio, 120
Bakhtin, Mikhail, 11, 132
Bambaglioli, Graziolo, 184n. 33
baptismal rite, 106
Baranski, Zygmunt G., 164nn. 9 and 11, 177n. 40
Barberino, Francesco da, 16, 66, 68, 184n. 31–3
Barbi, Michele, 28, 163n. 1, 165n. 14, 170n. 6, 189n. 21
Bariola, Felice, 183n. 29

Index

Bassi, Simonetta, 202n. 2, 205n. 16
Batkin, Leonid M., 164n. 12
Battaglia, Salvatore, 165n. 13, 175n. 36
Battera, Francesca, 193n. 3
Bausi, Francesco, 201n. 37
Beatrice, 25, 29–32, 36–9, 56, 60, 89–91, 95, 126, 165n. 14, 171nn. 9 and 11, 172nn. 19–20, 177n. 41, 189n. 22
Benivieni, Antonio, 96
Benivieni, Domenico ('Lo Scotino'), 96, 199n. 24
Benivieni, Girolamo, 17, 19, 67, 96–116, 121, 149, 165n. 16, 189n. 22, 193nn. 1–3, 194nn. 5–6, 195nn. 6–9, 196nn. 9–13, 197nn. 15 and 17, 198nn. 19, 21–2, 199nn. 22–5, 27–8, 200nn. 30 and 32, 202n. 37
Benjamin, Walter, 149, 167n. 24, 211n. 24
Benstock, Shari, 215n. 9
Benvenuto da Imola, 213n. 29
Bernardus Silvestris, 16, 68
Bible, 172n. 16, 207n. 4; Amos, 214n. 33; Apocalypse (apocalyptic angels, Book of Revelations), 20, 142–3, 145–7, 150, 210n. 17, 211n. 21; Corinthians, St Paul's Second Letter to the, 34, 58, 109; David, 152, 209–10n. 15; Exodus, 109–10, 200n. 30; Isaiah, 151; Jeremiah, 38–9, 91, 95, 152; John the Baptist, 138, 181n. 16; John the Evangelist, 18, 47–8, 50–1, 139, 147–8, 172n. 16, 177n. 45, 178n. 54; Jonah, 207n. 6; Joshua, 200n. 30; Lamentations, 38; Luke, 172n. 17, 172n. 21; Mark, 48–9, 136, 172n. 17, 173n. 21, 178n. 48; Matthew, 33, 37, 172n. 17, 173n. 21; Moses, 80, 82, 109–10, 137, 177n. 44, 200n. 30; Nathan, 209–10n. 15; New Testament, 146, 211n. 19; Old Testament, 39, 80, 122, 146, 177n. 43; Proverbs, 177n. 43, 178n. 53; Psalms, 112–13, 193n. 3, 200n. 30; Romans, St Paul's Epistle to the, 33, 178n. 51; Song of Songs (and Solomon), 121–3
Bigi, Emilio, 184n. 3
Billanovich, Giuseppe, 182n. 23
Boccaccio, Giovanni, 6, 9–10, 15, 17–18, **52–68**, 78, 150, 179nn. 1–5, 180nn. 8–10 and 12, 181nn. 19–21, 188n. 18, 207–8n. 7; as editor of Dante's *Vita Nuova*, 27–8, 168–9 n. 5, 170n. 7, 175n. 32, 181n. 19
Boethius, 6, 17, 30, 41, 48, 74, 76, 124, 166n. 18, 187n. 11
Bogue, Ronald, 208n. 8
Bolzoni, Lina, 206n.1, 211n. 20
Botticelli, Sandro, 79, 199n. 24
Brownlee, Kevin, 175n. 31
Bruno, Giordano, 11, 17, 20, 114, **119–33**, 135, 160–1, 202nn. 37 and 1–3, 203nn. 3–4, 6, 9–10, 204nn. 10–13, 205n. 15, 206nn. 18–20, 212n. 26
Burning of the Vanities, 97, 99, 111
Busnelli, Giovanni, 174n. 29
Buti, Francesco da, 213n. 29

Cain, Thomas H., 167n. 28
Calabrian uprising of 1599, 135, 139–40
Cambon, Glauco, 171n. 13, 178n. 50
Campagnola, Stanislao da, 146, 210n. 17
Campanella, Tommaso, 4, 7, 15, 17, 20, 67, 114, **134–52**, 155, 159, 161, 163n. 2, 184nn. 30, 203n. 7, 206n.1, 207nn. 1–3, 5–6, 208nn.

8–10, 209nn. 12–15, 210nn. 16 and 18, 211nn. 20–2 and 25, 212n. 26, 213nn. 28–33
Capella, Marianus, 16, 166n. 18, 168n. 30, 177n. 42
captatio benevolentia, 57, 78, 90
Cardini, Roberto, 182n. 23
Carducci, Giosuè, 8–9
Cassirer, Ernst, 159
Catholic Reformation, 20
Catullus, 188n. 18
Cavalcanti, Guido, 179n. 2
Celano, Tommaso da, 146
Cena de le cenere (*Ash Wednesday Supper* by Giordano Bruno), 202n. 1, 204n. 10, 205n. 15
Cerbu, Thomas, 208n. 8
Cervantes, Miguel de, 20
Cervigni, Dino S., 163n. 1
Charles VIII, King of France, 97
Charlewood, John, 120
Chaucer, Geoffrey, 53
Ciliberto, Michele, 202n. 2, 205n. 16
Ciociola, Claudio, 183n. 26
circle, centre point of, 32, 89, 92, 106, 127–8, 132
Città del sole (*City of the Sun*, by Tommaso Campanella), 135, 140, 144, 152, 208n. 9, 209n. 14
Clark, John R., 191n. 31
Clymene, 82–3, 151
Clytie, 84–8, 90, 191n. 29
coincidentia oppositorum, 126
Colie, Rosalie L., 190n. 25
Columbus, Christopher, 155
Colunga, Alberto, 172n. 16
Comedia delle ninfe fiorentine (*Comedy of the Florentine Nymphs* by Giovanni Boccaccio), 179n. 3, 180n. 12

Comento alli miei sonetti (by Lorenzo de' Medici), 18, **71–95**, 99, 106–7, 112, 115–16, 128, 164nn. 8 and 10, 168n. 31, 184n. 3, 185nn. 5 and 7, 186nn. 8–9 and 11, 187n. 16, 189n. 22, 192n. 36, 198–9n. 22, 201n. 37, 203n. 8; 'Quando il sol giù dall'orizzonte scende,' 84; 'O chiara stella, che coi raggi tuoi,' 79–80
comment (*cum-mente*), 26, 168n. 3, 179n. 56
Commento (also *Canzoni e sonetti con commento*, by Girolamo Benivieni), 17, 19, **96–116**, 121, 193n. 3, 195n. 7, 196n. 12–14, 198nn. 19, 21–2, 199nn. 22 and 25, 199n. 25, 200n. 32; 'Così volge Fortuna, o cure Humane,' 195n. 7; 'Lasso hor non veggio più in qual parte io vada,' 195n. 7; 'Se el cieco e debil sol, che in questa obscura,' 108; 'Signor mio dolce ovunche gli occhi gira,' 108; 'Venuto è el tempo hormai, hor el momento,' 195n. 7
Conrad of Hirsau, 41
Conti, Antonio (and his *Prose e poesie*), 20, 154, 158–9, 215n. 7
Contini, Gianfranco, 164n. 11, 170n. 9
Convivio, 25, 30, 34, 37, 40–51, 54, 60–2, 73, 78, 93, 99, 103, 114, 120–1, 138–9, 171n. 13, 173nn. 24 and 26, 174nn. 26–7, 175nn. 31 and 36, 176nn. 36–8 and 40, 178n. 50, 179n. 56, 184n. 2, 187n. 15, 192n. 36, 198nn. 19–21, 203n. 8, 207n. 4; 'quasi commento,' 8, 18, **40–51**, 173n. 24, 177n. 40
Cook, James Wyatt, 6, 72, 94, 164n. 8, 185nn. 5 and 7
Copeland, Rita, 195n. 8

242 Index

Copernicus, Nicolaus, 204n. 10
Cornford, Francis M., 216n. 12
Coward, Noel, 166n. 22
Crespi, Achille, 183n. 27
Croce, Benedetto, 28, 170n. 7
Cudini, Piero, 178n. 50
Curtius, Ernst Robert, 198n. 19

d'Andrea, Antonio, 28–9
Dante Alighieri, 4–7, 9, 13, 15–19, **25–51**, 52–6, 58–67, 71, 73–4, 76–9, 81–2, 89–95, 99–101, 103–4, 107, 111–14, 120–1, 124, 126, 128, 131, 136–9, 146, 153, 163n. 1, 164nn. 9 and 11, 165nn. 14, 15, and 16, 166n. 18, 168nn. 30 and 3, 169n. 5, 170nn. 6, 8, and 9, 171nn. 11–13, 172nn. 13–16 and 18–20, 173n. 23–4 and 26, 174nn. 26–7 and 29, 175nn. 31–2 and 34–6, 176n. 38, 177nn. 40–2, 178nn. 50 and 55, 179n. 56 and 2, 180nn. 10–11, 181nn. 19 and 22, 183nn. 25 and 27, 184nn. 33 and 2, 187n. 11, 188nn. 18–19, 189nn. 21–2, 191n. 32, 192nn. 35–7, 197nn. 15–16, 199n. 28, 200nn. 28 and 30, 201n. 33, 203n. 8, 207nn. 4 and 6, 213n. 29
Daphne, 19, 88
d'Aragona, Alfonso, 184n. 2
d'Aragona, Federigo, 184n. 2
d'Ascoli, Cecco (*pseud.* Francesco Stabili, and his *L'acerba*), 16, 66–7, 183nn. 26–7 and 29
Decameron (by Giovanni Boccaccio), 180n. 9, 181n. 19, 188n. 18
deconstruction theory, 7
De la causa, principio e uno (*On the Cause, Principle, and One*, by Giordano Bruno), 202n. 1

De l'infinito universo e mondi (*On the Infinite Universe and Worlds*, by Giordano Bruno), 202n. 1
della Robbia, Luca, 194n. 5
delle Bande Nere, Giovanni, 98
de Mattei, Rodolfo, 209n. 13
DeRobertis, Domenico, 168n. 1, 184n. 2
Derrida, Jacques, 149, 211n. 23
Descartes, René (Cartesian methodology), 13, 134, 154, 157–8
De sensu rerum (*On the Nature of Things*, by Tommaso Campanella), 144, 209n. 14
De vulgari eloquentia (by Dante Alighieri), 52–3, 77, 174n. 27, 192n. 36
Dialogo di Antonio Manetti, 197n. 15
dialogue, see poetic self-commentary, dialogic nature of
dignitas, 30–2, 34, 38, 73, 75, 77–8, 92, 105, 120, 133, 196–7n. 14
Dionysius the Areopagite, 158
Divina Commedia (*Divine Comedy*, by Dante Alighieri), 19, 47, 51, 67, 94, 99–100, 114, 173n. 23, 174n. 26, 183n. 27, 197n. 16; Cato d'Utica, 198n. 18; Francesca da Rimini, 55, 64, 101–2, 200n. 30; *Inferno*, 55, 64, 94, 101–3, 114, 184n. 33, 192n. 37–8, 197n. 15, 198n. 19; Lonza (leopard), 100, 105; *Paradise*, 137, 146, 177n. 40, 178n. 54, 210n. 18, 213n. 29; *Purgatory*, 180n. 10, 192n. 37, 198n. 18–19, 200n. 30, 213n. 29; Ulysses, 93–4, 101–3, 192n. 38, 198nn. 18–19, 199n. 25
divisio textus, 28, 37, 98, 172n. 18
dolce stil novo, 114, 116, 120, 171n. 13, 185n. 4

Dronke, Peter, 10–11, 15–16, 165n. 15, 166n. 18, 167n. 30, 171n. 12, 177n. 42, 184n. 33, 187n. 13
Dupré, Louis, 154
Durling, Robert M., 29, 66

Egloghe (*Bucoliche*), 195n. 6, 199nn. 22–3
E.K. (glosses by), 15, 167n. 28
Eliot, T.S., 14, 153
emblem, 120, 124–5, 161, 203n. 9
Enciclopedia dantesca, 172n. 19
Eroici furori (*Heroic Frenzies*, by Giordano Bruno), 11, 19–20, **119–33**, 160, 202n. 37 and 2–3, 203n. 4 and 6, 205n. 16, 213n. 31; 'Abbiate cura, o furiosi, al core,' 129; 'Amor, per cui tant'alto il ver discerno,' 130; Cicada, 128–30, 132–3, 204n. 13; Tansillo (*see also* Tansillo, Luigi), 128–33; 'Un tempo sparge, ed un tempo raccoglie,' 130; 'Venere, dea del terzo ciel, e madre,' 130
eroisatiricomica (heroisatiricomic), 155
Eucharist, 47, 151
exile, 39, 41, 43–6, 52, 63, 65, 139, 173n. 23

fedele d'Amore (the faithful of Love), 4, 33, 58–9, 76, 89, 121, 171n. 13
Ferruolo, A., 204n. 12
Ficino, Marsilio, 76, 78–9, 114–16, 186n. 11, 191n. 31, 193nn. 2, 195n. 9, 199nn. 25, 201n. 34, 207n. 3
Field, Arthur, 165n. 15, 200nn. 28–9
Filocolo (by Giovanni Boccaccio), 180n. 12
Firpo, Luigi, 209n. 12, 210n. 18, 211n. 21

Fletcher, Angus, 216n. 11
Florence, 38–9, 42, 44–5, 75, 78–9, 81, 91, 97–100, 104, 115–16, 186n. 8, 188n. 18, 193nn. 1 and 3, 199nn. 27–8
Folena, Gianfranco, 5
Foscolo, Ugo, 215n. 9
Foucault, Michel, 159, 208n. 8
Franke, William, 168n. 30
Freccero, John, 177n. 41, 198n. 19, 201n. 33
Frye, Northrop, 167nn. 23 and 25
Fubini, Mario, 185n. 6
Fulgentius, 74

Gadamer, Hans Georg, 166n. 21
Gallehault, 64, 181n. 19
Garbo, Dino del, 179n. 2
Garin, Eugenio, 186n. 9, 189nn. 19–20 and 23, 195n. 9
Genealogia deorum gentilium (*Genealogy of the Gentile Gods*, by Giovanni Boccaccio), 10, 58, 169n. 5
Genette, Gérard, 5
Gentile, Giovanni, 202n. 2, 204n. 12
Giovanni da Parma, 146
Goffen, Rona, 186n. 8
Gorni, Guglielmo, 163n. 1, 168n. 4
Gower, John, 15, 167n. 27 and 29
Grafton, Anthony, 20, 163n. 5, 166n. 22, 168n. 32, 215n. 9
Gregory, Horace, 190n. 26
Guarini, Battista, 166n. 20
Guerri, Domenico, 169n. 5, 170n. 7
Guglielminetti, Marziano, 211n. 22
Guzzo, Augusto, 212n. 26

Harrison, Robert Pogue, 171n. 11, 172nn. 19–20
Hegel, Georg Wilhelm Friedrich, 158
hermeneía, 12

244   Index

Hermes Trismegisto, 186n. 11
Hollander, Robert, 179n. 1, 180n. 8
Homer, 76
Homeric Hymn to Hermes, vii–viii
Horace, 182n. 23
Hugh of St Victor, 168n. 3
Huygens, R.B.C., 174n. 28

Iannucci, Amilcare A., 164n. 9
Iapetos, 151
imitation, 89, 120, 187n. 16
'intentional fallacy,' 167n. 23
interpretatio, 12; for *interpretatio nominis*, see Squilla, Settimontano
Isidore of Seville (and his *Etymologies*), 141, 181n. 15

Jacoff, Rachel, 174n. 27, 177n. 41, 198n. 19
Jayne, Sears, 201nn. 34–5
Joachim of Flora, 146–7, 210n. 18
John, Harry, 211n. 24
Joyce, James, 166n. 17, 215n. 9

Kantorowicz, Ernst H., 187n. 14
Kaske, Carol V., 191n. 31
katabasis narrative, 82
Kennedy, George A., 216n. 12
Kennedy, William J., 185n. 8
Kermode, Frank, 58, 177n. 44, 178n. 52
Kirkham, Victoria, 179n. 1
Kirkpatrick, Robin, 6
'know thyself,' 20, 85–6, 88, 90, 93, 95, 105, 132, 204n. 14

Lactantius, 180n. 8
Ladner, Gerhart B., 199n. 26, 200nn. 31
Lana, Jacopo della, 213n. 29
Lancelot and Guinevere, 64, 156

Landino, Cristoforo, 78, 89, 95, 187n. 16, 199n. 28, 200nn. 28–9
Lansing, Richard H., 173n. 24, 174n. 29, 176n. 38
Leibniz, Gottfried, 158
Leo the Jew, 147–8
Leocothoe, 84–5
Lewin, Jane E., 163n. 4
Limentani, Alberto, 6, 53, 164n. 6, 179nn. 1 and 4, 180n. 8
Lipari, Angelo, 72
Love, god of, 19, 33, 36, 39, 58, 60, 89–90, 92, 95, 128, 165n. 14, 177n. 47; faithful of (*see fedeli d'Amore*). See also *Vita Nuova*, Love's obscure words
Lucretius, 202n. 1
Lull, Ramón, 203n. 10
Luther, Martin, 111

Machiavelli, Niccolò, 150
MacLennan, L. Jenaro, 166n. 18
Malebranche, Nicholas, 158
Mandelbaum, Allen, 184n. 1
Marcus, Leah S., 15
Marshall, Donald G., 166n. 21
Martelli, Mario, 164n. 10, 184n. 3, 185n. 6
Martinez, Ronald L., 28
Mazzacurati, Giancarlo, 185n. 6
Mazzeo, Joseph Anthony, 170n. 7, 174n. 26
Mazzotta, Giuseppe, 168n. 3, 173n. 23, 177n. 41, 187n. 16, 207n. 6
McCoy, Bernadette Marie, 164n. 6, 179n. 4
McLaughlin, Martin L., 187n. 16
Medici, Cosimo de,' 193n. 2
Medici, Giuliano de,' 79, 194n. 6, 199n. 24

Medici, Lorenzo de,' 6–7, 17–19, **71–95**, 96–7, 99, 103–4, 106–7, 111–16, 123, 128, 151, 164nn. 8 and 12, 168n. 31, 184nn. 2–3, 185nn. 4–5 and 7–8, 186nn. 8–9 and 11, 187n. 16, 188nn. 18–19, 189nn. 21–2 and 24, 190nn. 24–5, 191nn. 28, 30–1, 33–4, 192nn. 35–6, 193n. 2, 198nn. 20 and 22, 199n. 24, 201n. 37, 203n. 8, 206n.20

Memmo, Jr, Paul Eugene, 202n. 2

Memory (also Book of), 26, 28, 30, 39, 55, 90–1, 104, 112, 168n. 2, 180n. 9, 194n. 5, 202n. 3

Menippean satire, 10

Menocal, María Rosa, 165n. 16, 172n. 20

Menzini, Benedetto (and his *Poetica e satire* and *Arte Poetica*), 20, 154, 158

Metafisica (*Metaphysics*, by Tommaso Campanella), 144, 152, 209n. 14, 212n. 26

Migliorini, Bruno, 180n. 15

Miller, Jacqueline T., 174n. 30

Minerva, 86, 181n. 16

Minnis, A.J., 167n. 27, 173n. 25, 174nn. 28 and 30, 175nn. 32–3, 179n. 1, 180n. 8

Montale, Eugenio, 3

Musa, Mark, 29, 171n. 11, 191n. 32

mystical body of Christ, 75

Narcissism, 105

Nardi, Bruno, 173n. 26

Nelson, John Charles, 10–11, 202n. 37, 203n. 6

Neoplatonism, 29, 77–8, 86, 93, 97–8, 109, 111, 202n. 37

Newton, Isaac, 158

Nicene Creed, 142

nominalism, 154

Oram, William A., 167n. 28

Orpheus (and Eurydice), 74, 82, 91; the 'other Orpheus' (*l'altro Orfeo*), 96, 114, 193n. 2

Orvieto, Piero, 186n. 11, 189n. 22, 190n. 25, 191n. 34

L'Ottimo commentatore, 213n. 29

Ovid (or his *Metamorphosis*), 19, 63, 71, 78, 82–6, 88–9, 93–4, 188n. 18, 190n. 27, 191n. 29, 202n. 1; Cupid, 88; King Minyas and his daughters, 86–8; Pyramus and Thisbe, 86; Python, 88; Salmacis and Hermaphroditus, 86

Ovide moralisé, 98, 167n. 23, 195n. 8

palinode, 47, 114, 187n. 16

parables, 207n. 5, 209–10n. 15; Christ's speaking in, 18, 33, 37, 48–9, 60, 62, 136, 160, 172n. 16, 178nn. 48–9

paradox, 81–2, 95, 126, 128, 190n. 25

paraphrasis, 46, 63, 73, 186n. 9

Parker, Deborah, 170n. 9

'Pater Noster' (Our Father), 208n. 10

Pazzi conspiracy, 7

periphrasis, 46, 60, 63, 68, 92

Peron, Gianfelice, 163n. 3, 183n. 26, 215n. 7

Perrin, N., 178n. 49

Petrarca, Francesco (or his *Canzoniere, Rerum vulgarium fragmenta*), 6, 65–6, 71, 75, 78, 81, 96, 98, 123, 156, 182n. 23, 183n. 25, 185n. 8, 186n. 8, 187n. 16, 188nn. 18–19, 213n. 29

Pflaum, Hans, 183n. 26

Phaeton, 71, 82–3, 85, 88, 93–5, 151, 192n. 37, 206n.20
Philosophia Realis (by Tommaso Campanella), 208n. 9
Philosophy, Lady, 106, 114
Piaia, Gregorio, 158–9
Pico della Mirandola, Giovanfrancesco, 99
Pico della Mirandola, Giovanni, 78–80, 82, 96–8, 103–4, 106, 114–16, 186n. 9, 188n. 19, 195n. 9, 196n. 12, 199n. 23, 202n. 37, 212n. 26
Picone, Michelangelo, 164n. 9
Pietrobono, Luigi, 170n. 8
pilgrims, 38–9, 42, 55, 63, 91, 110, 176n. 39, 197n. 17
Plato, 78, 96, 104, 110, 115–16, 127, 131, 160–1, 187n. 13, 199n. 25, 216n. 12
poetic self-commentary: as opposed to other forms of autoexegesis, 5, 52, 156–7, 166n. 17, 174n. 27, 183n. 27, 185n. 7, 186n. 8, 214n. 4; as opposed to standard commentary, 3–5, 19, 29–30, 40, 42–3, 65, 72, 74, 98, 126, 136, 154, 157, 167n. 23, 204n. 12, 214n. 5; authority of, 4, 6–9, 13, 18, 30, 37, 42–3, 54, 60–1, 65, 76, 104, 120, 145, 150, 159, 164n. 11, 172n. 18, 173n. 23, 174nn. 27 and 30, 175nn. 31–3, 180n. 8, 185n. 8, 187n. 16, 203n. 10, 215n. 6; Ciceronian mode of, 12; definition of, 5, 8, 29, 168n. 3; dialogic nature of, 11–12, 20, 119–20, 124–7, 130–2, 153, 159–60, 166n. 21, 202nn. 1 and 3, 204n. 13, 205n. 15, 215nn. 10–11; difficulty of, 41–3, 48, 49–50, 79, 81, 92–3, 139, 172n. 15, 174n. 29, 207n. 2; laconic mode of, 12, 163n. 2; not clarification, 5–6, 14, 28, 41, 43, 49, 58, 121, 136, 149, 156, 170n. 8, 172n. 18, 192n. 35; not self-centred, 13; pedagogical/didactic intent, 41, 43, 65, 68, 98, 100, 112, 127, 136, 158–9, 170n. 7, 175n. 33, 199n. 22; poet's absolute judgment in, 6–7, 14, 125, 164n. 9, 187n. 12 (*see also* poetic self-commentary, authority of); risks of overdetermination in, 9; satirical/parodic tones of, 20, 74, 155–8, 186n. 11; Socratic mode, 20, 127, 132; symbolic mode, 159, 216n. 11; truth in, 7, 138, 144–5, 149–50, 157, 166n. 21, 189–90n. 24, 206nn. 18–19, 207n. 7, 209–10n. 15, 211n. 25; utility of, 4, 167n. 28 (*see also utilitas*); poetic work: essence of, 32, 44–5, 49–51, 53, 62, 122–3, 148, 188n. 19; form of, 44–5, 48–53, 99–100, 105–6, 108, 110–12, 119–20, 124, 127–8, 134, 139, 154–5, 158, 160, 168n. 30, 171n. 12, 175n. 36, 188n. 19, 202n. 1, 204n. 14
Poetica (*Poetics*, by Tommaso Campanella), 144, 152
Poliziano, Agnolo Ambrogini detto il, 199n. 24, 201n. 37
Pomponazzi, Pietro, 151
Pope, Alexander, 154, 157
Porena, Manfredi, 182n. 23
Proclus, 186n. 11
Profezia di Cristo (*Prophecy of Christ*, by Tommaso Campanella), 152, 213n. 32
proleptic vision, 150
Prometheus, 151, 212n. 27
Propertius, 188n. 18
prophecy, 20–1, 39, 46, 48, 51, 64, 66, 95, 112, 122, 135, 137, 139–41, 143,

146, 149–52, 159–60, 207nn. 5–6, 208n. 11, 210n. 18, 213–14n. 33
prosimetrum (prosimetrical self-commentary), 10–11, 16–19, 61, 65–6, 68, 71, 75, 78, 112, 126–7, 158, 166n. 22, 167n. 29, 179n. 3, 184n. 2
Protestant reform, 111
Pugliese, Olga Zorzi, 193n. 3, 196nn. 9 and 13

Querengo, Antonio, 212n. 26
'Qui legit intelligat,' 67, 136. *See also* Parables, Christ's speaking in
Quint, David, 206n.19

Rabelais, François, 20
Raccolta aragonese, 71
Raffa, Guy, 177n. 41
Ranke, Leopold von, 166n. 22
Ranson, Daniel J., 177n. 42
Re, Caterina, 165n. 16, 193n. 1, 199nn. 23–4
reader reception theory, 7, 14
Rehm, Walter, 21, 168n. 32
retorica ornata, 31, 37
Ricci, Roberta, 181n. 20
Ridolfi, Roberto, 185n. 6
rima baciata, 53
Rime petrose (by Dante Alighieri), 201n. 33
Rochon, André, 184n. 3
Rossi, Giorgio, 214nn. 3–4
Rossi, Pellegrino, 214–15n. 6
Rossi, Valentina, 165n. 12
Ryan, Christopher, 173n. 24, 174n. 29, 176n. 36, 179n. 56

Saba, Umberto, 215n. 9
Sabbatino, Pasquale, 202n. 3, 204n. 13, 205n. 15

Sacrobosco, Giovanni di, 183n. 26
St Augustine, 25–6, 30, 41, 48, 76, 107–8, 138, 177n. 44
St Bonaventure, 146, 174n. 28, 196n. 13
St Bridgett, 210n. 18
St Francis of Assisi, 145–6, 210n. 17 and 19, 211n. 20
St Girolamo, 152
St John of the Cross, 15
St Paul, 200n. 30, 210n. 16
St Peter, 210n. 16
Salutati, Coluccio, 165n. 15, 182n. 24
Salviani, Gaspare, 155 (see also Tassoni, Alessandro), 214nn. 3–6, 215n. 6
Sanguineti, Edoardo, 170n. 9
Santagata, Marco, 182n. 23
satura, 16–17, 167–8n. 30, 177n. 42
Savonarola, Girolamo, 19, 97, 199n. 27, 200n. 32
Scaglia, Giacomo, 214n. 3
Scalzo, Joseph, 208n. 8
Scanferla, B.M., 184n. 2
Scelta di poesie filosofiche (by Tommaso Campanella), 19, **134–52**, 155, 203n. 7, 206n.1, 208n. 8, 210n. 16, 212n. 26, 213n. 32; 'Ai poeti,' 209n. 15; Antichrist, 145–6; Bocca, 137; 'Contra il proprio amore scoprimento stupendo,' 150; 'Fede naturale del vero sapiente,' 142; 'Sonetto sopra la congiunzion magna,' 140
Schnapp, Jeffrey T., 179n. 1, 181n. 21
Scholasticism, 37, 66–7, 90, 98, 129–30, 166n. 20, 175n. 33
Scioppio, Gaspare, 209n. 12
Scott, A.B., 167n. 27, 173n. 25, 174n. 28

248   Index

scriba Dei, 114
Scriblerians (and Marinus Scriblerus), 157
La secchia rapita, 154–5, 158, 214nn. 3, 5–6
self-gloss (glossorial self-commentary), 11, 16–18, 20, 53, 57, 65–7, 98–9, 108, 114, 135–6, 144, 149–50, 154, 158, 165n. 16, 166n. 22, 179nn. 2–3, 180n. 16, 182n. 24, 184nn. 30 and 32, 193n. 3, 207n. 1, 214n. 4
Settimontano, Temisquilla (pseudonym for Tommaso Campanella), 209n. 12
Shapiro, Marianne, 164n. 12, 192n. 36
Shuckburgh, Evelyn S., 203n. 5
Sibyls, 210n. 18
Sidney, Sir Philip (and his *Apologie for Poesie*), 120, 131, 203n. 5, 204n. 12, 205n. 17
Silenus topos, 165n. 15
Simonelli, Maria, 174n. 29
Simpson, James, 167n. 29
Singleton, Charles S., 28, 168n. 2, 172n. 14, 177n. 41, 178n. 54, 192n. 37, 197n. 16
Smarr, Janet Levarie, 63, 179n. 1, 180n. 12
Snyder, Jon R., 215nn. 10–11
Socrates, 127, 132, 160, 165n. 15, 201n. 34, 204n. 14, 209–10n. 15. *See also* Poetic self-commentary, Socratic mode of
Spaccio de la bestia trionfante (*Expulsion of the Triumphant Beast*, by Giordano Bruno), 120, 202n. 1
Spampanato, V., 204n. 13, 213n. 30
Spariosu, Mihai I., 208n. 8
Spenser, Edmund, 15

Squilla, Settimontano (pseudonym for Tommaso Campanella), 20, 143–5, 148–9, 152, 209n. 13, 210n. 16, 213n. 29
Statius (or his *Thebeid*), 54, 63, 90, 180n. 8
Steiner, George, 173n. 23
Sterne, Laurence, 166n. 17, 215n. 9
Stevens, Walter, 175n. 31
Stillinger, Thomas C., 172n. 18, 173n. 22
Swift, Jonathan, 157
Symonds, John Addington, 207n. 1

Tansillo, Luigi, 20, 120, 124, 202n. 1
Tasso, Torquato, 202n. 1
Tassoni, Alessandro (and his *Dichiarazioni alla* Secchia rapita), 20, 154–8, 214nn. 3–6, 215n. 6; Cesi, Countess Laura, 156; declarations, 156; Gemignani, 155; *L'oceano*, 155; Petroniani, 155
Teglia, Francesco del, 158
Telesio, Bernardino, 135, 140
Teseida delle nozze d'Emilia, 6, 15, 18, 52–68, 164n. 6, 179nn. 2–5, 180nn. 7 and 10; Arcita, 53, 60; Emilia, 53, 57, 59–60, 64; Fiammetta, 53–9, 61, 63–4, 180n. 12, 207–8n. 7; Hymen, 64; Jove, 64; Juno, 64; Mars, 58–9, 63; Palemone, 53, 59–60, 63–4; Theseus, 53. *See also* Venus
Tetel, Marcel, 186n. 8
Theophrastus, 37
Tibullus, 188n. 18
translation, 12–13, 26, 56, 94, 97, 149–50
Trask, Willard R., 198n. 19
Trattatello in laude di Dante (by Giovanni Boccaccio), 181n. 22

Trinity (trinitarian view of the text), 13–14, 26, 36, 49, 142, 146, 197n. 17
trobar clus, 31, 37, 171n. 13
troubadour *chansonnier*, 18
Turrado, Laurentio, 172n. 16

utilitas, 30, 32–3, 77, 100

Valéry, Paul, 215n. 10
Vallone, Aldo, 170n. 8
Vandelli, Giuseppe, 54, 174n. 29, 179n. 1
Varchi, Benedetto, 166n. 20
varietas, 74–5, 99, 188n. 18, 191n. 28
Vasoli, Cesare, 193n. 1
Vasta, Edward, 163n. 1
Vaticano latino 3196, 65, 182n. 23
veil (dressing of poetry), 32, 34–6, 42–3, 49, 51, 56–8, 81, 93, 108–9, 113, 115, 173nn. 20 and 23, 175n. 34, 199n. 27, 200n. 28, 201n. 33
Venus, 59, 63, 122, 130
Veronese riddle ('Se pareba boves ...'), 61, 180n. 14
Verzera, Antonino, 213n. 31
Vespucci, Simonetta Cattaneo, 79, 104, 189n. 22, 194n. 6, 199n. 24, 201n. 37
Vicecomite da Coreggio, Niccolò, 196n. 12, 199n. 25
vida and *razos*, 18
Virgil (or his *Aeneid*), 54, 63, 82, 95, 179n. 2, 182n. 23, 192n. 37, 199–200n. 28
Vita Nuova, 4–6, 13, 15–18, **25–40**, 54–5, 58–61, 78–9, 89–90, 92–4, 99, 104, 107, 111–12, 114, 120–1, 128, 131, 136, 163n. 1, 165n. 15, 168nn. 1, 2

and 4, 171n. 9, 175n. 34, 176n. 39, 177nn. 41 and 47, 180n. 11, 184n. 2, 189nn. 21–2, 191n. 32, 192n. 35; 'A ciascun'alma presa e gentil core,' 89; 'Amor e 'l cor gentil sono una cosa,' 32; *divisioni* (divisions), 9, 15, 18, 27–9, 31, 33, 35–7, 126, 165nn. 14 and 16, 168–9n. 5, 170nn. 7–9, 171n. 11, 18–19, 172n. 20, 175n. 36; 'Donne ch'avete intelletto d'amore,' 31, 39; Giovanna, 79, 189n. 22; Love's obscure words, 32–3, 89, 92, 128, 171n. 13, 172n. 15; 'Piangete, amanti, poi che piange Amore,' 189n. 22; 'Sì lungamente m'à tenuto Amore,' 38; 'widowed' poems, 37–8, 126, 165n. 14

Walker, D.P., 207n. 3
Walter of Châtillon (or his *Alexandreis*), 54
Wetherbee, Winthrop, 179n. 5
Wilkins, Ernest Hatch, 182n. 24
William of Conches, 74
Wincheimer, Joel, 166n. 21
witness (testimony), 48, 52, 56–7, 60, 65, 138–9, 161, 174n. 31, 190n. 24, 207–8n. 7
Witt, Ronald G., 186n. 8
Wutrich, Timothy Richard, 212n. 27

Yates, Frances A., 203n. 8, 204n. 11, 205n. 15

Zanato, Tiziano, 164nn. 8 and 10, 185nn. 5–7
Zingarelli, Nicola, 197n. 15
Zohn, Harry, 167n. 24

OHIO UNIVERSITY LIBRARY
Please return this book as soon as you have finished with it. In order to avoid a fine it must be returned by the latest date stamped below. All books are subject to recall after two weeks or immediately if needed for reserve.

CF